MW00987153

A BOOK
OF
NOVENAS

By
Raymond Edwards
Glynn MacNiven-Johnston
Fr Philip G. Bochanski
The National Service Committee for
Catholic Charismatic Renewal in England
Fr Walter Macken
Miguel Cuartero Samperi

Compiled & edited by
Raymond Edwards

*All booklets are published thanks to the
generous support of the members of the
Catholic Truth Society*

CATHOLIC TRUTH SOCIETY
PUBLISHERS TO THE HOLY SEE

A Book of Novenas, first published 2017 by The Incorporated Catholic Truth Society, 40–46 Harleyford Road London SE11 5AY Tel: 020 7640 0042 Fax: 020 7640 0046. Copyright © 2017 The Incorporated Catholic Truth Society.

Cover image: *The Church Militant and Triumphant*, 1365-1367. Fresco by Andrea di Bonaiuto (Andrea da Firenze). Spanish Chapel, Santa Maria Novella, Florence, Italy. © Bridgeman Images.

ISBN: 978 1 78469 171 4

CONTENTS

INTRODUCTION

PART I: NOVENAS THROUGH THE CHURCH'S YEAR

4

PART II: SCRIPTURAL NOVENAS

PART III: FOUR LONGER NOVENAS

INTRODUCTION

WHAT IS A NOVENA?

A novena is a way of praying, often for a particular need or grace. It consists of a prayer or prayers said over nine days. The word *novena* is originally Latin, and means "in a group of nine".[1] This is because a novena lasts for nine consecutive days; on each day, there is a particular prayer to be said, or devotional practice to be made.

The original novena, the model for all the rest, is the nine days between Christ's Ascension and the descent of the Holy Spirit at Pentecost, when, as we read in the Acts of the Apostles, "all these [Apostles] joined in continuous prayer, together with several women, including Mary the mother of Jesus".[2] The Church still asks Christians to pray with particular intensity between these two feast days for the Holy Spirit to renew the Christian community.[3]

There are many different sorts of novena; you can make a novena using any prayer you want: the main thing is to pray it regularly for nine days in a row. Nevertheless most people will make a novena using a prayer composed for the purpose. Some novena prayers are long, and may include litanies, or meditations; others are short. You can make a novena using the same prayer nine times, or nine

---

[1]   The official Latin equivalent is *novendialis prex,* "nine days' prayer".

[2]   Acts 1:14.

[3]   In 1897 Pope Leo XIII asked that this practice, which was of long custom, should be celebrated by all Catholics worldwide. The official *Handbook of Indulgences* states that "a *partial indulgence* is granted the Christian faithful who devoutly take part in a publicly celebrated novena before the solemnity of Christmas, Pentecost, or the Immaculate Conception of the Blessed Virgin Mary" (3rd edition 1986, English edition 1991, par. 33 (p. 72 in the edition published by the Catholic Book Publishing Corporation of New York)).

different prayers, one for each day. There are no rules; what follows are only suggestions.

PART I: NOVENAS THROUGH THE CHURCH'S YEAR

The novenas in **Part I** of this book are of two sorts.

Some are addressed to individual saints, asking their intercession for whatever our intention may be. As well as interceding (praying) on our behalf, the saints are also examples of how the Christian life has been lived. Each saint experienced different events, and responded to them in different ways; we can see in their lives examples of how embracing God's will for us, whatever our individual circumstances, always brings the grace and strength from God we need to do what he asks us. To use religious language, the saints are examples of particular virtues. In the novena prayers to saints, we have tried for each day to take one particular virtue or quality that a saint has shown, and to ask God to make it our own too, according to our needs and circumstances, and in this context to make our prayer for any particular intention we may have, whether for ourselves or for another. The tradition and experience of the Church is that certain saints are especially powerful intercessors in a particular area, or for a particular need (St Anthony for things that have been lost, or St Gerard Majella for motherhood, for instance). We have given some brief indication of these areas at the start of each novena. This may sound like superstition, but in fact it is founded on the long experience of praying Christians. For some reason, which is sometimes obvious but sometimes not, certain saints are especially helpful for particular types of need or intention. We should not be ashamed to have a devotion to a particular saint who has helped us or others with their prayers; after all, praying for each other, and for the world, is an especial charism and duty of the Christian, and one that (surely) does not end when we die. The saints have passed to a life that is fuller and richer than ours is now, or theirs was during their time on earth, and so we may rely on their prayers more than on our own; and there is surely no mystery if, after death as in this life, they, like us, have fields of particular interest or expertise.

The other novenas in Part I are slightly different. They take for their theme not a particular person's witness to God's work in them, but some of the great feasts and seasons of the Christian year. When we pray in this way, we are placing ourselves within the great rhythm of the Church's journey within time. All time is Christian time; that is to say, since God began his journey with his people, and more so since he took our human condition upon him in a physical way by being born of a woman (the great event we call the Incarnation), we experience God's work in us, his presence alongside and within us, through the medium of time. All times are one for God, to be sure: he is not bound by time in the same way that we are, and he sees and causes things in a way we cannot properly imagine, from the viewpoint of his simultaneous presence to all times and places (what, in religious language, we call his eternity); but he has chosen to make time, the ongoing progression of days and seasons that are both the same as what we have known before, and yet somehow always new. This time, then, he has made the vehicle and the means of our salvation – that is to say, the way through which we experience this world as his world, and our days lived in it as not meaningless or random but always charged with his presence.

The Church from its earliest days has discerned particular characters in certain times and days within the yearly round.

Some of these are taken up from the Jewish tradition, from which Christianity was born; others express the new events and developments specific to Christianity. These seasonal characteristics are expressed in the different texture we experience in the Church's worship, its liturgy, throughout the year. Advent, Lent, Eastertide, the great feasts of Jesus's life and the life of his mother Mary: all have their own particular flavour, if you like, by which the Church opens to us some aspect of the life of Christ's body that is her own, and our own, and invites us to live this aspect of the Christian life in a particular way during this season or on this feast.

The primary way we are called to do this is through the public liturgy of the Church: the Eucharist, and the Divine Office (the breviary). By praying as the Church prays throughout the year, we can enter more fully into the various aspects of the Christian life – which is, no more and no less, the life of God-with-us. These novenas have been composed with the intention of helping us to enter into various liturgical times more consciously, and to bring our prayers of intercession – that is, when we pray for God to give us some particular thing or virtue or help, or in some especial need, for ourselves or for another – within the circle of the Church's year. All of our needs, let us remember, all the things we ask for and the events we may find difficult or baffling, all these things happen within time: and time is God's. Whenever we pray, we pray at a particular time, during some part of the Christian year; perhaps we may be helped to pray if we place our intercessions consciously within this cycle, which, day in and day out, maps and records and celebrates God's saving work with his people. The works he has done for our ancestors in the faith he will do again for us; we have only to ask.

PART II: SCRIPTURAL NOVENAS

The novenas in **Part II** of this book are different again. They focus on particular figures from the Bible, most from the Old Testament (the Hebrew Scriptures) because, from the start, the Christian life has been lived after the model of the Old Covenant.[4] Scripture is a record of God's mighty deeds with his people, which are the pattern for his deeds with us today. Biblical figures are given to us for our imitation, not in all the details of their lives (King David was a murderer and an adulterer, Jacob deceived his father and cheated his brother, Jonah was grumpy and rebellious) but rather in one particular – their ability to accept, often after a struggle, the action of God in their lives, and his will for them. This acceptance, however it was mediated and however it played out, allowed their lives to assume a particular shape and conform to the providential pattern God intended. In this way, they become images – icons, types – of particular virtues or characteristics – Abraham of faith, Job of perseverance amidst suffering – and it is their whole-hearted, even if grudging and gradual, giving permission for God's act that makes them not just characters in a historical narrative (although they retain that historical identity and function) but exemplars of a living faith for us today.

By bringing our own questions, troubles, needs, despair or hope to God in the context of these patterned lives,

---

[4] This is primarily true of Jesus Christ: "The forty days of Jesus represent the forty years of Israel's wandering in the desert; the whole of Israel's history is concentrated in him.... the history of Israel, which corresponds to our life's history, finds its ultimate meaning in the Passion that Jesus undergoes." Congregation for Divine Worship and the Discipline of the Sacraments, *Homiletic Directory*, par. 59 (CTS, 2015, p. 40).

we are inviting God to act with us as he did for them. Sometimes our circumstances may be similar to theirs – Job despairing in the ruins of his life, Hannah asking for children; sometimes our apparent circumstances may be very different, but underneath this, our disposition may be identical. We are unlikely to find ourselves actually stuck between an Egyptian army and the impassable waters of the Red Sea, but we may well find ourselves trapped between apparently inescapable problems. God opened a way for Moses and the Israelites; he will open one for us, if we ask him with faith. God keeps his promises; and he is stronger than death.

In the novena prayers in Part II, like those to the saints in Part I, we have tried for each day to take a particular virtue or quality or response that a scriptural character (or characters) has shown, and to ask God to make it ours too, according to our circumstances; and in this context, again, we can pray for any particular intention we may have, for ourselves or for others.

PART III: FOUR LONGER NOVENAS

Part III of this compilation consists of four longer novenas: two devotions to the Holy Spirit that might be said between Ascension and Pentecost; another to the Virgin Mary that can be said in the context of any of the great Marian feasts, especially before the Immaculate Conception (8th December); and, last, the particular devotion to Our Lady, Untier of Knots. The first three are written by, respectively, an Oratorian, members of the charismatic movement, and a priest of Opus Dei, and well illustrate the characteristic spirituality that their respective religious movements have given to the Church at large.

The fourth is associated with a well-known picture of the Virgin Mary, and is a favourite devotion of Pope Francis, who first encountered it whilst studying in Germany.

HOW TO USE THIS BOOK

On each day of the novena, say the short prayer for that day, and add your intention (if any); then say the *Our Father*, the *Hail Mary*, and the *Glory Be*. Do this on each of the nine days.

Some of the novenas have only one prayer, which you should say each day for the nine days.

Often people making a novena to a saint will start a novena eight days before a saint's feast day, so that the last day of the prayer falls on the feast itself: so you might begin a novena to St Joseph on 11th March in order to finish on his feast day, 19th March. You could also start a day earlier to finish on the eve, or vigil, of the feast. Where appropriate, the dates of feast days, or suggested start days, are given at the start of each novena. But, again, there are no hard and fast rules here; you can make a novena whenever you want.

NOTE

Please note that none of these novena prayers has any official liturgical authorisation; they are intended for private use only.

ADVENT SEASON ❧ ST ANDREW ❧ BLESSED
CHARLES DE FOUCAULD ❧ THE IMMACULATE
CONCEPTION ❧ CHRISTMAS SEASON ❧
THE EPIPHANY ❧ ST THOMAS AQUINAS
❧ ST JOSEPHINE BAKHITA ❧ ST DAVID ❧
ST JOHN OF GOD ❧ ST PATRICK ❧ ST JOSEPH
❧ ST BENEDICT ❧ ANNUNCIATION ❧ EASTER
SEASON ❧ ST GEORGE ❧ ST PEREGRINE ❧
THE ENGLISH MARTYRS ❧ ST DAMIEN OF
MOLOKAI ❧ ST DYMPHNA ❧ ST RITA ❧

❧ *NOVENAS* THROUGH *THE CHURCH'S YEAR* ❧

PENTECOST ❧ ST ANTHONY OF PADUA
❧ ST THOMAS MORE ❧ ST JOHN FISHER ❧
THE SACRED HEART ❧ ST CHRISTOPHER ❧
ST ANNE ❧ ST MARTHA ❧ TRANSFIGURATION
❧ ST TERESA BENEDICTA OF THE CROSS
(EDITH STEIN) ❧ ST MAXIMILIAN KOLBE ❧
ASSUMPTION ❧ ST HELENA ❧ ST MONICA
❧ EXALTATION OF THE CROSS ❧ ST JOSEPH
OF CUPERTINO ❧ ST PIO OF PIETRELCINA
❧ ST RAPHAEL ❧ ST THÉRÈSE OF LISIEUX
❧ ST GERARD MAJELLA ❧ ST JUDE ❧
ST MARTIN DE PORRES ❧ CHRIST THE KING ❧

PART I: NOVENAS THROUGH
THE CHURCH'S YEAR

*A*dvent

On the last days of Advent, the Church turns our eyes and hearts to the coming of Christ in an especially focussed way. One means of doing this is by what are known as the "O Antiphons". This is not some obscure Irish family, but a series of seven short scriptural sentences that the Church uses as part of Vespers (Evening Prayer) between the 17th and 23rd of December. Each announces one of the names of Jesus, who is called Christ. We can make our prayer at this time in light of these names.

Light and darkness are very frequently mentioned in these texts. Our condition is seen as one sunk in darkness, without light, without hope, bound in prison in the depths of a night without dawn. This may not be our own experience, not now at any rate; but we will probably have at some point in our lives felt like this, or known someone who has. Darkness and captivity can take many forms; all can crush the spirit. From all of these, the light of Jesus Christ, small and weak in the form of a new-born baby (and new-born babies are very small, and very vulnerable), will set us free: for even the smallest light is stronger than darkness, which flees away from it. God is stronger than death. We need only ask.

FIRST DAY: O SAPIENTIA | 17TH DECEMBER

O Wisdom, you come forth from the mouth of the Most High. You fill the universe and hold all things together in a strong yet gentle manner. O come to teach us the way to truth.

The last-written books of the Old Testament – the prophet Baruch, the Book of Wisdom – speak often of the Wisdom of God. This is a mysterious figure, often personified as a woman, who is a tangible presence of God in our world, who knows and understands all things, who can guide us, and guard us with her glory. The Prologue of St John's Gospel takes this enigmatic figure and identifies it with Jesus, the man who was born in Bethlehem and grew up in Nazareth, and who was anointed as the one to save God's people from their sins. The Greek word used is *Logos*, which is usually translated "Word", but means something far richer and more complex in the Greek philosophy of its time: an overmastering pattern, the very matrix of all things, by which all things are created and sustained, which enfolds and encompasses all things (Chinese thought speaks of the Tao in comparable terms). This is what is born in Jesus: the primordial pattern and vessel of all things, something as gentle as water and as stupendous as the starlit sky at night. We are called to bring his very life and being into our lives and selves.

Father, help me to know you and follow you.
I ask you especially for [*here name your intention*]

Our Father - Hail Mary - Glory Be

SECOND DAY: O ADONAI | 18TH DECEMBER

O Adonai and leader of Israel, you appeared to Moses in a burning bush and you gave him the Law on Sinai. O come and save us with your mighty power.

This identifies the coming Christ with the deliverer God of the Hebrew Scriptures: Adonai, the Lord God who with mighty hand and outstretched arm opened the Red Sea to the children of Israel, and will open for us a way through all that bars our way, even death itself.

Father, help me to believe you have power over all things. I ask you especially for [*here name your intention*]

Our Father - Hail Mary - Glory Be

THIRD DAY: O RADIX JESSE | 19TH DECEMBER

O stock of Jesse, you stand as a signal for the nations; kings fall silent before you whom the peoples acclaim. O come to deliver us, and do not delay.

The royal house of King David, whom God set over Israel for ever, had seemed to be destroyed by the broils of history and the ambition of powerful neighbours. Yet here it is named as the root from which God will raise a new king for his people, a king above all other kings of the earth; and, more, this withered stump, this apparently dead tree, is to be a beacon of hope for all who see it. Jesus is the one through whom God can raise up out of all our dead hopes and apparent disasters a salvation that will not just bring us joy, but also be a saving sign to the world around us: God makes all things new.

Father, help me to trust you even if I cannot see your plan for me.
I ask you especially for [*here name your intention*]

Our Father - Hail Mary - Glory Be

FOURTH DAY: O CLAVIS DAVID | 20TH DECEMBER

O key of David and sceptre of Israel, what you open no one else can close again; what you close no one can open.
O come to lead the captive from prison; free those who sit in darkness and in the shadow of death.

Here, Jesus is named the key that opens all doors, unchains all prisoners and lets light into all dark places. There is no lock or bar or prison-house that can stand against him. We may not be literally in prison, although we might be; but all of us have known, or will some time know, the tomb-like prison of our thoughts, our circumstances, our sins. Jesus Christ can unlock all of these prisons; he can shed light where we are certain no light can ever come. He can lead us into the light, and set us free.

Father, unlock for me all that bars my way; free me from all my imprisonments.
I ask you especially for [*here name your intention*]

Our Father - Hail Mary - Glory Be

18

FIFTH DAY: O ORIENS | 21ST DECEMBER

O Rising Sun, you are the splendour of eternal light and the sun of justice. O come and enlighten those who sit in darkness and in the shadow of death.

Even in the depths of winter, or perhaps especially then, the breaking light of dawn brings forgotten colours and brilliant light to a world long grey. The morning sun transforms the world. During the long night, we may have become unable to imagine anything except unchanging and unending blackness; but dawn shatters this illusion, and brings light into our eyes and our hearts. So does Jesus Christ work in the long night of our sin and hopelessness.

Father, shed light in my darkness.
I ask you especially for [*here name your intention*]

Our Father - Hail Mary - Glory Be

SIXTH DAY: O REX GENTIUM | 22ND DECEMBER

O King whom all the peoples desire, you are the cornerstone which makes all one. O come and save man whom you made from clay.

A true king is one who stands as a father to all his people, and is merciful to all; he brings all together, like the cornerstone that binds together a building. Jesus Christ gathers all our hopes and aspirations into his kingdom, and will bring all to fulfilment. We may be clay, weak and malleable; but once fired by his spirit, and together with our neighbours, we can be strong bricks in a mighty building.

Father, strengthen my weakness; have mercy on my hopes. I ask you especially for [*here name your intention*]

Our Father - Hail Mary - Glory Be

SEVENTH DAY: O EMMANUEL | 23RD DECEMBER

O Emmanuel, you are our king and judge, the One whom the peoples await and their Saviour. O come and save us, Lord, our God.

Emmanuel is a Hebrew name that means "God is with us". The birth of Jesus makes this literally true: God has taken on our human condition in all its weakness and its glory, and stands now eternally on our side. All human hopes and aspirations throughout history find their completion in him; all our needs and yearnings are taken up into God's hands, and in Jesus Christ they are transfigured. God is on our side, always.

Father, help me to know you are with me. I ask you especially for [*here name your intention*]

Our Father - Hail Mary - Glory Be

EIGHTH DAY: CHRISTMAS EVE

When the sun rises in the heavens you will see the king of kings. He comes forth from the Father like a bridegroom coming in splendour from his wedding chamber.

Here, the words of Psalm 18 are applied to Christ coming in splendour like the sun at dawn; but the splendour is that of a human child, a baby, weak and apparently helpless. This paradox of strength shown in weakness is one of the core truths of the Christian life: it is when we freely admit our own absolute inability to do what we must do that God is most able to act in us: to lend us the strength, and the love, that we know for certain we cannot find in ourselves.

Father, help me not to be afraid of my weakness; help me to trust in your strength.
I ask you especially for [*here name your intention*]

Our Father - Hail Mary - Glory Be

NINTH DAY: CHRISTMAS DAY

Today Christ is born, today the Saviour has appeared; today the angels sing on earth, the archangels rejoice; today upright men shout out for joy: Glory be to God on high, alleluia.

These words are so familiar to us that we may find them hard to grasp. But all creation, men and women and angels and archangels, and even the watching beasts in the stable or on the hillside, all living things are somehow filled with a joy, a happiness, that wells from the very depths of their being. God has come to make good all that we lack, to repair all that is broken, restore all that is lost, and give us new eyes to see him at work in us and around us, and new hearts to praise him. We may not feel the truth of this, or see what it has got to do with our lives in the here and now. Nevertheless, we live in a world renewed, and its song of joy can be sung by our voices too, if we will let it.

Father, help me to be joyful; help me not to be afraid to be happy.
I ask you especially for [*here name your intention*]

Our Father - Hail Mary - Glory Be

Novena Prayer to St Andrew

FEAST DAY: 30TH NOVEMBER

The Apostle St Andrew, brother to Simon Peter, has been invoked as intercessor and patron since the early years of the Church. After the Resurrection, according to legend he preached the gospel in Scythia (north of the Black Sea), in Asia Minor and in Greece. He is traditionally said to have been martyred in Patras on the Gulf of Corinth, crucified on a "saltire" cross (hence the well-known flag of St Andrew); relics of him are still found there, and also in many other places, including, at one time, St Andrews in Scotland. As well as being Scotland's patron, he is also patron of Greece, Russia, the Ukraine, Romania and various European towns and cities.

NOVENA PRAYER TO ST ANDREW

St Andrew, you were the first to recognise and follow the Lamb of God. With your friend St John, you remained with Jesus for that first day, for your entire life, and now throughout eternity. As you led your brother St Peter to Christ, and many others after him, draw us also to him. Teach us to lead others to Christ solely out of love for him and dedication to his service. Help us to learn the lesson of the Cross and to carry our daily crosses without complaint so that they may carry us to Jesus.

Amen

Novena to Blessed Charles de Foucauld

FEAST DAY: 1ST DECEMBER

As a young man, Charles de Foucauld was rich and privileged. He ran through a small fortune on high living and mistresses, and sought adventure in the army and in exotic travel. Eventually, God touched his heart, and he gave up his old life to enter a monastery. But this was not enough for him; he returned to the deserts of North Africa, where as a young soldier he had been impressed by the religious devotion of the Muslim tribesmen, and lived amongst them as a hermit, witnessing to Christ without words, but simply by his way of life. He was shot to death by robbers in 1916, when after fifteen years in the desert he had made only one convert. But, despite appearances, his life and witness was not in vain: after his death, his example has brought many to God, and inspires the Little Brothers of Jesus and the Little Sisters of Jesus, religious communities which follow Charles's example by living in "the lowest place" and seek to bring God's love to others in a silent and hidden way.

FIRST DAY

You knew what it is like to be burdened by many sins. Help us not to despair in the face of our sins, especially our habitual sins, but really to believe in God's power to change us.

I ask you especially for [*here name your intention*]

Our Father - Hail Mary - Glory Be

SECOND DAY

You turned to God, and knew his mercy on your sins. Help us to hear his call to repent the evil we have done, and to welcome the grace to return to our loving Father as you did.

I ask you especially for [*here name your intention*]

Our Father - Hail Mary - Glory Be

THIRD DAY

You heard God's call to follow him in a particular way. Help us, too, to hear God's call to us to love him and our neighbour in the vocation he has planned for us.

I ask you especially for [*here name your intention*]

Our Father - Hail Mary - Glory Be

FOURTH DAY

You lived amongst strangers and saw God's hand at work in them. Help us to find God wherever we are, especially in the places we might not think to look for him.

I ask you especially for [*here name your intention*]

Our Father - Hail Mary - Glory Be

FIFTH DAY

You lived in the desert and found God in solitude and silence. Help us to make space for God in our lives.

I ask you especially for [*here name your intention*]

Our Father - Hail Mary - Glory Be

SIXTH DAY

You gave witness to God most of all by what you did, rather than by what you said. Pray for us, that we, too, may be a sign of God's love to those around us, more by how we live than by what we say.

I ask you especially for [*here name your intention*]

Our Father - Hail Mary - Glory Be

SEVENTH DAY

Your mission seemed to be a failure and your life's work to have come to nothing, yet you did not give up. Help us to persevere in doing God's will, even if – especially if – we can see only failure and defeat: help us to know that, in God's sight, the only important thing is to do his will in love, and to live in hope, not discouragement.

I ask you especially for [*here name your intention*]

Our Father - Hail Mary - Glory Be

EIGHTH DAY

You abandoned your whole life to God's will. Pray for us, that we may have something of the faith you had.

I ask you especially for [*here name your intention*]

Our Father - Hail Mary - Glory Be

NINTH DAY

You loved God until the end, and even in your death you praised him. Intercede for us, that death may find us blessing God for all his mercies.

I ask you especially for [*here name your intention*]

Our Father - Hail Mary - Glory Be

The Immaculate Conception

FEAST DAY: 8TH DECEMBER

The Immaculate Conception is a title given to the Blessed Virgin Mary. We have been freed from sin by Christ but we were conceived and born bearing the sin of Adam – rebellion against God. Mary, however, was redeemed by Christ before she was conceived (God is not constrained by time) and was never separated from God's will. She can teach us how to live in God's will, which we fear may only limit or judge us, but which is in fact perfect freedom.

Many of the authorised apparitions of the Virgin Mary (such as that to St Bernadette at Lourdes) have been under this aspect, of her who is the Immaculate Conception.

To finish this novena on the eve of the feast, you should begin it on 29th November; to finish it on the feast itself, begin on 30th November.

FIRST DAY

Mother, sin never separated you from God. I ask you to help me want this union too. May I see that my true happiness lies in the plan God has lovingly created for each of our lives.

I ask you especially for [*here name your intention*]

Our Father - Hail Mary - Glory Be

SECOND DAY

When the angel announced God's will to you, you accepted it, trusting in God's love. Help me to believe that the Lord wants to do marvels for me.

I ask you especially for [*here name your intention*]

Our Father - Hail Mary - Glory Be

THIRD DAY

You gave birth to the Light of the World. May I be enlightened to see my life as God sees it and not as it is shown to me by Satan, the father of lies.

I ask you especially for [*here name your intention*]

Our Father - Hail Mary - Glory Be

FOURTH DAY

You are the one who crushes the head of the serpent. Help me to want to crush the evil in my heart. May I call on your help when the devil calls me to sin or despair.

I ask you especially for [*here name your intention*]

Our Father - Hail Mary - Glory Be

FIFTH DAY

When you appeared to St Catherine Labouré you showed yourself standing on the world and ready to pray for all who ask you. I ask your intercession for all my needs and for the needs of the world.

I ask you especially for [*here name your intention*]

Our Father - Hail Mary - Glory Be

SIXTH DAY

St Bernadette was not educated or important but you called her to be your messenger. I pray that you help me to announce the love of God in my life, asking him to show me how and where.

I ask you especially for [*here name your intention*]

Our Father - Hail Mary - Glory Be

SEVENTH DAY

At Lourdes you show your concern for the sick and suffering. Help me to enter the sickness and sufferings of my life, believing the Father allows this in love, and help me to offer my sufferings, believing that this can save the world.

I ask you especially for [*here name your intention*]

Our Father - Hail Mary - Glory Be

EIGHTH DAY

St Maximilian Kolbe dedicated his life to you and in this relationship was able literally to offer his life for another. I pray that you help me to offer up my life for my neighbour in whichever way I am asked.

I ask you especially for [*here name your intention*]

Our Father - Hail Mary - Glory Be

NINTH DAY

You are the first and perfect disciple. May I imitate you in your love for your Son. Help me to see how to take you as my Mother.

I ask you especially for [*here name your intention*]

Our Father - Hail Mary - Glory Be

Christmas

The feast of Christmas extends over eight days, in what the Church calls an octave. Only the very greatest feasts of the year are like this.

The Christmas octave runs from Christmas Day itself until 1st January, when we mark the feast of his mother Mary, under her title Mother of God. In between, the Church opens for us the Gospels of the very earliest days of Jesus's life; but it also shows us three feasts of saints whose very different lives were marked with persecution for the sake of Jesus's name. These are not melancholy days, though, for brooding on suffering and opposition; rather, let us recognise how the transforming presence of God in the world and in the lives of human beings brings joy and lightness into the darkest places, and allows forgiveness and mercy to find a home in us, whose nature is often so unforgiving.

FIRST DAY: 25TH DECEMBER | MIDNIGHT

Lk 2:1–14

Luke locates Jesus's birth at a precise historical moment (although he may have got some of his dates wrong) and repeatedly stresses that Jesus comes of the royal line of King David. Yet the news comes first not to the great men of Israel, but to shepherds, poor and outside the town on the cold hills. So, whilst it is important to acknowledge that Jesus's coming to us is an historical fact – something that really happened – and that he has all the proper credentials of the promised Messiah, the one whom the people of Israel were expecting to deliver them from their enemies, the central message here is that God comes first to the poor, the neglected, the marginalised, however this poverty and neglect is manifest (and it may not be physical). This remains true today.

Lord, come to me in my poverty; help me to bring you to others.

I ask you especially for [*here name your intention*]

Our Father - Hail Mary - Glory Be

SECOND DAY: 25TH DECEMBER | DAWN

Lk 2:15–20

The shepherds hurry to the stable to see the sign they have been promised. When they arrive, their news causes astonishment and leaves their hearers bewildered. Babies are born all the time, in all sorts of unlikely places; what is so unusual about this birth that God's own angels are so excited about it? Awe at the revealed glory of God is surely combined with puzzlement. What is all this about? Mary carefully keeps these events in her memory, to reflect on later.

We know this scene so well that it is unlikely to have the same sort of impact on us; we need to imitate Mary, and guard these things in our hearts. A saviour has come into the world, as a human child; what does this mean for me? From what oppression do I need to be set free? Do I trust that God will keep his promises, and fulfil the signs he has given me (if I have even recognised them)?

Lord, help me to see my need of you; help me to
welcome your coming into my life, and to bring this news
to others.
I ask you especially for [*here name your intention*]

Our Father - Hail Mary - Glory Be

THIRD DAY: 26TH DECEMBER | ST STEPHEN

Mt 10:17–22

It seems strange, perhaps, that the day after Christmas
is dedicated to the first Christian martyr, St Stephen,
stoned to death for witnessing to Jesus. This reminds
us, maybe, that one of the possible reactions to the
baffling arrival of the Messiah amongst us is fear,
uncomprehending opposition, and even anger and
violence. We may feel these reactions ourselves; we
should certainly, the Gospel warns us, expect to meet
them in others. But we need not worry about this. God's
Spirit will be with us in our need, and will lend us the
words and strength we need. St Stephen prayed for those
who killed him, but also knew they did not know what
they were doing.

Lord, help me not to fear you, and not to let my fear
become anger; help me to forgive, and be forgiven.
I ask you especially for [*here name your intention*]

Our Father - Hail Mary - Glory Be

FOURTH DAY: 27TH DECEMBER | ST JOHN THE EVANGELIST

Jn 20:2–8

Now we are somewhere different again: the empty tomb on Easter morning. The Church today celebrates the feast of the Apostle John, author of the Gospel, and traditionally identified with the unnamed "beloved disciple" of this passage. The paramount witness of his life, this Gospel suggests, is this moment, when he first knows that God has passed through death and destroyed it. This is the ultimate end and purpose of the birth of Jesus; this baby will become the one who is tortured and dies for his people – who by his own suffering transforms all the pain and death of the world. No longer is it meaningless, but a way for the world to be saved.

Lord, be with me in all I experience; help me to know you have defeated death and pain.
I ask you especially for [*here name your intention*]

Our Father - Hail Mary - Glory Be

FIFTH DAY: 28TH DECEMBER | HOLY INNOCENTS

Mt 2:13–18

Even closer to the birth of Jesus is the brutal massacre of the male children of Bethlehem (whom the Church calls the Holy Innocents). There is a peculiar horror and shock produced by the deliberate killing of a child. How can God allow such things? In our day, the horror of abortion, which has destroyed millions of unborn lives, probably evokes similar bafflement (if we consider it at all. Most people do not).

But perhaps we should ask ourselves, instead, not why God allows such things, but why human beings permit them. This Gospel also shows us St Joseph acting to save Mary and Jesus from Herod; and the Church, in remembering these nameless children as holy, assures us that God has them in his hand. We should look, first, to our own hearts.

Lord, help me to protect the innocent.
I ask you especially for [*here name your intention*]

Our Father - Hail Mary - Glory Be

SIXTH DAY: 29TH DECEMBER

Lk 2:22–35

From his earliest days, Jesus is enfolded by the customs and observances of the Mosaic Law. He is taken to the Temple, the heart of Jerusalem, the holy city. There he is to be presented to the Lord, as the Law decrees every first-born male child must be. And there again, as in Bethlehem, Mary and Joseph are confronted with a baffling event: an old man comes over and claims their child is the one God has sent to save Israel and overturn the settled order of things. Making this announcement crowns his life's work. In one sense, we too are called as Christians to be like Simeon, to announce Jesus to others and leave the rest to God. But this happens in God's time, and not ours.

Lord, teach me to be patient, to wait for you; and help me to recognise you when you appear, in however unexpected a guise.
I ask you especially for [*here name your intention*]

Our Father - Hail Mary - Glory Be

SEVENTH DAY: 30TH DECEMBER

Lk 2:36–40

We can easily overlook or make fun of pious old
ladies, who like Anna daughter of Phanuel seem to be
constantly in church, praying for something or other,
lighting candles, running mysterious errands in the
sacristy. Even when they are not actively mad (and many
of them are), they can be a nuisance or a distraction. Yet
whatever their faults or foibles, their short temper or
uncertain personal hygiene, they give an undeniable and
constant witness of prayer. We would do well, perhaps,
to imitate more than we judge.

Lord, help me to see others as you see them.
I ask you especially for [*here name your intention*]

Our Father - Hail Mary - Glory Be

EIGHTH DAY: 31ST DECEMBER

Jn 1:1–18

After the various circumstantial details of Jesus's birth,
and the events of his first months, the Church's camera
tracks back and gives us a look at the big picture. The
Prologue to John's Gospel can seem like a forbidding
and rather opaque philosophical tract, but at its heart is
a simple assertion: the Word was made flesh, and dwelt
amongst us. God has lived amongst his people, and all
we know and are he has known too and been. Nothing
now need daunt or frighten us; the primordial light, the
pattern and energy of all things, him through whom all
came to be: this Word of God we know as Jesus, born as
a human baby, just as we were.

Lord, help me to know your glory.
I ask you especially for [*here name your intention*]

Our Father - Hail Mary - Glory Be

NINTH DAY: 1ST JANUARY | MARY, MOTHER OF GOD

Lk 2:16–21

On this last day of the octave, which is also the first day
of the calendar year, we return to where we began, with
the shepherds visiting the stable. There is, however, one
small but important addition: the child is now named:
Jesus, which means "God saves". In the Judaism of this
time, only the father names a son; so by naming Jesus as
part of the rite of circumcision, Joseph adopts him into
the line and house of David. But they are poor: when
Jesus is presented at the Temple, Joseph and Mary bring
only the poor man's offering of two doves. Mary is not
now named the mother of a king, but Mother of God.

We, like Mary, should gather in our hearts what we
have seen and experienced, and we will see, perhaps,
that much looks the same as before; but now, at the
centre of the picture, is the man Jesus.

Lord, let me in my weakness know your saving power.
I ask you especially for [*here name your intention*]

Our Father - Hail Mary - Glory Be

*E*piphany

The Gospels of the days of Christmastide are a sort of overture to the public ministry of Jesus. They fall into two halves, either side of the feast of Epiphany on 6th January. That feast, which means "The Revealing" or "The Making Known" is the point at which Jesus's birth, which has already been announced to the Jewish people in the person of the shepherds, is now made known to the rest of the world. The wise men, however, have already got an inkling of the event; indeed, they are rather better informed than Herod and his learned advisers. This reminds us not to scorn the wisdom and insight of those apparently outside the Church; God has ways to make himself known to them too.

Before the Epiphany, John the Baptist announces that Jesus is coming; after the Epiphany, we have a sort of whirlwind summary of Jesus's preaching and healing.

The feast of the Epiphany is the first sign that Jesus's mission is not just to the people of Israel, the bearers of the promise, but also to all the children of Adam and Eve. This remains true. God's love and mercy extend to all people, no matter how far away they may seem – whether physically, in those parts of the world remotest from where the Church has historically flourished, or in terms of their way of life. Jesus Christ came to call sinners, and associated with outcasts and the morally compromised: prostitutes, tax-collectors (who were the hated collaborators of an occupying power), lepers. No one is outside God's mercy; however far we may feel ourselves from "proper Christian behaviour" in whatever way, God remains close to us. He shows himself to us in his vulnerability; we in our turn should feel able to share with him our deepest fears and anxieties, our failures and shame, our concern for those we know who seem to live as if nothing matters very much. These are exactly the situations where Jesus is most present.

FIRST DAY | 2ND JANUARY

Jn 1:19–25 (A voice crying in the wilderness)

The religious authorities in Jerusalem do not understand who this man, John the Baptist, is, nor why he is acting as he does. Immersing in the river people who came to him, in answer to his call to repent, to mark a change in their lives and their undertaking to live again by God's Law, was a powerful sign associated with the Messiah, the king whom Jewish tradition expected to come and rescue his people from oppression and sin. Was John claiming to be the Messiah? He was not; he was, he declared, merely a forerunner, a sign of the one whom God was about to send.

We may have similar questions for the Church. What is the point of it all? What is the purpose of the sacraments we are invited to, especially Confession and the Eucharist? These are not done primarily for the sake of the Church, to gain it status or our dutiful obedience, or the reflected glory of pomp and ceremonial, although sometimes people within the Church act as if this were so. No: the Church's aim in all this is to make us ready to receive Jesus – to prepare our hearts for the arrival of God. All of our questions are best answered by the person of Jesus, the Christ: the Messiah.

Father, help me to make a path for Jesus to come to me.
I ask you especially for [*here name your intention*]

Our Father - Hail Mary - Glory Be

SECOND DAY | 3RD JANUARY

Jn 1:29–34 (Behold the Lamb of God)

When John sees Jesus, he recognises him as the One he
has been announcing, even though he did not know him
by sight (Luke's Gospel makes the two cousins, but we
may suppose they had not seen one another much since
early childhood). He is the one who will baptise with
the Holy Spirit – that is, who can produce a real change
of heart in us. When we meet him, we will know him,
because the Holy Spirit is with him. The undying life,
the joy that is not destroyed by the great or small deaths
we encounter each day, this is the Spirit in us. When we
meet this, we will know that Jesus is there.

Father, send me your Spirit, so I may know Jesus.
I ask you especially for [*here name your intention*]

Our Father - Hail Mary - Glory Be

THIRD DAY | 4TH JANUARY

Jn 1:35–42 (We have found the Messiah)

Again, John points Jesus out to others. This time, two of
them, hitherto his own disciples, follow Jesus, and make
a formal request to become his disciples instead (this
is the meaning of their question, "Rabbi, where do you

live?"). In turn, one of them tells his brother "we have found the Messiah", and this brother, Simon, is given a new name – which means, in scriptural terms, a new identity in God's eyes. When we are brought to Jesus, he gives us a new identity, too: this is most obviously symbolised in the new name we are given in baptism, but at a deep level means that only by meeting Jesus can we come to know our true selves, who we really are in God's eyes, rather than the various masks and roles we sedulously assume for our own purposes. Only by living in this our true self can we be happy.

Father, tell me my true name; help me to be my true self, as you alone know me.
I ask you especially for [*here name your intention*]

Our Father - Hail Mary - Glory Be

FOURTH DAY | 5TH JANUARY

Jn 1:43–51
(You are the Son of God, you are the King of Israel)

This is a strange and slightly puzzling passage. Why is Nathanael so amazed that Jesus saw him under a fig tree? And why does this mean Jesus knows he is a righteous man, "incapable of deceit", a model Israelite? We have a sense that more is going on than we are ever likely to understand. But whatever the undisclosed meanings here, they lead Nathanael, like Philip before him, to recognise Jesus as the Messiah, the one who is sent by God to free them and rule over them in God's name. Jesus tells him then that he will see angels going up and down from him to heaven. This is an echo of the dream that came to Jacob, who became Israel, the father of the Twelve Tribes, as recorded in Genesis 28. Jesus is claiming to be the new Israel, the renewer of God's holy people.

The signs by which God speaks to us may be opaque or trivial-looking to others; but they are the exact way God has for talking to our hearts, and we should not despise them because they do not look like what we expected. Jesus comes to make all things new: to renew in us the promise of God.

Father, help me to listen when you speak to me.
I ask you especially for [*here name your intention*]

Our Father - Hail Mary - Glory Be

FIFTH DAY | 6TH JANUARY: THE EPIPHANY

Mt 2:1–12 (The wise men come to pay homage)

In Jesus's time, as in ours, the mysterious East was the expected home of inscrutable but often accurate spiritual insight. God's message announcing freedom for humanity has come a good deal more clearly to the Magi (magician-astronomers, if you like, who practised their art in the service of religion) than to the professional experts of Herod's court, or the Jerusalem Temple. This may well be in part because the substance of the message (that salvation will come in the shape of a child born in an obscure small town, far from the centres of influence and learning) is so unexpected, and on the face of it frankly ridiculous. How can this event make any sort of difference to us? Yet the Magi, in a matter-of-fact way, walk easily in this dream-like world of visions and celestial signs, and give their gifts, precious and symbolic, before vanishing as silently as they appeared. In their wake, the politico-religious establishment is profoundly disturbed, even though all the child has done so far is be born.

God is not constrained by what we expect, or disturbed by our panicked reactions to his appearance in our lives. Let us try to welcome him, and offer him what we have, rather than trying to second-guess what he is about before we will give him house-room.

Father, help me to find Jesus and not be afraid.
I ask you especially for [*here name your intention*]

Our Father - Hail Mary - Glory Be

SIXTH DAY | 7TH JANUARY

Mt 4:12–17, 23–25
(John is arrested; Jesus begins to preach)

Only when John is arrested does Jesus begin to preach. His message is identical to John's: repent, because God's kingdom is very near. But Jesus, unlike John, accompanies words by signs: he heals those who are sick or afflicted; nor does he stay in one place and allow people to come to him, as John did. Instead, he goes throughout Galilee, to those who dwell in shadow and darkness, and seeks out those who are lost, to bring them light and healing.

God does not expect us to do everything, or indeed very much. He comes to find us wherever we are, however dark or obscure the place we find ourselves in. All he asks is that we turn to him when we hear his voice.

Father, help me to hear you and turn to you.
I ask you especially for [*here name your intention*]

Our Father - Hail Mary - Glory Be

Mk 6:34–44
(The feeding of the five thousand)

The crowds who come to find Jesus are lost and helpless, like a mob of sheep; they have come after him without bothering to think about obvious things like food or shelter, or what time it is. His disciples, too, are also pretty hopeless: their main goal is to be reassured that this is someone else's problem, and nothing they need be worried about. Jesus does not let them off the hook; but he at the same time provides all that they need to do what he asks them, in a way that goes beyond anything they could have expected.

We very often try to find reasons not to do anything to help, to avoid a situation that God presents us with. We can't possibly do anything, we reckon, so it must be someone else's problem, not ours. Jesus does not work like this. He tells the disciples what to do, and then gives them what they need to do it.

Father, help me not to look for excuses but instead to trust that you will provide what I need.
I ask you especially for [*here name your intention*]

Our Father - Hail Mary - Glory Be

Mk 6:45–52
(Jesus walks on the lake – do not be afraid)

Now the disciples are trying to cross a lake at evening, against a headwind, after Jesus has insisted they make the crossing. He comes past them, walking on the waves, but stops to help them only when in their fear and distress they call out to him. Then the wind drops, and their fear is replaced by utter bewilderment. What on earth is going on? Who is this? Feeding five thousand men and uncounted women and children with five loaves has clearly not made any lasting impression on them.

Like the disciples, sometimes we find ourselves out on a limb – in the middle of a metaphorical (or perhaps an actual) lake, in a high wind, far from shore, after doing something that Jesus has appeared to tell us to do. The sight of him passing by at a distance, defying what we reckon are the settled laws of existence, is no obvious comfort to us; in fact, it may make our distress only deeper. Like the disciples, at these moments we must call out to him; and he will come to us. Unlike the disciples, we must remember what he has already done in our lives. He will not abandon us now.

Father, help me to call to you in my distress; help me to remember your mighty works.
I ask you especially for [*here name your intention*]

Our Father - Hail Mary - Glory Be

Lk 4:14–22
(This text is being fulfilled today even as you listen)

Now Jesus returns to his home town, and goes to the
synagogue. There he reads a passage from Isaiah that
more or less openly declares he is the promised Messiah:
"the Lord has anointed me ... This text is being fulfilled
today even as you listen". But it is the details of his
mission that are important. He is not a triumphant king,
driving the Roman oppressor out of the Holy Land
and restoring the Kingdom of Israel to the glory it had
under David and Solomon; he brings sight to the blind,
freedom to the imprisoned, good news to the poor and
downtrodden. A good king might do some of these
things; but only after his enemies were overthrown and
his rule re-established. Jesus promises these things first;
and from this beginning, God's kingdom will grow. It is
not limited by the covenant with Israel, but is open to
the whole world.

We need Jesus to open our eyes, free us from
imprisonment, bring joy to our poor and downtrodden
hearts; then we, too, may help bring these things to
others. Jesus's example suggests another profound truth:
it is by bringing these things (light, freedom, consolation)
to others first, not to ourselves, that our own hurts may
be healed.

Father, help me to hear your good news, and to bring it
to others.
I ask you especially for [*here name your intention*]

Our Father - Hail Mary - Glory Be

$\mathcal{N}$ovena to St Thomas Aquinas

A famous theologian, Thomas Aquinas (his surname means "from Aquino", his birthplace) was the son of an Italian nobleman. He became a member of the Dominican Order (Order of Preachers), and died in 1274 aged about fifty. Although he seemed a slow learner at first (he was fat, and habitually silent, and so was nicknamed the "dumb ox"), his teachers eventually realised he was an enormously talented theologian; he was also a man of deep prayer. He is best known for his voluminous writings, which include theological works, commentaries on Scripture, and some well-known prayers and hymns. His most famous work is the *Summa Theologiae* (*Compendium of Theology*), a systematic treatise covering the whole of Christian theology, which was a standard textbook until the 1960s. He was declared a Doctor of the Church in 1567. He is often considered a patron saint of study, and of education in general.

FIRST DAY

You experienced the mockery and misunderstanding of others; teach us to bear with patience, as you did, those times we receive the scorn or ridicule of others.

I ask you especially for [*here name your intention*]

Our Father - Hail Mary - Glory Be

SECOND DAY

Those who noticed only your body were surprised to learn of the great knowledge of and love for God it concealed; help us not to judge others by outward appearance, but to remember that all men and women are made in God's image and likeness.

I ask you especially for [*here name your intention*]

Our Father - Hail Mary - Glory Be

THIRD DAY

You had a great knowledge of and love for the Scriptures; help us to hear God's Word and respond to it as you did.

I ask you especially for [*here name your intention*]

Our Father - Hail Mary - Glory Be

FOURTH DAY

You had a profound love for Christ in the Eucharist;
help us, too, to experience this same reverence and love
for the God who comes to us so humbly, under the forms
of bread and wine.

I ask you especially for [*here name your intention*]

Our Father - Hail Mary - Glory Be

FIFTH DAY

You did not despise the learning of the pagans, and
of those of other faiths, but drew it into the service
of knowing and loving the one true God, the God of
Abraham, Isaac and Jacob; help us to see God's truth
wherever it is to be found, and his hand at work in all
he has made.

I ask you especially for [*here name your intention*]

Our Father - Hail Mary - Glory Be

SIXTH DAY

You gave glory to God by your writing and thought; help
us to place all the works of our hands and minds at the
service of God and his Church.

I ask you especially for [*here name your intention*]

Our Father - Hail Mary - Glory Be

SEVENTH DAY

You delighted to teach, and to learn; teach us to know and love God as you did, and to recognise in all we experience the signs of his overwhelming love for us.

I ask you especially for [*here name your intention*]

Our Father - Hail Mary - Glory Be

EIGHTH DAY

You were above all a man of prayer; help us to discover that it is only in a relationship of prayer that we can come to know him, who is the heart and goal of our Christian life.

I ask you especially for [*here name your intention*]

Our Father - Hail Mary - Glory Be

NINTH DAY

You knew that, however great our intellectual knowledge of God, it is like straw compared to the experience of his love. Help us not to let our own thoughts, concepts and plans become idols standing between us and the Father's overwhelming love for us.

I ask you especially for [*here name your intention*]

Our Father - Hail Mary - Glory Be

Novena to St Josephine Bakhita

FEAST DAY: 8TH FEBRUARY

Josephine Bakhita was born in Sudan in around 1869 but was abducted by slave traders at a young age and was so traumatised she forgot her own name. She is known by the cynical name given to her by her abductors – Bakhita, which means "Lucky". Bakhita was passed around from "owner" to "owner" and one of them had her body scarred with intricate patterns. Eventually she ended up with an Italian family who sent her to school with the Canossian sisters in Schio, Venice. There she was baptised Josephine. Contrary to the wishes of the family, she remained with the Canossians and became a religious. She was the doorkeeper of the order and was well loved by the local people for her deep compassion and sweetness, which she didn't lose even during the long, painful illness which preceded her death. Josephine Bakhita was canonised in 2000.

FIRST DAY ✓

St Josephine, you were taken from your family at an early age and lost your entire identity. We pray for all those children who have been abducted and for their parents and families, who suffer not knowing what has become of them. Send your Holy Spirit to comfort them; and may they one day be reunited.

I ask you especially for [*here name your intention*]

Our Father - Hail Mary - Glory Be

SECOND DAY

You knew what it was to be a slave, to have no rights, to have lost even your name. We pray for the victims of people traffickers and all those in any kind of slavery. May this evil be wiped out from our world.

I ask you especially for [*here name your intention*]

Our Father - Hail Mary - Glory Be

THIRD DAY

St Josephine, one of your owners had your whole body scarred. You knew this terrible pain. We pray for all victims of torture. Help them to heal in body, mind and spirit. May all governments abandon this practice.

I ask you especially for [*here name your intention*]

Our Father - Hail Mary - Glory Be

FOURTH DAY

Even in the terrible suffering of your life, you saw beauty in the world and believed there must be a God because of that beauty. May we, too, have something of your love for beauty and the natural world.

I ask you especially for [*here name your intention*]

Our Father - Hail Mary - Glory Be

FIFTH DAY

When the family that had rescued you wanted you to leave the Canossians, you had the courage to refuse, even though you were truly grateful to them. Help us to put God's will above all things, even above our natural affections.

I ask you especially for [*here name your intention*]

Our Father - Hail Mary - Glory Be

SIXTH DAY

St Josephine, you were so grateful to know God and to be part of his Church that you often kissed the baptismal font. May we never take for granted the faith we have been offered and may you give us something of your humility and gratitude for all God does.

I ask you especially for [*here name your intention*]

Our Father - Hail Mary - Glory Be

SEVENTH DAY

Your sufferings gave you great compassion for others and you were constantly smiling and always open to those who came to you, no matter how inconvenient it was. St Josephine, may we have something of your sweetness and openness, something of your joy.

I ask you especially for [*here name your intention*]

Our Father - Hail Mary - Glory Be

EIGHTH DAY

In your last painful illness you relived your slavery, begging the nurse to loosen your chains. We pray for all those who are weighed down by pain, and we ask that we, too, may enter the sufferings of our lives where God seems to have abandoned us. May we have the faith to know he has not.

I ask you especially for [*here name your intention*]

Our Father - Hail Mary - Glory Be

NINTH DAY

Your last words were "Our Lady, Our Lady". May we, too, know the comfort of the Mother of God, now and at the hour of our death.

I ask you especially for [*here name your intention*]

Our Father - Hail Mary - Glory Be

ovena to St David

We know almost nothing about the life of St David, who was a monk and bishop in south Wales in the late sixth century. He was widely venerated from the eighth century onwards, and his sanctity officially recognised by the Pope in 1120. There are many stories about his life, but it is not clear how many of them are historical. He is best known as the patron saint of Wales. He is also patron of vegetarians and poets.

This prayer to St David can be said over nine days as a novena.

PRAYER TO ST DAVID

O God, who raised Blessed David to be an apostle and patron for your people in Wales, grant, we implore, that through his prayers the people may be restored to the truth which he taught, and to attain to everlasting life. Through Jesus Christ our Lord.

Amen

Novena to St John of God

When John was eight years old he ran away from his home in Portugal and turned up in the Castile region of Spain, where he worked as a shepherd. When he was old enough he became a mercenary and for the next eighteen years fought in various wars. He lost nearly all moral sense, but when he was injured falling from his horse whilst out looting he called on the Virgin Mary to save him – and he was saved. This made an impression, and when his mercenary company was disbanded – when he was forty years old – he sought to put his life right with God. He wanted to be punished for his past life so pretended to be insane, since the "treatment" for that at the time was flogging. It was only when Blessed John of Avila intervened that he gave up the idea. He then started looking after the sick and set up several hospitals which he supported through work and begging. Others joined him and the Hospitaller Order began. He died aged fifty-five in 1550, his heart worn out in the service of the sick. He is patron of heart sufferers because of both his death through a weakened heart, and the great love he had for his neighbour. He was canonised in 1690 and declared patron of the dying and of hospitals in 1898.

FIRST DAY

You are the patron of all who suffer heart disease. We pray for them that they may find help for their illness. We also pray for all who are sick of heart whether through sin or unrequited longing. May they find and follow God's will.

I ask you especially for [*here name your intention*]

Our Father - Hail Mary - Glory Be

SECOND DAY

You ran away from home when you were young. We ask you to intercede for all runaways, that they may meet those who might help them, not those who might harm them. May we, too, not try to run away from the realities of our lives.

I ask you especially for [*here name your intention*]

Our Father - Hail Mary - Glory Be

THIRD DAY

You were a penitent sinner. We pray to know our sins and to repent of them and to know God's love and forgiveness. Awake in us a true love for the Sacrament of Penance and the courage to begin again.

I ask you especially for [*here name your intention*]

Our Father - Hail Mary - Glory Be

FOURTH DAY

You listened to Blessed John of Avila when he told you to stop punishing yourself. May we also hear the voice of holy men and women in our lives and especially the voice of the Church, believing that is how God speaks to us. Grant us the humility to be able to obey.

I ask you especially for [*here name your intention*]

Our Father - Hail Mary - Glory Be

FIFTH DAY

You worked tirelessly for the sick, spending your life in the service of others. We ask that you intercede for us that we may be healed of our spiritual sicknesses.

I ask you especially for [*here name your intention*]

Our Father - Hail Mary - Glory Be

SIXTH DAY

You founded hospitals and worked to support them. We pray for all who work in hospitals, especially in areas where there is no funding. May they always trust in God and see him in their patients.

I ask you especially for [*here name your intention*]

Our Father - Hail Mary - Glory Be

SEVENTH DAY

You said, "Labour without ceasing to do all the good works you can while you still have the time". Grant us the grace to convert today.

I ask you especially for [*here name your intention*]

Our Father - Hail Mary - Glory Be

EIGHTH DAY

Before you worked for the sick, you sold religious books. We ask your blessing on all who make the Word known through the written word or other media.

I ask you especially for [*here name your intention*]

Our Father - Hail Mary - Glory Be

NINTH DAY

We pray for the dying, especially those who are dying alone. We ask you, their patron, to intercede for them before God.

I ask you especially for [*here name your intention*]

Our Father - Hail Mary - Glory Be

Novena to St Patrick

FEAST DAY: 17TH MARCH

Although best known as patron saint of Ireland, St Patrick was in fact born in what is now England, son of a minor Roman official in (probably) the mid-fourth century. He was kidnapped by pirates as a boy, and taken as a slave to Ireland. He escaped after six years, but on his return to Britain discerned a call from God to bring Christ to the island of his captivity. The details of his later career are surrounded with many fabulous and legendary accretions, but we can be certain that he preached the gospel widely in Ireland, was bishop to the Christian community there and took a central role in the conversion of Ireland from paganism to Christianity. Devotion to him soon became very widespread, and from the eighth century onwards he was considered patron of Ireland.

This prayer to St Patrick can be said over nine days as a novena.

PRAYER TO ST PATRICK

God our Father, you sent St Patrick to preach your glory to the people of Ireland. By the help of his prayers, may all Christians proclaim your love to all men. Grant this through our Lord Jesus Christ, your Son, who lives and reigns with you and the Holy Spirit, one God, for ever and ever.

Amen

Novena to St Joseph

FEAST DAY: 19TH MARCH; 1ST MAY
(ST JOSEPH THE WORKER)

Joseph, [Mary's] husband, ... was a righteous man (Mt 1:19).

St Joseph, husband of the Virgin Mary and foster-father of Jesus Christ, is one of the best-loved and most powerful intercessors. He is particularly invoked by husbands and fathers, by men in general, by those looking for work, by those with problems at work and by those looking for somewhere to live. St Joseph is also known as the Protector of the Holy Church, since he was entrusted by God with the care of the Virgin Mary (who is an image of the Church) and the child Jesus. He is also a strong guard against the assaults of the Enemy. Not least, he is the patron of a holy death, and so is often invoked by wthe dying.

62

FIRST DAY ✓

As husband to Mary and foster-father to Jesus, you are an example of chastity, humility, faithfulness, and obedience to the Word of God; intercede for us so that we, too, may be given these virtues in our lives, and may witness to God's power working in our weakness.

I ask you especially for [*here name your intention*]

Our Father - Hail Mary - Glory Be

SECOND DAY ✓

You were chosen by God to be guardian and protector of Jesus and Mary; protect our homes and families. We ask your intercession for husbands and fathers, and for all those who bear responsibility for others.

I ask you especially for [*here name your intention*]

Our Father - Hail Mary - Glory Be

THIRD DAY ✓

You know what it is like to have your own plans and expectations overturned by God's plans; help us to trust that he knows better than we do what we really need.

I ask you especially for [*here name your intention*]

Our Father - Hail Mary - Glory Be

FOURTH DAY ✒️

You knew what it was like to be exiled from your homeland, to be without a stable place to live; we ask your intercession for those who are looking for somewhere to live, and for those who are far from home.

I ask you especially for [*here name your intention*]

Our Father - Hail Mary - Glory Be

FIFTH DAY ✒️

When the child Jesus went missing, and was found in the Temple, you knew the pain of loss, and the joy of finding again; intercede for all who suffer the anguish of separation or bereavement, and help them to know that, like Jesus, we may all be found safe in our Father's house.

I ask you especially for [*here name your intention*]

Our Father - Hail Mary - Glory Be

SIXTH DAY ✒️

As you watched over Jesus and Mary on earth, now you are the Protector of the Universal Church; we ask your intercession for all who bear the name of Christian.

I ask you especially for [*here name your intention*]

Our Father - Hail Mary - Glory Be

SEVENTH DAY

In the silent witness of your life in Nazareth, the Church sees in you the model of our interior life with Christ; help us to pray, and to put our relationship with Jesus in prayer at the heart of our lives.

I ask you especially for [*here name your intention*]

Our Father - Hail Mary - Glory Be

EIGHTH DAY

You know what it is to work; help us to see the dignity and value of the tasks entrusted to us, and to believe that by humbly and faithfully doing what we have to do, we too may give glory to God whether the world recognises us or not.

I ask you especially for [*here name your intention*]

Our Father - Hail Mary - Glory Be

NINTH DAY

You are the model and patron of Christian death; we ask your intercession for all those who are close to death, and the grace of a holy death for them and for ourselves.

I ask you especially for [*here name your intention*]

Our Father - Hail Mary - Glory Be

Novena to St Benedict

FEAST DAY: 21ST MARCH; 11TH JULY
(AS PATRON OF EUROPE)

Benedict was a learned Roman of the fifth–sixth century who, inspired by the great monastic saints of Egypt, left public life to seek God in the wilderness (the closest equivalent to the Egyptian desert), living in community with others who felt a similar calling. They lived under a Rule which Benedict drew up, balancing work and prayer in solitude with a dedication to the great "work of God", the daily round of common prayer based on Scripture, especially the Psalms.

Like the saints of the desert, he was constantly aware of the attempts of the devil to destroy his life with God, and was constant in his prayer to God against this peril. His powerful protection against the Enemy continues, and is often symbolised by the Benedictine Medal or Cross.

Benedict is regarded as the father of all monastic orders in the Western Church, and is one of the patrons of Europe. The monasteries that drew their life from his *Rule* played an essential, and providential, role in preserving and transmitting the learning and culture of the classical world, and in forming the religious life of Western Christendom. Most monks in the West today still live by a version of the *Rule* Benedict compiled almost a millennium and a half ago.

FIRST DAY

You were clear in your resolve to seek God alone, to be detached from anything that might impede this, and to persevere in these intentions. Help us to have the same determination to become the people – the saints – God sees us truly to be.

I ask you especially for [*here name your intention*]

Our Father - Hail Mary - Glory Be

SECOND DAY

You found God by being obedient to a rule of life, and in love for your brothers in Christ. Help us to keep our lives according to God's plan, and to love especially those we find most difficult.

I ask you especially for [*here name your intention*]

Our Father - Hail Mary - Glory Be

THIRD DAY

You were a father to the monks of your community, and remain the spiritual father of the whole Benedictine family. Help all Christian fathers – whether physical or spiritual – and all who exercise authority, to be icons of God's loving fatherhood.

I ask you especially for [*here name your intention*]

Our Father - Hail Mary - Glory Be

FOURTH DAY

You drew up a Rule for the common life of your brothers to help them love God and their neighbour; help us to be lovingly obedient to those over us, firm yet kind to those in our charge, and thus to grow in love of God and of our brothers and sisters in Christ.

I ask you especially for [*here name your intention*]

Our Father - Hail Mary - Glory Be

FIFTH DAY

Through you, God worked miracles of healing and deliverance; help us to recognise God's mighty deeds in our lives and in the world around us, and to be ourselves a sign to others of God's love and power, and to make this love present in God's world.

I ask you especially for [*here name your intention*]

Our Father - Hail Mary - Glory Be

SIXTH DAY

You were granted even in this life a vision of God's glory, and were able to see both the insignificance of much that we worry about, and our supreme value in God's eyes. Help us to see with the eyes of faith, especially the loving care with which our Father treats us.

I ask you especially for [*here name your intention*]

Our Father - Hail Mary - Glory Be

SEVENTH DAY

You spread the gospel by fearless preaching and your evident holiness of life. Help us to lead others to Christ by what we do as much as by what we say.

I ask you especially for [*here name your intention*]

Our Father - Hail Mary - Glory Be

EIGHTH DAY

You remain a strong protector against all the assaults and wiles of the Evil One. Strengthen us against his deceits and attacks, and help us not to believe the lying tales he spins around the facts of our lives, but to see in them only the hand of God, our loving Father.

I ask you especially for [*here name your intention*]

Our Father - Hail Mary - Glory Be

NINTH DAY

You held fast to God to the end, sustained by your faith in his promises, particularly by the promise of true happiness in the life that does not end or fail. Help us, too, to hear God's promises to us, and know that he will never cheat us, but desires only our true happiness.

I ask you especially for [*here name your intention*]

Our Father - Hail Mary - Glory Be

*A*nnunciation
25TH MARCH

For much of Christian history, this feast – celebrated on 25th March, nine months before Christmas – marked the beginning of the year. This may seem odd at first sight, and our modern adoption of 1st January much more obvious and straightforward, but there is a profound truth here: the Annunciation, the visit of the angel Gabriel to the young girl, Mary of Nazareth, and her response to his offer from God, is the very turning-point of human history. At this moment, when Mary says "yes" to God, the Incarnation – God's life with us, as one of us – begins, in the womb of a virgin. From this moment, everything is different. God is amongst us; God is on our side. Just as Jesus grew slowly in the months before his human birth, so he grows in us – God's gift of undying life – slowly, once we accept his word into our hearts.

Every time we say the *Hail Mary*, we remember, and make present, the message of God to Mary, given through the angel; and we ask that this come to pass in us, too, in God's time and with the watchful prayers of the Virgin to help us.

To finish this novena on the eve of the feast, you should begin it on 16th March; to finish on the feast itself, begin on 17th March.

No one addresses anyone today using the greeting "Hail!", except humorously or in badly scripted historical drama ("Hail Caesar! The Armies of the North salute you!", and so on). But originally it was a quite normal greeting; it is from the Old English *Wes thu hael*, "May you be well". Here it translates a Greek word, χαιρε, which is the corresponding normal greeting amongst speakers of New Testament Greek, and means "Rejoice, be glad". Both the English and the Greek words share a basic sense of wishing for another person wholeness and fulness of life: health and happiness, broadly understood, are two ways of expressing the same thing. "May you be the person God knows you to be" is a cumbersome way of expressing this, but might be the best way to look at the ultimate implications of these greetings. For Mary, the fulness of life lies in accepting the role God has chosen her for, as mother of his Son; for us, too, true life is in saying yes to God and his plans for us, however unlikely or plain ridiculous these may seem.

Father, help me to accept the fulness of life.
I ask you especially for [*here name your intention*]

Our Father - Hail Mary - Glory Be

SECOND DAY: MARY ✓
....

The name Mary is our form of the Aramaic name
Maryam, which derives from the Hebrew *Miriam*. Its
Latin and Greek form is *Maria*. The meaning of the
name is obscure; it may be related to an Egyptian root
mr, "love", or *myr*, "beloved", but other etymologies
have been suggested.

   The first Miriam found in Scripture is the elder sister
of Moses, who hid him in the bulrushes where he was
found by Pharaoh's daughter; she also suggested Moses's
mother as a nurse for the infant. Later, Miriam sings the
song of triumph over Pharaoh's army drowned in the
Red Sea, a song we still sing each year at the Easter Vigil
(see *Ex* 15:20–21). Mary, mother of Jesus, echoes these
later roles: she takes the child Jesus into safety in Egypt
from Herod; she sings her *Magnificat* celebrating God's
triumph through the poor and unregarded.

Father, help me to know Mary as my mother.
I ask you especially for [*here name your intention*]

Our Father - Hail Mary - Glory Be

The next three words in English, "full of grace", are two words in Latin (*gratia plena*) and in Greek, only a single word: κεχαριτωμένη. This has been sometimes translated "highly favoured" (which, in at least one well-known Christmas carol, has become "highly flavoured (gravy)" to generations of schoolboys), but "full of grace" brings out the sense well enough.

Full: empty of self-will and her own plans, Mary is able to be filled by God. His life takes root in her to such an extent that, uniquely, she becomes physically fruitful: God comes forth from her in the person of the child Jesus. We, too, are called to be filled with God, although in our case the birth this presages is that of God's life in us – the life of undying love, of love that death cannot conquer, of life that death cannot quench. We, too, are to bring Christ to the world, but not as a physically separate person like Mary's son, the child Jesus, but through the medium of our own minds and bodies, our own joys and sorrows and kindnesses, which allow us to be in a strong sense Christ for those around us.

Father, let Jesus be born in me.
I ask you especially for [*here name your intention*]

Our Father - Hail Mary - Glory Be

FOURTH DAY: OF ✓

This is a small and usually overlooked word, but it
is charged with mystery. If one thing is "of" another,
it is somehow enfolded in it, it belongs to it, it issues
from it, and yet it has its own separate being. Things
both belong to each other – are included in each other
– and are yet distinct one from another. We are both
one and many. This may sound hopelessly vague and
"mystical", but in fact we are all of us, even those who
think of ourselves as ruthlessly pragmatic and practical,
effortlessly comfortable with this concept, since we
have been unconsciously deploying it, since childhood,
whenever we say "of". This relationship, encompassing
both inclusion and separateness, may stand as a type, a
pattern, of our relationship with God. We are "of" God;
God is "of" us.

Father, help me to know that you are with me.
I ask you especially for [*here name your intention*]

Our Father - Hail Mary - Glory Be

FIFTH DAY: GRACE ✓

Theologians have made much of the concept of grace,
analysing it into various technical categories (created
and uncreated, prevenient, habitual and actual,
sufficient and efficacious) that most will find either
baffling or pernickety. In sum, though, grace means
the action or presence of God in the Christian life.
Some writers talk about "graces", meaning by that a
particular manifestation of God's presence or action in
the experience of the Christian. In both senses, Mary

is full of grace: God is present and acts through her, and she witnesses God's action and presence in all she experiences. We are called to be like her, who "stored up all these things in her heart" (*Lk* 2:51).

Father, help me to be alive to your presence in my life. I ask you especially for [*here name your intention*]

Our Father - Hail Mary - Glory Be

SIXTH DAY: THE LORD

The Jewish people reckoned the name of God, as told to Moses, too holy to be spoken aloud; only once a year, in the Holy of Holies in the Temple on the Day of Atonement (Yom Kippur), might the High Priest utter this name. When reading any passage of Scripture in which this name (the Holy Tetragrammaton, the four letters) appears, one says instead another title of God, most usually *Adonai*, "the Lord". *Adonai*, which in Greek is rendered *kyrios*, is the one to whom all things belong, for whom all things are made, to whose ends all things work, knowingly or not. God is Lord of all things: everything we are, have, experience or witness, all these things belong to him, and reveal his hand to the eye and heart willing to see it; and all things ultimately do his will, whether they know it or not.

Father, let me welcome you as Lord of my life. I ask you especially for [*here name your intention*]

Our Father - Hail Mary - Glory Be

SEVENTH DAY: IS

This is another small word of immense importance.
Gabriel declares to Mary that "the Lord is with thee":
"is" signifies that the presence of God is not something
in our memory (although we should remember his
mighty deeds with us and throughout salvation history)
or in some wished-for future, but something that
happens now, at the very moment I am writing this
sentence, or you are reading it. In all the events, great
or small, of our daily lives, God is there; God sends us
all these things to touch our hearts through them, if
only we are willing to see it. God's time is always now.
By saying the Lord "is" with her, the angel declares
that God is present and acting at that very moment. He
joins together two things, God and the Virgin Mary, by
naming them and joining those names with "is". Words,
we should remember, are potent things; we should not
use them lightly.

Father, help me to be present in this moment, which is
your moment.
I ask you especially for [*here name your intention*]

Our Father - Hail Mary - Glory Be

EIGHTH DAY: WITH

God is "with" Mary: he is both intimately present to
her, as he is to us all, but in her case, with the added
dimension of the physical presence of Jesus in her womb,
and also "with" her in the related sense that he is on her
side: God stands "with" her in all the events of her life,
and lends her his strength and love. So it is for us: God is

with us, in our hearts and in all the people and events we meet; but he is also with us, on our side, a strong helper in distress and the one who rejoices in our happiness. God is not neutral or indifferent; he is our passionate advocate and defender, and the merciful father who welcomes us home.

Father, be with me all the days of my life.
I ask you especially for [*here name your intention*]

Our Father - Hail Mary - Glory Be

NINTH DAY: THEE

We may imagine the old second person pronouns "thee" and "thou" are somehow ceremonious or formal, and belong to high etiquette and stilted courtesy. In fact almost the opposite is true. These were intimate forms, words used between parent and child, husband and wife, brother and sister. In many languages even today, asking someone to address you by the less formal pronoun (for which the French, for example, even have a particular word: *tutoyer*) is a strong gesture of friendship. So when the angel calls Mary "thee" rather than "you", he is showing her and us that God is as close to us as a mother or father is, as a sibling, as a beloved friend. This is not an archaism preserved out of unthinking reverence for what is old and accustomed, but a sign of God's loving closeness to Mary, and to each of us.

Father, help me to know you love me.
I ask you especially for [*here name your intention*]

Our Father - Hail Mary - Glory Be

Easter

Easter is the centre of the whole Christian year, the point around which all the Church's worship and belief turns. To bring out the riches of this feast, it is extended into an "octave" – that is, the following week, which together with Easter Sunday itself makes eight days, a number that to the ancients signified completion or fulfilment. During these days, the Gospels at Mass present the various appearances of the risen Jesus after his Resurrection, and show the ways he transforms the lives of his disciples, who (unsurprisingly) were confused and distraught after his crucifixion and death. Jesus, risen from the dead, comes to them and renews them; he grants them a share in his new life, the life of Easter, life that has passed through death and destroyed it. This life, eternal life, he offers to us, too, not merely in some abstract future state, but here and now, as we are, in all our defeats and confusions. During this octave, we can place ourselves within these Gospels, and allow Jesus to come to us, as he came to his first disciples.

The last day of the Easter Octave, known as the Second Sunday of Easter, was named by St John Paul II as the Sunday of the Divine Mercy. We are invited to make our own the doubts and fears of the disciples, and to offer them to God our Father, who is rich in mercy, and who, through Jesus, sends us the Spirit that allows us to know ourselves forgiven, and in our turn to have mercy on others.

FIRST DAY: THE EASTER VIGIL

Mt 28:1–10; *Mk* 16:1–7; *Lk* 24:1–12
(The women go to the tomb)

It is dawn, the day after the Sabbath, and the women who followed Jesus are on their way to the tomb. They are coming as early as they can without breaking God's Law of Sabbath rest. The angel tells them, "Do not be afraid. He is not here, he is risen". Then, when they meet Jesus himself, he repeats the message: "Do not be afraid".

Father, often I put off or delay what I need to do; help me to have the same zeal as these disciples, and not to be mastered by my fears.
I ask you especially for [*here name your intention*]

Our Father - Hail Mary - Glory Be

SECOND DAY: EASTER DAY

Jn 20:1–9
(Peter and John run to the tomb)

When they hear the baffling news that Jesus's body has disappeared, Peter and John run to see for themselves. There is a strong emphasis on the factual nature of their witness: first one looks in, then the other goes in, and they see specific cloths in particular places. The Church has always insisted on the physical fact of the Resurrection, but also on its mysterious nature. The life that Jesus passes to, the life we are offered, is rich and strange, but rooted in the same physical world we know.

Father, help me not to be slow to follow the truth; help me to live the life you promise.
I ask you especially for [*here name your intention*]

Our Father - Hail Mary - Glory Be

THIRD DAY: EASTER MONDAY ✔️

Mt 28:8–15
(Jesus meets the women in the garden)

After meeting the angel, the women set off to tell the others. Almost at once, they run into Jesus himself. He gives them another message for the disciples. Meanwhile, the chief priests and soldiers come up with a cover story about a stolen body: "to this day that is the story among the Jews".

We can be very ready to explain away the apparently clear action of God in our lives. Human beings are very good at refusing to see the big picture. We should not be credulous or gullible, or see extraordinary miracles everywhere: God generally works through "ordinary" things (what the philosophers call "secondary causes"). But we should not dismiss events lightly; God is at work in exactly the small and overlooked things; the day-to-day action of our lives is charged with his presence, if only we have eyes to see it.

Father, help me to see your work.
I ask you especially for [*here name your intention*]

Our Father - Hail Mary - Glory Be

FOURTH DAY: EASTER TUESDAY

Jn 20:11–18
(Mary of Magdala meets Jesus)

In the story given in John's Gospel, whilst Peter and
John are running back with their shocking news, Mary of
Magdala is still hanging about the garden. She despairs
of finding Jesus's body; and when she meets him "she
did not recognise him". Only when he calls her by
name does she know him. Then she seems to want to
take physical hold of him, which he gently discourages.
Perhaps we should see here that what is most important
is not the precise physical character of the Resurrection,
but the way in which we find ourselves truly only when
named by God. Only God knows us; only he can help us
to know ourselves, and thus be ourselves, and be capable
of true joy and true sorrow.

Father, help me to meet you and recognise you.
I ask you especially for [*here name your intention*]

Our Father - Hail Mary - Glory Be

FIFTH DAY: EASTER WEDNESDAY

Lk 24:13–35
(The road to Emmaus)

We don't know exactly where Emmaus is, but we do
know that when the disciples were on their way there,
they were going the wrong way. Jesus falls into step
with them, and eventually turns them around. He turns
them, in fact, both in the literal sense that they retrace
their steps back to Jerusalem, and in the metaphorical
sense that he takes their depression, their frustration and

disappointment, and turns them into joy and zeal. Their encounter culminates, and Jesus is revealed, when he breaks bread with them. Until this moment, the fact that they had already heard the news about the Resurrection had made no difference to them.

If we have taken a wrong turning, Jesus comes to us in the Scriptures, in the Eucharist, in a chance encounter with an apparent stranger, to set us on the right path again. No amount of factual knowledge of itself will do this: only meeting the Risen Lord.

Father, help me to see things as they truly are, not as they suit my own narrative, especially if that is one of despair or self-pity.
I ask you especially for [*here name your intention*]

Our Father - Hail Mary - Glory Be

SIXTH DAY: EASTER THURSDAY ✔

Lk 24:35–48
(Jesus is not a ghost)

This Gospel follows immediately on from the previous one. The news from the road to Emmaus is corroborated by the news from Jerusalem itself: Jesus has appeared to Peter. But none of this prevents a similar collapse of nerve when Jesus himself comes amongst them all. He has to take strong steps to prove he is really there. Touch me, he says; watch me eat. Jesus is not a ghost. He opens the Scriptures to them: all that has happened is set out there – and also what must happen now. The call to repent and be forgiven must be brought to the whole world, beginning right there, where they are, in Jerusalem.

Sometimes, even after repeated evidence, we cannot believe in a God who loves us and takes an interest in what we do, who wants to save us from our sins and mistakes and fears. Jesus shows us here that God is patient, that if we open the Scriptures, he will speak to us there. And he also tells us that the good news of forgiveness needs to be heard, first of all, where we ourselves are.

Father, help me to know forgiveness; help my disbelief. I ask you especially for [*here name your intention*]

Our Father - Hail Mary - Glory Be

SEVENTH DAY: EASTER FRIDAY

Jn 21:1–14
(The disciples go fishing on the Sea of Tiberias)

This story is tacked on to the end of John's Gospel in a sort of appendix. It shows us, again, how hard it is for Jesus's disciples to stay persuaded of anything. After all the excitement of the garden, Emmaus and the Upper Room, Simon Peter and the rest have gone back to their old life on the seashore. They spend a fruitless night fishing, probably because they can think of nothing else to do. Then a stranger calls out instructions, they make a huge catch, and they realise it must be Jesus. He cooks them breakfast.

We see, again, how easily we can slip back into our old ways, our old habits and niggles and sins. But we see, also, how Jesus comes to find us, and makes himself known in the most apparently ordinary events. The turning-point of the Gospel passage is the disciple's cry "It is the Lord!" After that, the whole encounter is charged with meaning (breakfast is more than just breakfast).

Father, help me not to lose heart; come to find me when
I lose my way.
I ask you especially for [*here name your intention*]

Our Father - Hail Mary - Glory Be

EIGHTH DAY: EASTER SATURDAY

Mk 16:9–15
(A summary of Jesus's appearances)

This passage is thought by most scholars to be something
added to Mark's Gospel at some point after it was first
written. This doesn't make it any less a text through
which God speaks to us. It gives a brisk and telling
summary of Jesus's appearances and his disciples'
reactions. First, they didn't believe Mary Magdalene;
then they didn't believe the disciples coming back from
Emmaus. So Jesus appears to them all in person. He tells
them off for being so pig-headed and distrusting. Then
he tells them to "proclaim the Good News to
all creation".

Like the disciples, I sometimes refuse to believe, and
discount others' testimony. Father, be patient with my
obstinacy; help me to hear the Good News, and share it
with others.
I ask you especially for [*here name your intention*]

Our Father - Hail Mary - Glory Be

Jn 20:19–31
(Jesus gives them the Holy Spirit. Doubting Thomas)

We end, on Divine Mercy Sunday, with another example of God's patience. Jesus first dispels the fears and doubts of the assembled disciples; then he comes back a week later, on the octave day of his Resurrection, to do the same for Thomas, who is sulking and sceptical.

First, Jesus gives his disciples his own spirit, the Spirit that allows us to love and forgive where we know for a certain fact no forgiveness or love is possible. God, the merciful Father, loves us and forgives us in this way, no matter what we have done or how little we think of ourselves. In God's eyes, we are, all of us, beyond price. He loves us, who feel ourselves unlovable, so we may love others. Like Thomas, we can refuse to believe this on the testimony of others; God will give us proof, if we have the courage to ask for it: and that means, perhaps, acting as if we can do what we know we cannot.

Father, help me to know myself loved and forgiven; help me to love and forgive others, as you have loved me. I ask you especially for [*here name your intention*]

Our Father - Hail Mary - Glory Be

Novena Prayer to St George

We all know St George as patron of England and tamer of dragons. The facts of his life are obscure, but he seems to have been a Roman soldier, probably of the late third century, who was martyred at Lydda in Palestine during the great persecution by the Emperor Diocletian, probably for refusing to renounce Christ and worship the Emperor as a god. His cult was very widespread in the east from that time on; when English soldiers went to the Holy Land on Crusade, they were inspired by this warrior saint; Richard the Lionheart put himself and his army under St George's protection. From then on his popularity in England only grew: Edward III founded the Order of the Garter, with St George as patron, in 1348; Henry V called on St George for aid before the great victory of Agincourt in 1415. Thereafter he was secure as patron of England (although the patronage of two Anglo-Saxon Saint-Kings, Edward the Confessor and Edmund of East Anglia, was not neglected), and his popularity survived the spoliation and wreckage of the Reformation.

This prayer to St George can be said for nine days as a novena.

PRAYER TO ST GEORGE

Faithful servant of God and invincible martyr, St George, inflamed with a burning love of Christ, you fought against the dragon of pride, falsehood and deceit. Neither pain nor torture, nor the sword nor death could part you from the love of Christ.

I implore you for the sake of this love to help me by your intercession to overcome the temptations that surround me, and to bear bravely the trials that oppress me, so that I may patiently carry my cross and let neither distress nor difficulty separate me from the love of our Lord, Jesus Christ.

Amen

Novena to St Peregrine

FEAST DAY: 1ST MAY

Peregrine Laziosi was born in 1265 in Forlì, a small town north-east of Florence now probably most familiar as the destination of budget flights to Bologna (which is in fact forty miles away). In the late thirteenth century, however, Forlì was best known as a stronghold of opposition to the Papacy. In 1282, Pope Martin IV excommunicated the whole town. In an effort to resolve this situation, the Pope sent Fr (later St) Philip Benizi, who was head of the Servites, a newly founded order of friars who were much involved in caring for the sick, to preach to the townsfolk. Philip's visit was not a success: he was roughed up by a mob and thrown out of the town. One of those who assaulted him was the young Peregrine Laziosi.

This incident was a turning-point for Peregrine. He was gradually overcome with remorse for what he had done, and this led him to turn to God. He eventually joined the Servites, Philip's own order, as a lay-brother, when he was thirty years old.

He threw himself into their work of caring for the sick, especially during the frequent outbreaks of plague. Sometime later, Peregrine himself fell ill, but not with the plague. He had a malignant growth on his leg that was so severe that the doctors proposed to amputate the whole limb. Peregrine spent a night in prayer before a crucifix, after which he was miraculously cured. As a result, he is considered a patron of cancer patients. Very many people can witness to the results of his intercession, whether physical healing or the ability to accept their sufferings in peace. Peregrine died of old age in 1345; he was canonised in 1726.

This prayer to St Peregrine can be said over nine days as a novena.

✒ PRAYER TO ST PEREGRINE

God our Father, you are a God who loves me. I thank you for the many blessings you have given me. In loving trust I place myself before you. Let your healing love fill my life.

Give me the strength to understand my illness. Forgive my failures in carrying the cross. In St Peregrine you give us an example of patient suffering. Supported, then, by his prayers, I ask that the suffering I endure may be a source of life both now and for ever. I make this prayer through Christ, your Son.

Amen

Novena to the English Martyrs

✓ FEAST DAY: 4TH MAY; (FORMERLY 25TH OCTOBER)

The English Martyrs are those English Catholics who suffered death for the faith between the time of Henry VIII's breach with Rome in the early 1530s and the late seventeenth century. During this time, it was illegal even to attend Mass; priests celebrating the sacraments could be executed for treason. It was impossible to be educated as a Catholic, let alone train as a priest, in England; so thousands of English Catholics went abroad as exiles, to Italy, Spain, Portugal and the Low Countries, so as eventually to return to England to keep the faith alive.

The exact number of martyrs for the faith in England during these years is known only to God. Of those of whom we have record, over forty have been canonised, and several hundred beatified. There are some hundreds more whose causes are still open, or have been postponed owing to incomplete evidence.

They were a very disparate group of people – many were priests executed for saying Mass, others laity who helped them or simply refused to deny their faith under persecution. They came from all classes of society, rich and poor, educated and unlettered; but they were alike in placing their faith above any material advantage, and indeed valuing it more than life itself. Their witness to Christ is one of the glories of the Church in England, and their intercession for us now one of its greatest treasures.

FIRST DAY

You endured exile from your country and your families for love of God and the faith. Help all who live in exile today; and help us to value our faith above our securities.

I ask you especially for [*here name your intention*]

Our Father - Hail Mary - Glory Be

SECOND DAY

You had the courage to witness for Christ before men without counting the cost. Help us to have this same courage in our day.

I ask you especially for [*here name your intention*]

Our Father - Hail Mary - Glory Be

THIRD DAY

You loved England, your country, enough to suffer exile, persecution and death in order to proclaim Jesus Christ here. Intercede for England, and for all who are called to proclaim Christ here today.

I ask you especially for [*here name your intention*]

Our Father - Hail Mary - Glory Be

FOURTH DAY ✓

You had a great love of the sacraments, especially the Eucharist, for which you were ready to give up your lives. Help us to have something of this same love, and never to take for granted these great gifts of God.

I ask you especially for [*here name your intention*]

Our Father - Hail Mary - Glory Be

FIFTH DAY ✓

You had a profound love of truth, and would not deny it even though this meant suffering and death. Give us the same love of truth, and zeal for the faith, that you had.

I ask you especially for [*here name your intention*]

Our Father - Hail Mary - Glory Be

SIXTH DAY ✓

At the heart of all you did and endured was the love of God. Help us to know this love, and to pass it to our neighbour.

I ask you especially for [*here name your intention*]

Our Father - Hail Mary - Glory Be

SEVENTH DAY ✓

You had such compassion for sinners that you risked all that they might be converted and live. Help us not to judge others, but to show God's merciful love to all; help us, too, not to despair of our own sins, but to lay them humbly before the Father who loves us.

I ask you especially for [*here name your intention*]

Our Father - Hail Mary - Glory Be

EIGHTH DAY

You readily forgave those who persecuted you, and offered your sufferings for their conversion. Intercede for us to have something of the same spirit in the face of injustice or persecution.

I ask you especially for [*here name your intention*]

Our Father - Hail Mary - Glory Be

NINTH DAY

You persevered in your witness to the end, and joyfully accepted the sufferings that opened to you the Kingdom. Intercede for us, and for those who are near to death, or undergoing a trial of faith, that we, too, may have the grace of final perseverance.

I ask you especially for [*here name your intention*]

Our Father - Hail Mary - Glory Be

Novena to St Damien of Molokai

FEAST DAY: 10TH MAY

Damien de Veuster was born in Belgium in 1840 into a Flemish-speaking family of grain merchants. His parents wanted him to go into the family business but when he wanted to join the Congregation of the Sacred Hearts of Jesus and Mary, like his older brother, they did not stand in his way. Damien's older brother was meant to go to Hawaii to the missions, but when he became ill Damien arranged to take his place. Once ordained and given his own parish, Damien was full of energy – evangelising, building churches, farming, ministering to his parishioners and debunking voodoo. Later he volunteered to be the resident priest on Molokai, a horrific leper colony, where he set about the physical and spiritual care of the sufferers, changing their lives until he himself died of the disease sixteen years later. He was only forty-nine. He was beatified in 1995 and canonised in 2009. He is considered patron of those with leprosy, those suffering from HIV/AIDS and all those cast out by society. He is also patron of the American state of Hawaii.

FIRST DAY

You were sent away to school in a region where you didn't speak the language and people tried to bully you because of it. We pray for those who are bullied whether at school or at work or in whatever situation. May they emulate you in not accepting it.

I ask you especially for [*here name your intention*]

Our Father - Hail Mary - Glory Be

SECOND DAY

You loved your parents but you loved God more. You knew God was calling you to the priesthood and you answered that call although you knew your parents had other hopes for you. May we put God first and never refuse his call because of any other attachment.

I ask you especially for [*here name your intention*]

Our Father - Hail Mary - Glory Be

THIRD DAY

You gave up family, country and language to go and evangelise, knowing that you would never see your home or family again. Accord us something of your courage and clear-sightedness.

I ask you especially for [*here name your intention*]

Our Father - Hail Mary - Glory Be

FOURTH DAY

In Hawaii you worked tirelessly, giving everything to make Christ known. We pray that we can value our faith as much as you did.

I ask you especially for [*here name your intention*]

Our Father - Hail Mary - Glory Be

FIFTH DAY

When you went to Molokai you were prepared to give up your life to serve others. Help us to understand this Christian love and to begin to desire it for ourselves.

I ask you especially for [*here name your intention*]

Our Father - Hail Mary - Glory Be

SIXTH DAY

When you first arrived in the leper colony you were revolted by the patients, but you didn't let them see this and continued to work for them. We pray to have this spirit so we can put others first, thinking of their needs and feelings rather than our own.

I ask you especially for [*here name your intention*]

Our Father - Hail Mary - Glory Be

SEVENTH DAY

You didn't deal well with bureaucracy and often offended people by your brusqueness. You had to learn to ask forgiveness. May we never think God cannot use us because of our character, and may we, too, have the humility to ask pardon of those we have offended.

I ask you especially for [*here name your intention*]

Our Father - Hail Mary - Glory Be

EIGHTH DAY

You suffered greatly on Molokai because you were cut off from the sacraments, especially the Sacrament of Reconciliation. May we understand the importance of this sacrament and have recourse to it often.

I ask you especially for [*here name your intention*]

Our Father - Hail Mary - Glory Be

NINTH DAY

You suffered terrible loneliness and turned to the Blessed Sacrament for comfort. We pray for all who are lonely. Help us to give time to anyone we know who is lonely, and to give time to Christ in the Blessed Sacrament.

I ask you especially for [*here name your intention*]

Our Father - Hail Mary - Glory Be

Novena to St Dymphna

FEAST DAY: 15TH MAY

Tradition says St Dymphna was a seventh-century Irish princess, daughter of a Christian mother and a pagan father. Tragically her mother died when Dymphna was a young teenager, and Dymphna's father, the balance of his mind disturbed, tried to marry his own daughter. Dymphna went for help to a priest, Fr Gerebran, who, understanding that the king, her father, had the power to do whatever he wanted, advised her to flee the country. Fr Gerebran and two others escaped with Dymphna to Gheel in modern-day Belgium. Her father tracked her down, however, and when she refused to return with him he killed Fr Gerebran and Dymphna, cutting off their heads with his sword. They were buried in tombs by the local people and soon there were reports of the miraculous healing at Dymphna's tomb of the mentally ill and those suffering from epilepsy. More and more mentally ill people came to the shrine and the local people began to look after them in their homes, a tradition which continues today. St Dymphna is patron of those suffering mental illness or epilepsy, and also patron of family harmony.

To help the family to love one another. Please Someday Soon

FIRST DAY

St Dymphna, one of your parents was Christian but the other was not and you lived with two different views of the world. We pray for all families that are divided by religion. Intercede for them and bring harmony; help them to live together in love and respect.

I ask you especially for [*here name your intention*]

Our Father - Hail Mary - Glory Be

SECOND DAY

You lost your mother when you were a young teenager. We pray for all children who have lost one or both parents through death, divorce or other separation. We ask you to comfort them and help them to experience God's love for them.

I ask you especially for [*here name your intention*]

Our Father - Hail Mary - Glory Be

THIRD DAY

Your father was destroyed by grief. We pray for all those who grieve, especially those who do not know the hope of eternal life or those whose grief is affecting their sanity. Intercede for them that they can receive hope and comfort.

I ask you especially for [*here name your intention*]

Our Father - Hail Mary - Glory Be

FOURTH DAY ✓

You had to flee your homeland. We pray for all refugees and those escaping from danger, especially danger in their own families. Intercede that they may find people to help and succour them.

I ask you especially for [*here name your intention*]

Our Father - Hail Mary - Glory Be

FIFTH DAY ✓

You had to run away from home to avoid incest. We pray for all those who have been sexually abused, especially those who have been abused in their own families. We pray for the healing of their self-worth.

I ask you especially for [*here name your intention*]

Our Father - Hail Mary - Glory Be

SIXTH DAY ✓

You are the patron of those with mental illness. We pray for all those who suffer from mental illness and for their families. We pray that they do not lose hope or sight of God.

I ask you especially for [*here name your intention*]

Our Father - Hail Mary - Glory Be

SEVENTH DAY

As the sick came to your shrine to be cured, people began to care for and look after them. We pray for all those who work with the mentally ill. We pray that they see in their charges the face of Christ, and always guard their dignity.

I ask you especially for [*here name your intention*]

Our Father - Hail Mary - Glory Be

EIGHTH DAY

You lost your mother to death but your father to mental illness and abuse. We pray for all those who have lost their parents to mental illness or addiction, and for all whose parents have treated them badly. Intercede for them that they may be able to forgive.

I ask you especially for [*here name your intention*]

Our Father - Hail Mary - Glory Be

NINTH DAY

We ask you to intercede for us all, that we might be cured of our delusions and misconceptions, whether about ourselves or others. We pray for a healing of our family history.

I ask you especially for [*here name your intention*]

Our Father - Hail Mary - Glory Be

Novena to St Rita

Rita Lotti was born to elderly parents near Cascia, in the Italian region of Umbria, around 1381. She wanted to join the convent and become a nun, but instead obeyed her parents and got married. Her marriage was a difficult one and her husband was eventually killed in a vendetta. When her sons planned to avenge their father, Rita prayed that they would not commit murder, even if it meant they die first. Both of them died from illness soon afterwards. Rita then tried to enter the convent, but the community was reluctant to take her. She did not give up, and waited for God to make it possible. In the meantime, she brokered peace between her husband's family and that of his murderer, thus ending the vendetta. Finally she was accepted into the convent.

One day, when she was praying for a share in Christ's sufferings, a thorn from Christ's crown of thorns pierced her forehead. She suffered the pain of the resulting suppurating wound for the rest of her life. She is known to be effective in making peace, especially in families, and is called the saint of things despaired of.

FIRST DAY ✓

You wanted to enter the convent but your parents arranged a marriage for you. We pray for those whose hopes have been frustrated.

I ask you especially for [*here name your intention*]

Our Father - Hail Mary - Glory Be

SECOND DAY ✓

You lived for many years with a difficult husband at a time when there was no escape. You never stopped praying for him. We pray for all those fleeing from or experiencing domestic violence.

I ask you especially for [*here name your intention*]

Our Father - Hail Mary - Glory Be

THIRD DAY ✓

You wanted the best for your sons even if it meant their death. Help all mothers of difficult children to pray for them, and to entrust them to God's providence and mercy.

I ask you especially for [*here name your intention*]

Our Father - Hail Mary - Glory Be

FOURTH DAY

You brokered peace between your husband's family and the family of his murderer. We ask you to intercede anywhere in our lives there is discord and hatred.

I ask you especially for [*here name your intention*]

Our Father - Hail Mary - Glory Be

FIFTH DAY

You did everything God asked of you, but he did not give you your heart's desire. Help us not to become bitter if God has not rewarded us as we think we deserve. May we humbly ask his will.

I ask you especially for [*here name your intention*]

Our Father - Hail Mary - Glory Be

SIXTH DAY

You persevered in your desire to enter the convent, waiting on God's time. Eventually everything became easy and you were able to enter. Help us to persevere in prayer for our intentions and trustingly accept God's will, whatever the outcome.

I ask you especially for [*here name your intention*]

Our Father - Hail Mary - Glory Be

SEVENTH DAY

You endured painful illness and the rejection of your
sisters because of the terrible stench of your wound.
You accepted this in peace. May we, too, learn to accept
suffering and rejection, knowing God will never reject us.

I ask you especially for [*here name your intention*]

Our Father - Hail Mary - Glory Be

EIGHTH DAY

You were famed for your compassion and wisdom and
many people came to ask your help. Intercede for us that
we can be open to others.

I ask you especially for [*here name your intention*]

Our Father - Hail Mary - Glory Be

NINTH DAY

You are the saint of things despaired of. We pray that you
intercede for us in this thing which seems impossible.

I ask you especially for [*here name your intention*]

Our Father - Hail Mary - Glory Be

Pentecost

Pentecost, the Feast of Weeks, marks the fiftieth day after Passover in the Jewish calendar (a week of weeks is forty-nine days, plus one for the feast itself). The Church celebrates on this day the descent of the Holy Spirit on the disciples, locked by their fears into the virtual prison of the Upper Room, but suddenly given the same zeal and fire as came down on the Elders of Israel when Moses received the Law on the Holy Mountain, which the Jewish Pentecost or Shavuot called to mind. The Church, it is often said, was born on the day of Pentecost; but it is also a day that reminds us strongly of our enduring ties with the People of the Covenant.

To finish on the feast, begin the novena on the Saturday of the Sixth Week of Easter; to finish on the eve of the feast, begin on the Friday of the Sixth Week.

FIRST DAY

Acts 1:9

Although the disciples had lived with Christ and seen his Resurrection and Ascension with their own eyes, their lives had not yet changed. Help me not to live as if faith were only a Sunday obligation, but to see what you have done in my life.

I ask you especially for [*here name your intention*]

Our Father - Hail Mary - Glory Be

SECOND DAY

Acts 1:14

The disciples were with Mary and were praying constantly. I ask you to give me this grace of prayer. I ask you for hope and for the consolation of the love of the Blessed Virgin Mary.

I ask you especially for [*here name your intention*]

Our Father - Hail Mary - Glory Be

THIRD DAY

Acts 1:21–26

After referring to the Scriptures, the disciples chose a replacement for Judas. Matthias joined the Apostles later than the original Twelve, but was not less than the others. Help me to see that no matter how late I come to you, you are waiting for me.

I ask you especially for [*here name your intention*]

Our Father - Hail Mary - Glory Be

FOURTH DAY

Acts 1:24

Before deciding who should take Judas's place, the disciples prayed together to understand your will. Help me to remember that I am not alone; you are there to help me make decisions and know your will for me. Give me gratitude for the Church where we gather to pray together.

I ask you especially for [*here name your intention*]

Our Father - Hail Mary - Glory Be

FIFTH DAY

Acts 2:1

The disciples had come together to celebrate the Jewish feast of Shavuot. This feast marks the giving of the Ten Commandments and is on the fiftieth day after Passover, which recalls the freeing of the slaves from Egypt, just as the Christian Pentecost marks fifty days from the Resurrection that breaks our slavery to sin and death. Jewish tradition speaks of the Spirit of God coming down like fire on the seventy elders who accompanied Moses to Mount Sinai (see *Ex* 18–19); they were symbols of the whole human race, which was reckoned to be made up of seventy nations. The account in Acts renews this encounter as the Spirit comes down like fire on the disciples, who then go out and preach in all the languages of the known world.

You always help us to understand new things by using what we already know. Help me to trust that.

I ask you especially for [*here name your intention*]

Our Father - Hail Mary - Glory Be

SIXTH DAY

Acts 2:2–4

The disciples' lives changed in a moment when they were filled with the Spirit which pushed them to share the gospel. Help me to recognise the impulses that come from you and not to be afraid of what people think of me.

I ask you especially for [*here name your intention*]

Our Father - Hail Mary - Glory Be

SEVENTH DAY

Acts 2:5

Shavuot was a pilgrim festival and people had come to Jerusalem from many other places to celebrate the feast. Help me to know that you never forget any details; that everything that happens does so at the appointed time. Give me the grace to trust in your love.

I ask you especially for [*here name your intention*]

Our Father - Hail Mary - Glory Be

EIGHTH DAY

Acts 2:6–12

When the disciples spoke, each person heard the word in their own language. You know me better than I know myself and you speak to me in my own language. Help me to do the same with others. Help me to speak to them in ways they can understand; help me to accept putting their needs before my own.

I ask you especially for [*here name your intention*]

Our Father - Hail Mary - Glory Be

NINTH DAY

Acts 2:14

Peter took the place Christ had prepared for him. The Church was built on him as the Lord had intended. I ask you for love for your Church. Give me the grace to pray with and for the Holy Father, the Pope.

I ask you especially for [*here name your intention*]

Our Father - Hail Mary - Glory Be

Novena to St Anthony of Padua

St Anthony of Padua was actually born in Portugal, towards the end of the twelfth century. He joined the new order of friars that had recently been founded by St Francis, and moved to Italy. He was a very famous preacher, and was known for his great love for the poor – many churches still collect money for "St Anthony's Bread", for the poor and hungry. He is usually shown with a book, on which the child Jesus is seated. This shows his strong love for Christ as he is present in the proclaimed Word of the Scriptures.

He is very well-known as an intercessor for those who need to find something that has been lost. This apparently stems from a time when one of the friars borrowed his prayer-book without asking, and Anthony appeared to him in a fearsome vision. Whatever the origin of this, St Anthony is undeniably effective in finding lost items – whether physical objects (anything from car keys upwards) or spiritual things, including faith, hope, and love.

The best-known novena to St Anthony is known as the Nine Tuesdays, because it is usually said (as the name suggests) on nine successive Tuesdays; however you could certainly make it on nine consecutive days instead. We give a version of it here.

FIRST DAY

Blessed St Anthony, I greet you in the name of the Virgin Mary, Queen of the Angels. I ask you, with her, to bring my request before Almighty God.

I ask you especially for [*here name your intention*]

Our Father - Hail Mary - Glory Be

SECOND DAY

Blessed St Anthony, I greet you in the name of the patriarchs and prophets. Like them, you were given the gift of knowledge, even knowledge of the future. I ask you, with them, to bring my request before Almighty God.

I ask you especially for [*here name your intention*]

Our Father - Hail Mary - Glory Be

THIRD DAY

Blessed St Anthony, I greet you in the name of all Christ's holy apostles and disciples. God chose you, too, to preach the gospel and spread the faith. I ask you, with them, to bring my request before Almighty God.

I ask you especially for [*here name your intention*]

Our Father - Hail Mary - Glory Be

FOURTH DAY

Blessed St Anthony, like the martyrs and saints who proclaimed Christ, you were always ready to suffer persecution for his sake.

I ask you, with them, to bring my request before Almighty God.

I ask you especially for [*here name your intention*]

Our Father - Hail Mary - Glory Be

FIFTH DAY

Blessed St Anthony, I greet you in the name of all holy bishops and priests. Like them, you were given the grace to convert many to Christ. I ask you, with them, to bring my request before Almighty God.

I ask you especially for [*here name your intention*]

Our Father - Hail Mary - Glory Be

SIXTH DAY

Blessed St Anthony, I greet you and bless God for you, because he gave you the grace to spend your life in good works, like so many holy monks and hermits. You, too, kept vigil, prayed, fasted and denied yourself. May your prayers and theirs rise before God on my behalf.

I ask you especially for [*here name your intention*]

Our Father - Hail Mary - Glory Be

SEVENTH DAY

Blessed St Anthony, I greet you in the name of all holy
virgins and innocents. Like them, you led a life of purity
and overcame temptations against it. I ask you, together
with them, to pray to God for me.

I ask you especially for [*here name your intention*]

Our Father - Hail Mary - Glory Be

EIGHTH DAY

Blessed St Anthony, I greet you in the name of all holy
widows, and all holy husbands and wives, and I bless
God for all of your virtues. You, like these holy men and
women, served God faithfully here on earth; I ask you
and them to pray for me now.

I ask you especially for [*here name your intention*]

Our Father - Hail Mary - Glory Be

NINTH DAY

Blessed St Anthony, I greet you in the name of St Joseph,
most chaste husband of the Blessed Virgin Mary. I greet
you in the name of all holy men and women now living.
I bless the most high God for giving you so much of his
love and grace. I ask you, and them, to speak to God for
me; may my request be granted if it is for God's greater
glory, and for my salvation.

I ask you especially for [*here name your intention*]

Our Father - Hail Mary - Glory Be

Novena to St Thomas More

Thomas More was born in London in 1478. He married and had four children and after the death of his first wife married again. More was a devoted father who made sure his daughters were educated as well as his son – unusual in those days. He was also very successful in his career, being a lawyer, then a judge known for his fairness and incorruptibility and finally becoming Lord Chancellor. As well as this he was a theologian, author and personal friend of the king. But when he had to choose between all of this and faith, he chose faith, entering into the consequences of that with his eyes wide open. He could not in conscience say that Henry VIII's marriage to Catherine of Aragon was not valid, or that the king was head of the Church in England, and he was imprisoned and executed for treason because of this. He was canonised in 1935 and shares a feast day with St John Fisher, a bishop martyred for the same reasons. He is often seen as patron of politicians and all those in public life, and of all trying to live Christian lives in the world.

FIRST DAY

You were a devoted family man, lovingly involved in the lives of your children, providing security for them and making sure they were well equipped for life. We pray for all fathers that they may give time to their children and show interest in their lives.

I ask you especially for [*here name your intention*]

Our Father - Hail Mary - Glory Be

SECOND DAY

You were successful in your career, but were also known for your integrity. Intercede for us that we may be honest and hard-working in our professions.

I ask you especially for [*here name your intention*]

Our Father - Hail Mary - Glory Be

THIRD DAY

As a lawyer, judge and statesman you were known for your fairness and incorruptibility. We pray for all those in the law and in politics, that they may be motivated not by greed or personal gain but by honesty and altruism.

I ask you especially for [*here name your intention*]

Our Father - Hail Mary - Glory Be

FOURTH DAY

You were well-known for your sense of humour and love of life. You were even able to make jokes on the scaffold. Intercede for us that we may learn truly to enjoy life and to learn how to be happy in all situations.

I ask you especially for [*here name your intention*]

Our Father - Hail Mary - Glory Be

FIFTH DAY

You knew your faith and learned how to defend it. Help us to learn to do the same, so that we can have a solid foundation on which to base our lives and a way of passing the gospel to others.

I ask you especially for [*here name your intention*]

Our Father - Hail Mary - Glory Be

SIXTH DAY

You were not afraid to be the lone voice of truth even when you knew it could cost you everything. Intercede for us that we may be able to stand up for the teachings of the Church even when they are unpopular.

I ask you especially for [*here name your intention*]

Our Father - Hail Mary - Glory Be

SEVENTH DAY

You were finally betrayed by someone you had helped. May we, too, learn to forgive those who have betrayed our trust.

I ask you especially for [*here name your intention*]

Our Father - Hail Mary - Glory Be

EIGHTH DAY

You submitted to God's will and had faith that even if you betrayed him in your anguish, he would pull you up again as he did St Peter. Help us to learn the humility of accepting failure, and to trust in God's will.

I ask you especially for [*here name your intention*]

Our Father - Hail Mary - Glory Be

NINTH DAY

You went to your death in the sure hope of eternal life. Give us, too, something of your faith, your hope and your courage.

I ask you especially for [*here name your intention*]

Our Father - Hail Mary - Glory Be

Novena to St John Fisher

Like St Thomas More, St John Fisher was martyred for refusing to put his conscience, and his love for truth and the Church of Christ, second to the demands of the secular power, in the person of King Henry VIII. Fisher was the only one of the English bishops who was brave enough to do this; the others were intimidated into submission, or were willing to compromise in the fond belief that the matters of the king's divorce and the governance of the Church were ultimately secondary or unimportant.

John Fisher was a Yorkshireman, born in 1469, and had a successful academic career (he was central to the renewal in England of scholarship in the ancient languages of Greek and Hebrew) before he was made Bishop of Rochester, England's smallest and poorest see, in 1504. He refused to move to a richer or more important diocese, and was diligent in his pastoral duties. He was also a world-famous theologian, and confessor to the queen, Catherine of Aragon, whom Henry VIII wanted to repudiate. Henry went to great lengths to persuade Fisher to support him, but the saint refused to put his own advantage before the truth – that the marriage was valid and no amount of the king's bullying could make it otherwise. He was imprisoned on a trumped-up charge, and then executed on 22nd June 1535, not before the then Pope had made him a cardinal. Four hundred years later, another Pope declared him a saint.

This prayer, composed by St John Fisher himself, can suitably be said over nine days as a novena.

PRAYER OF ST JOHN FISHER

I know, most gracious Father, that thou
art here present with me albeit I see thee
not. But thou both seest me and hearest me
and no secrecy of my heart is hid from thee.
Thou hearest that I now ask thine Holy Spirit
and thou knowest that I now pray therefore
and that I am very desirous to have the same.
Lo! Dear Father, with all the enforcement
of my heart I beseech thee to give thine
Holy Spirit unto me. Wherefore unless thou
wilt disappoint the promise of thy son Jesu
thou canst not but give me this Holy Spirit;
so by this means I shall be fully relieved of
that misery whereof I complained unto thy
goodness at the beginning. Thy most Holy
Spirit he shall make me to love thee with all my
heart, and with all my soul, with all my mind,
with all my power, for he is the author of all
good love, he is the very furnace of charity and
he is the fountain of all gracious affections and
godly desires.

Amen

The Sacred Heart ✓

The modern feast of the Sacred Heart of Jesus derives mainly from a series of visions experienced by a French nun, St Margaret Mary Alacocque, in the latter part of the seventeenth century. Her visions included a series of twelve "promises" made concerning the graces that would be given to those who practised devotion to Jesus under this aspect. Her near contemporary, the French priest St John Eudes, also wrote much on this devotion.

The feast of the Sacred Heart is celebrated on the Friday after the second Sunday after Pentecost (the first Sunday after Pentecost is always Trinity Sunday; the second, in many places including England & Wales, is the feast of Corpus Christi). This means a novena, to end on the feast itself, should begin on the Thursday after Trinity Sunday; or to end on the eve of the feast, the Wednesday after Trinity Sunday.

St John Eudes taught that Jesus is at the centre of everything and his love, his heart, holds us all. He also saw how much Jesus's mother's love helps us. He wrote: "So closely are Jesus and Mary bound up with each other that whoever beholds Jesus sees Mary; whoever loves Jesus, loves Mary; whoever has devotion to Jesus, has devotion to Mary."

Lord, may I come to know your love for me and also the help of your Blessed Mother in all the difficulties of my life. Help me to know how to live a life devoted to you and to find the peace only you can give.

St Margaret Mary's visions of you brought her great
suffering. Her sisters and superiors were saddened
and exasperated by her. Doctors found her silly and
attention-seeking. One even told her that if she ate
properly these visions would go away.

Help me, when I speak out and speak the truth to
defend you, to have the courage she had, even in the face
of people who laugh at me. But let me also speak with care
and love, remembering your love and care for all people.

Lord Jesus, let my heart never rest until it finds you who
are its centre, its love and its happiness.

By the wound in your heart, pardon the sins I have
committed whether out of malice or evil desires.

Place my weak heart in your divine heart, continually
under your protection and guidance, so that I may
persevere in doing good and in fleeing evil until my last
breath. Amen

(*St Margaret Mary*)

I ask you especially for [*here name your intention*]
Our Father - Hail Mary - Glory Be

My God, I offer you all my prayers, works, joys and
sufferings in union with the Sacred Heart of Jesus, for
the intentions for which he pleads and offers himself
in the holy sacrifice of the Mass, in thanksgiving for
your favours, in reparation for my sins, and in humble
supplication for my temporal and eternal welfare,
for the needs of our holy Mother the Church, for the
conversion of sinners, and for the relief of the poor souls
in purgatory.

SECOND DAY

Lord, you promised through your Sacred Heart *all things
needed for daily life* and *blessings on our undertakings*
(1st and 5th Promises).

I ask for your blessings on my life and all that I do, but
also to know that you lead me. You know what is best for
me. May I always join myself to you so that I am yours
and live in you. Let me recognise your hand in my life,
see when you are guiding me, and trust in your will for
my life, knowing that all things work for good for those
who love God.

Lord Jesus, let my heart never rest ...

I ask you especially for [*here name your intention*]

Our Father - Hail Mary - Glory Be

My God, I offer ...

THIRD DAY

Peace and blessings will be showered on the home dedicated to the Sacred Heart (2nd and 9th Promises).

May I pray and work every day for harmony and love in my home and in my family. May I be a sign to others of your love. Give me a heart like yours. Help me to love, to ask pardon, to forgive and to help others to reconcile. Let me recognise and be grateful for the times when your spirit appears in the family, and always put you at the centre.

Lord Jesus, let my heart never rest ...

I ask you especially for [*here name your intention*]

Our Father - Hail Mary - Glory Be

My God, I offer ...

FOURTH DAY

You have promised *comfort in suffering* and *refuge in danger* (3rd and 4th Promises).

In any suffering and cross in my life you are there, waiting to comfort and console me. I know I can always find you if I call on you and wait to hear your voice. Help me, too, to turn to you when I am in danger of sin, knowing you can break this attraction – that you can rescue me before I am lost.

Lord Jesus, let my heart never rest ...

I ask you especially for [*here name your intention*]

Our Father - Hail Mary - Glory Be

My God, I offer ...

FIFTH DAY

Through your Sacred Heart you promise *mercy for sinners* (6th Promise).

I ask for mercy for my sins and for the gift of showing mercy to others. You said sinners will find your heart an ocean of mercy for those who seek it. I ask to trust in this and be truly grateful. May my gratitude for your forgiveness of my sins spill over into forgiveness for anyone who has wronged me.

Lord Jesus, let my heart never rest ...

I ask you especially for [*here name your intention*]

Our Father - Hail Mary - Glory Be

My God, I offer ...

SIXTH DAY

Lord, you promise help both *for the tepid* and *for the fervent* (7th and 8th Promises).

I know I can be both of these things, but also how easily I become lukewarm in everything, but especially in living as a Christian. May I rediscover the joy of your love and live my life in hope. When I live according to your will, such a burden is lifted from me. You alone can give this fervour. Give me the desire to ask for it, and in my fervour give me discernment not to discourage or alienate others.

Lord Jesus, let my heart never rest ...

I ask you especially for [*here name your intention*]

Our Father - Hail Mary - Glory Be

My God, I offer ...

SEVENTH DAY

Through your Sacred Heart, *priests will be given help to reach hearts* (10th Promise).

May I always remember to pray for priests I know. They are the head of the body that is your Church and the Evil One targets them. If it is in my power to encourage them, help me to do that. Give your priests courage in their daily lives and hope in you and in your Blessed Mother who loves them. May they not become cynical or sad, remembering that with you all things are possible. May they speak the truth in mercy and show their faith, hope and trust in you, believing you can reach all hearts.

Lord Jesus, let my heart never rest ...

I ask you especially for [*here name your intention*]

Our Father - Hail Mary - Glory Be

My God, I offer ...

EIGHTH DAY

Through your Sacred Heart you promise that I can have a true relationship with you (11th Promise).

Help me to wish for and accept a true relationship with you; to have love for you and to know happiness in your presence; to be able to feel you in my heart as St Margaret Mary did. Give me the grace to receive communion often, as you have asked us to, and especially on the first Fridays.

Lord Jesus, let my heart never rest ...

I ask you especially for [*here name your intention*]

Our Father - Hail Mary - Glory Be

My God, I offer ...

NINTH DAY

Through your Sacred Heart you promise us your *grace at the moment of our death* (12th Promise).

I ask this grace of you and also the grace to live each day in the fulness you want to give me. May I be a person who gives life and not death. Give me especially a guard over my tongue so I do not destroy others with my words but instead show them kindness and encouragement. Help me not to fear death and not to find life purposeless, but instead to know death as a passage to eternal life.

Lord Jesus, let my heart never rest ...

I ask you especially for [*here name your intention*]

Our Father - Hail Mary - Glory Be

My God, I offer ...

O most holy heart of Jesus, fountain of every blessing, I adore you, I love you, and with sorrow for my sins I offer you this heart of mine. Make me humble, patient, pure and wholly obedient to your will. Grant, good Jesus, that I may live in you and for you. Protect me in the midst of danger. Comfort me in my afflictions. Give me health of body, assistance in my temporal needs, your blessing on all that I do, and the grace of a holy death.

Amen

Novena Prayer to the Immaculate Heart of Mary

O most Blessed Mother, heart of love, heart of mercy, ever listening, caring, consoling, hear our prayer. As your children, we implore your intercession with Jesus your Son. We are comforted in knowing your heart is ever open to those who ask for your prayer. We entrust to your gentle care and intercession those whom we love and who are sick or lonely or hurting. Help all of us, Holy Mother, to bear our burdens in this life until we may share eternal life and peace with God forever.

Amen

$\mathcal{N}$ovena Prayer to St Christopher

FEAST DAY: 25TH JULY

St Christopher (whose name means "the one who bears Christ") seems to have been martyred for being a Christian some time before the mid-fifth century, probably in the third century, in the Roman province of Bithynia (where we know there were Christian communities at the start of the second century) in Asia Minor. He is best known because of a story in a medieval version of his life, which says that he was a giant who had been a pagan, and who, after becoming a Christian, served the community by carrying travellers on his back across a wide river. One day he carried a child who, despite his small size, was so heavy Christopher barely made it safely across. The child was Christ, and the weight was that of the whole world and its creator. Whatever we may think of this as history, it is a powerful reminder that Christian service to others is also service to Christ. St Christopher is very well-known as patron of travellers in general, of all who have journeys to make, and of motorists especially.

PRAYER TO ST CHRISTOPHER

St Christopher, you gained a beautiful name, Christbearer, from the wonderful legend that while carrying people across a raging stream, you also carried the Child Jesus. Teach us to be true Christbearers to those who do not know him. Protect drivers, and all who transport those who bear Christ within them. Keep safe all who travel, especially [make your request], and bring us all safe to our final journey's end, in God.

Amen

Novena to St Anne

FEAST DAY: 26TH JULY

Anne is the name tradition gives to the mother of the Blessed Virgin Mary. It is said that she and her husband Joachim were a good and holy couple who were unable to have children for many years and suffered humiliation because of this. Finally the Virgin Mary was born to them, and they brought her up to love God, and found a man of faith, St Joseph, for her to marry.

Again as tradition has it, she had much to do with the bringing up of Jesus himself, and after the death of Joachim she followed the Holy Family to Egypt. Tradition says also that when Martha, Mary and Lazarus went to France after Christ's death and Resurrection, they took with them the bones of St Anne.

A legend says St Anne was married three times, and this is why many people pray for her intercession to find a good husband. This is the origin of the humorous prayer, "Holy St Anne, Holy St Anne, find me a man, as fast as you can". Whether or not this legend is true, St Anne is known to help in these cases, finding good husbands for women, as she did for her own daughter.

FIRST DAY

You and your husband truly loved God but it seemed your piety went unrewarded. We pray to persevere, and not to lose hope in God's love.

I ask you especially for [*here name your intention*]

Our Father - Hail Mary - Glory Be

SECOND DAY

You had to see your husband's humiliation without being able to do anything. Help us not to be shocked or scandalised by the sufferings of our loved ones, and to believe God also loves them.

I ask you especially for [*here name your intention*]

Our Father - Hail Mary - Glory Be

THIRD DAY

When you finally had a child, you did not make her an idol but brought her up to love God. Help all Christian parents to bring up their children in the faith.

I ask you especially for [*here name your intention*]

Our Father - Hail Mary - Glory Be

FOURTH DAY

When your daughter was pregnant before being married, it seemed she had betrayed everything you taught her. Help us, when we are disappointed in people, not to judge too quickly.

I ask you especially for [*here name your intention*]

Our Father - Hail Mary - Glory Be

FIFTH DAY

You were a loving grandmother. We pray for all grandparents, that they may bring love and wisdom to their grandchildren's lives.

I ask you especially for [*here name your intention*]

Our Father - Hail Mary - Glory Be

SIXTH DAY

You followed the Holy Family into exile in Egypt. We pray for all older people who are uprooted later in life, and for all older people whose families live far away.

I ask you especially for [*here name your intention*]

Our Father - Hail Mary - Glory Be

SEVENTH DAY

You were so inspiring that Martha, Mary and Lazarus took your bones with them on their missionary journey. Help us to see that older people still have much to offer us.

I ask you especially for [*here name your intention*]

Our Father - Hail Mary - Glory Be

EIGHTH DAY

You are known to help those looking for husbands. We ask you to intercede for all those looking for Christian husbands or wives.

I ask you especially for [*here name your intention*]

Our Father - Hail Mary - Glory Be

NINTH DAY

You are also patroness of women in labour. We pray for all women giving birth, for all children born today, and for all those who have been aborted.

I ask you especially for [*here name your intention*]

Our Father - Hail Mary - Glory Be

Novena to St Martha

St Martha lived with her brother Lazarus and sister Mary in Bethany. Jesus often visited them there. Martha was the one who looked after the house, and is therefore the patron of cooks and homemakers. The Gospels record an incident where Martha complained to Jesus that he had not told her sister Mary to help her with serving their guests, but let her sit and listen to him. Jesus told Martha not to worry about so many things, and that her sister was right to put listening to him first.

Martha later recognised Jesus as the Messiah, and witnessed him raise her brother Lazarus from the dead. After the Resurrection of Jesus, it is said that she and her brother and sister evangelised in France, where Martha converted many people through her preaching, calling them away from the worship of a dragon god.

FIRST DAY

Yours was a home that Christ himself was comfortable in. We ask you to help us to be hospitable and open and to make our homes a place where Christ can be present.

I ask you especially for [*here name your intention*]

Our Father - Hail Mary - Glory Be

SECOND DAY

You worked hard in your house. Help us to give value to housework and the routine tasks of life. Intercede for us so that we can look after others' needs with serenity and joy.

I ask you especially for [*here name your intention*]

Our Father - Hail Mary - Glory Be

THIRD DAY

You served Christ. Help us to serve him in our own lives.

I ask you especially for [*here name your intention*]

Our Father - Hail Mary - Glory Be

FOURTH DAY

Help us to work for the good of others – but always to put Christ first. Help us also to learn from Christ, as you did, not to worry and fret, but to trust in God's all-powerful providence.

I ask you especially for [*here name your intention*]

Our Father - Hail Mary - Glory Be

FIFTH DAY

The Lord rebuked you for your judgement, anger and self-importance and you accepted it. You knew he loved you. We ask that we may be able to accept criticism without remaining resentful and without being destroyed by it.

I ask you especially for [*here name your intention*]

Our Father - Hail Mary - Glory Be

SIXTH DAY

You recognised Jesus as the Christ when he came to your house after your brother's death. Help us to recognise Christ in our lives and to know his love and power.

I ask you especially for [*here name your intention*]

Our Father - Hail Mary - Glory Be

SEVENTH DAY

You saw Christ raise your brother from the dead. Intercede for us so our eyes can be opened to the miracles Christ has done in our lives.

I ask you especially for [*here name your intention*]

Our Father - Hail Mary - Glory Be

EIGHTH DAY

Christ changed your life. Tradition says that you evangelised in France with your brother and sister. Help us not to be disappointed with our lives but to believe that life can be much more than we ever imagined, in ways we never thought possible.

I ask you especially for [*here name your intention*]

Our Father - Hail Mary - Glory Be

NINTH DAY

Tradition says you tamed a dragon, turning people away from worshipping a dragon god by your inspired preaching. Help us to see how God can do great things with small people if only we are open to his will.

I ask you especially for [*here name your intention*]

Our Father - Hail Mary - Glory Be

*T*ransfiguration

On his way to Jerusalem, Jesus goes up the mountain with Peter and John and there appears to them transfigured, in glory. This is usually reckoned to be a glimpse of the Uncreated Light, the divine presence that in the Hebrew Scriptures is called the Shekinah: that brightness which our eyes cannot bear nor our hearts conceive, but is the aboriginal nature of the Godhead, here glimpsed, and promised to us in the resurrection that, at the End, will renew our bodies too.

As well as on the feast of the Transfiguration, the high feast of summer, this Gospel is also read on the Second Sunday of Lent. This reminds us that the glory of new life that comes with Easter is born from the Cross, that we should not think that suffering is the end, or the only thing there is, but that it always points us forward to resurrection, and to the resplendent glory of a renewed creation.

To finish the novena on the feast, you should begin on 29th July; to finish on the eve of the feast, begin on 28th July.

The Gospel accounts of the Transfiguration are: *Mt* 17:1–8; *Mk* 9:2–8; *Lk* 9:28–36.

FIRST DAY

In the Transfiguration, heaven and earth meet, humanity and divinity, time and eternity. Give me the grace to see how powerful you are. You are master of the universe. If my prayer is not answered, it is not because you cannot do what I want but that you have a different and better plan for me.

I ask you especially for [*here name your intention*]

Our Father - Hail Mary - Glory Be

SECOND DAY

The prophet Malachi promised that Elijah would return as a sign the Messiah had arrived. Elijah and Moses appeared with Christ in his Transfiguration. Open our eyes to see how you speak to us in history and throughout our lives. You always keep your promises. Help us learn to read the signs of the times.

I ask you especially for [*here name your intention*]

Our Father - Hail Mary - Glory Be

THIRD DAY

Peter blurted out the first thing that came into his head, as we often do. Help me to keep a guard on my mouth: not to gossip or criticise, not to be hurtful or rude. Help me also to be careful if I tell other people how they should be living their lives.

I ask you especially for [*here name your intention*]

Our Father - Hail Mary - Glory Be

FOURTH DAY

Finally, Peter said, "Lord, it is good to be here". Give me the grace to be with you and to be glad to be with you, trusting you with my life; to know I am not alone in life; that you love me and have a wonderful plan for me if I trust you.

I ask you especially for [*here name your intention*]

Our Father - Hail Mary - Glory Be

FIFTH DAY

At the Transfiguration, Jesus tried to prepare his disciples for the crucifixion. You tell us that if we want to follow you we should take up our cross; but we always hope that the cross will go away. Give me the courage to believe that you carry my cross with me and that it will not crush me.

I ask you especially for [*here name your intention*]

Our Father - Hail Mary - Glory Be

SIXTH DAY

In the Transfiguration there is a glimpse of your glory, a glimpse of your divine nature. Give me this grace: to see your power in my life and have a desire for holiness. Help me to believe I will not lose myself if I follow your teachings.

I ask you especially for [*here name your intention*]

Our Father - Hail Mary - Glory Be

SEVENTH DAY

The disciples who saw your Transfiguration were terrified, but you told them to stand up and not to be afraid. Help me remember this. When life knocks me down and when I am afraid, help me to stand up and walk onward with you.

I ask you especially for [*here name your intention*]

Our Father - Hail Mary - Glory Be

EIGHTH DAY

Moses and Elijah are living in the presence of Christ in the Transfiguration. All who face death with faith in you will live in your presence for ever. Help us not to fear death.

I ask you especially for [*here name your intention*]

Our Father - Hail Mary - Glory Be

NINTH DAY

As in eternal life I will see your glory, so at the resurrection of the dead I, too, will be glorified. This life is only a small part of my life in you. Help me to look forward in hope to heaven and to the resurrection of the dead.

I ask you especially for [*here name your intention*]

Our Father - Hail Mary - Glory Be

Novena to St Teresa Benedicta of the Cross (Edith Stein)

FEAST DAY: 9TH AUGUST

Edith Stein was born into a prosperous Jewish family in what is now Poland. She was a well-known philosopher and teacher who converted to Catholicism, became a Carmelite nun, and was murdered in Auschwitz, a martyr for the Jewish people.

PRAYER TO ST TERESA BENEDICTA OF THE CROSS

God of our fathers, at the hour of her martyrdom you brought St Teresa Benedicta to the fulness of the knowledge of the cross. Fill us with that same knowledge and may we, through the intercession of St Teresa Benedicta, always seek you, the Supreme Truth, and remain faithful to the covenant of love ratified in the blood of your Son.

Amen

Novena to St Maximilian Kolbe

FEAST DAY: 14TH AUGUST

Maximilian Kolbe was born in 1894 of a Polish mother and ethnic German father. In 1914 his father was hanged by the Russian army after fighting for an independent Poland. As a child, Maximilian had a vision of the Blessed Virgin who offered him the crown of purity or the crown of martyrdom. He chose both. He initially thought of joining the army but instead became a Franciscan priest. He founded a "village" of religious dedicated to Mary Immaculate and a small religious newspaper which became hugely influential in Poland. In 1930 he and four companions went to Japan where they worked for six years. Maximilian suffered poor health all the time he was there but did not think of giving up. Soon after his return to Poland, the country was invaded by the Nazis and he was arrested, and was eventually sent to Auschwitz. He ministered to his fellow prisoners before finally offering his life in exchange for that of a married man who was one of ten prisoners sentenced to be locked up and left to starve to death. Fr Maximilian encouraged the other prisoners in his death cell, and announced the gospel even as they all starved to death. Finally only he was left alive, and was murdered by lethal injection, accepting death with peace.

FIRST DAY

When still a child you entrusted your future to the Mother of God and accepted the crowns of purity and martyrdom. Help us to learn to be generous with our lives in the service of God.

I ask you especially for [*here name your intention*]

Our Father - Hail Mary - Glory Be

SECOND DAY

You had a great love of the military and you thought of joining the army but instead founded the *Militia Immaculatae* to work for the conversion of sinners. We remember all those who serve in the armed forces and their families.

I ask you especially for [*here name your intention*]

Our Father - Hail Mary - Glory Be

THIRD DAY

You began a small religious newspaper which led to an upsurge of faith amongst your countrymen. May we, too, realise that nothing we do is too small for God to use.

I ask you especially for [*here name your intention*]

Our Father - Hail Mary - Glory Be

FOURTH DAY

You had such zeal for the proclamation of the gospel that you went to Japan with no money and not one word of the language; and what you built is now the centre of the Franciscan province there. May we share in your zeal to announce the Good News through our words and our lives.

I ask you especially for [*here name your intention*]

Our Father - Hail Mary - Glory Be

FIFTH DAY

When the Nazis had invaded your country and you were under suspicion you said, "No one in the world can change truth". May we hold firm to the one who is the Truth, Jesus Christ.

I ask you especially for [*here name your intention*]

Our Father - Hail Mary - Glory Be

SIXTH DAY

In prison you were asked whether you believed in Christ and were beaten every time you said you did. You persevered in your witness. May we still hold fast to Christ even in suffering or pain, and if we are persecuted for that belief may we have the courage not to desert him.

I ask you especially for [*here name your intention*]

Our Father - Hail Mary - Glory Be

SEVENTH DAY

Even when you were sent to Auschwitz you did not abandon your vocation as priest. Although you were beaten almost to death you still heard confessions and spoke of Christ's love. We ask you to give us something of your conviction and courage in front of the sufferings of our lives.

I ask you especially for [*here name your intention*]

Our Father - Hail Mary - Glory Be

EIGHTH DAY

When a fellow prisoner was sentenced to death by starvation, you volunteered to take his place: to die so that he had a chance of life. May we always remember the words of Our Lord, "He who loses his life for my sake will find it", and may you give us the courage to lose our lives in whatever way is asked of us.

I ask you especially for [*here name your intention*]

Our Father - Hail Mary - Glory Be

NINTH DAY

Because you were killed by an injection of carbolic acid, you are the patron of drug users. We pray for all those who suffer this terrible addiction and for their families. May they have the courage and help they need to turn their lives around.

I ask you especially for [*here name your intention*]

Our Father - Hail Mary - Glory Be

*A*ssumption

For centuries the Church has celebrated the passage of the Virgin Mary from this life to the fuller life with the Father, calling the mystery of her going-out the Dormition or Assumption. This was only formally defined as a certain truth of the Christian Faith in 1950, by Pope Pius XII, to the dismay of some non-Catholics.

The feast of the Assumption celebrates not just the unique role and eminence of the Virgin Mary, but also points towards the fulfilment that, please God, awaits us all. Mary, the Church declares, was assumed body and soul into heaven; our own promised life with God, this reminds us, will be one in which our physical self will play a full part. Heaven is not some ethereal fiesta of clouds and bodiless contemplation, but a life in all ways richer and fuller than, but in all ways also contiguous with, the life we live now. This is a feast of hope and promise.

To finish the novena on the feast itself, you should begin on 7th August; to finish on the eve of the feast, begin on 6th August.

FIRST DAY

Lord, we long to be able to reach out to you and to each other, but original sin prevents us from risking this. Our Blessed Mother was free from this sin from the very moment of her conception. She is our model of how to live fully and entirely in your will. I pray for the grace to know your will for my life and the courage to enter into it with joy and hope.

I ask you especially for [*here name your intention*]

Our Father - Hail Mary - Glory Be

Magnificat

SECOND DAY

Mary was given the grace to become *theotokos* (Mother of God). You made yourself vulnerable, and gave yourself into her motherly care. You entrusted everything to her but still left her free. Help me to see what you have entrusted to me and to value it. Help me, too, to be worthy of that trust. May I learn to love and trust you as Mary did and know that this kind of communion with you is possible.

I ask you especially for [*here name your intention*]

Our Father - Hail Mary - Glory Be

Magnificat

THIRD DAY

Even in agony on the cross you thought of us. You gave your mother to John and to the whole Church. You have crowned her Queen of Heaven so that she can intercede for us. May I know Mary, who knows and loves me as a mother does; may I know her as someone who is interested in me, who wants to help and comfort me. Give me the grace to call on her help.

I ask you especially for [*here name your intention*]

Our Father - Hail Mary - Glory Be

Magnificat

FOURTH DAY

Mary remained with the disciples and witnessed the Resurrection, the Ascension and the descent of the Holy Spirit with them. Her love and faith helped give them strength. Everything she did was from love. St Francis de Sales said that Mary's death (or passing from this life) was in love, from love and through love, and that, Father, she died of love for you. May I have this same desire to love you and my neighbour. Give me a heart that desires to perform the works of mercy.

I ask you especially for [*here name your intention*]

Our Father - Hail Mary - Glory Be

Magnificat

FIFTH DAY

Legend says that when Our Lady was about to depart
this life, all the Apostles were transported from where
they were preaching the gospel to her bedside – all
except Thomas; but when he arrived too late to witness
the Assumption, Our Lady dropped her belt from
heaven as a sign he was not forgotten. Lord, help me to
know your mother as my mother even when I am slow
to love.

I ask you especially for [*here name your intention*]

Our Father - Hail Mary - Glory Be

Magnificat

SIXTH DAY

Icons of the Dormition show Christ holding a baby
which represents Mary's soul. He holds her as once she
held him as a baby. Father, you have a plan for every
person. No one is forgotten and you are always faithful
even when we are not. You hold everything in being
while still giving us free will. I know that I am safe in
your love no matter what happens: in the end all will
be well.

I ask you especially for [*here name your intention*]

Our Father - Hail Mary - Glory Be

Magnificat

SEVENTH DAY

Mary was assumed into heaven body and soul. Help me to appreciate my body, given by God, and treat it with the dignity it deserves. We are part of the created order. Help me to understand what that means. Let me seek to discover the theology of the body and help me to live the fulness of my life as a Christian man or woman, embracing all that that means.

I ask you especially for [*here name your intention*]

Our Father - Hail Mary - Glory Be

Magnificat

EIGHTH DAY

Help me to know that in heaven I will be the fulness of myself. May I seek to become what you created me to be; may I see the importance of this. You love me as I am and for what you know I can become within the plan you have for me.

I ask you especially for [*here name your intention*]

Our Father - Hail Mary - Glory Be

Magnificat

NINTH DAY

Our Lady, Queen of Heaven, cares for us like the indulgent mother she is. Lord, give me the grace to follow her example and intercede with you for the needs of others. Help me to take time to pray for them and to care about their lives.

I ask you especially for [*here name your intention*]

Our Father - Hail Mary - Glory Be

Magnificat

Novena Prayer to St Helena

St Helena was Empress of Rome and mother of the Emperor Constantine, who in AD 313 gave the Christian faith official standing within the Roman Empire. Legend makes Helena a British princess, perhaps daughter to Coel, King of the Trinovantes ("Old King Cole" of the nursery rhyme); certainly, she became a Christian before her son did. In her old age, she made a tour of the Holy Land, visiting the places associated with Christ's life, death and Resurrection. During this visit she found the relics of the True Cross, long hidden in Jerusalem, many of which have survived and are venerated even to this day.

She is the patron of archaeologists and her tomb is in the church of St Maria in Aracoeli on the Capitoline hill in Rome.

St Helena witnesses to the historical reality of Jesus, the Incarnate God, in an age when many were confused by theological speculation and fashionable "gnostic" religions, similar to the "new age" notions of today. She also shows us that holiness is not confined to those who are literally poor or obscure, but can be found by anyone, whatever their state in life, who is ready to do God's will as it is given to them.

There is a superb life of St Helena, in a fictionalised form, by the English Catholic writer Evelyn Waugh.

A TRADITIONAL PRAYER TO ST HELENA

*H*oly St Helena, with the anguish and devotion with which you sought the Cross of Christ, I plead that you give me God's grace to suffer patiently the labours of this life so that through them, and with your intercession and protection, I may seek and carry the cross that God has given me, so that I can serve him in this life and be with him in the next.

Amen

From Evelyn Waugh's *Helena*, a prayer made by the Empress to the Three Wise Men before finding the Cross (which could also be used as a novena prayer before the Epiphany, 6th January):

*L*ike me, you were late in coming. The shepherds were here long before; even the cattle. They had joined the chorus of angels before you were on your way. For you the primordial discipline of the heavens was relaxed and a new defiant light blazed amid the disconcerted stars.

How laboriously you came, taking sights and calculating, where the shepherds had run barefoot! How odd you looked on the road, attended by what outlandish liveries, laden with such preposterous gifts!

You came at length to the final stage of your pilgrimage and the great star stood still above you. What did you do? You stopped to call on King Herod. Deadly exchange of compliments in which began that unended war of mobs and magistrates against the innocent!

Yet you came, and were not turned away. You too found room before the manger. Your gifts were not needed, but they were accepted and put carefully away, for they were brought with love. In that new order of charity that had just come to life, there was room for you, too. You were not lower in the eyes of the holy family than the ox or the ass.

You are my especial patrons, and patrons of all late-comers, of all who have a tedious journey to make to the truth, of all who are confused with knowledge and speculation, of all who through politeness make themselves partners in guilt, of all who stand in danger by reason of their talents.

For His sake who did not reject your curious gifts, pray always for the learned, the oblique, the delicate. Let them not be quite forgotten at the Throne of God when the simple come into their kingdom.

$\mathcal{N}$ovena Prayer to St Monica

FEAST DAY: 27TH AUGUST

Monica was the Christian wife of a difficult husband and mother of two sons, one of whom lived a dissolute life and then joined a cult. She never stopped praying for him and eventually he converted and became the great St Augustine of Hippo. She is the especial patron of those who have difficult marriages or wayward children.

PRAYER TO ST MONICA

Holy St Monica, troubled wife and mother, many sorrows pierced your heart during your lifetime but you never despaired or lost faith. With confidence and persistence you prayed for the conversion of your husband, and of your son Augustine. Your prayers were answered. Grant me that same patience, fortitude and trust in the Lord. Intercede for me before the Lord [make your request] and grant that I may have the grace to accept his will in all things.

Amen

*E*xaltation *of the Cross*

This feast is sometimes called Holy Cross Day. It marks various events in the history of the (still surviving) relics of the True Cross, which the Church believes to be the physical remains of the cross on which Jesus was put to death.

The most important event is the finding of the Cross, in AD 326, by the Empress Helena, mother of the Emperor Constantine. Only two years previously, Constantine had become sole ruler of the Roman world, something he attributed to his use of the cross as a battle sign. His victory established Christianity as the public faith of the Empire, put an end to the sporadic persecutions it had endured, and allowed the Church to emerge from its long hiding. The physical places and things that reminded Christians of the life and death of Jesus, and of his earliest followers, were now generally made known (they had often been previously concealed, either by Christians to keep them safe from the authorities, or by the authorities themselves to try and scotch the growing Christian cult).

Helena had been divorced by Constantine's father so he could make a political marriage, and had lived much of her life in comparative obscurity. Legend makes her a British princess, and there is no good reason not to believe this, although other stories about her parentage are found. At any rate, she was not of the Roman aristocracy, and was not felt to be quite the right sort of wife for an emperor. At some stage she had become Christian. By the time her son became Emperor, she was an old woman. He quickly rehabilitated her and declared her Empress Dowager; almost her first official act was to hurry off to the Holy Land to look for the relics of the Cross. They were found, and identified, after a series of events that look like miracles.

So why does the Church make such a fuss about what are, after all, just some old pieces of wood?

One reason is that the relics of the Cross anchor the Christian story firmly in history. Unlike the other mystery religions popular in the late Roman Empire (and their "new age" analogues today), the Church insists that the great drama of human salvation – the events that show us that God is, indisputably and irrevocably, on our side – issues from a series of historical occurrences, which have left tangible remains we can still see and touch.

Secondly, the Cross of Jesus Christ, which is the fulcrum of human history, is also the pattern of all the crosses we ourselves experience: those sometimes agonisingly painful events that God sends us, not to punish us or discourage or destroy us, but to allow us to enter the mystery of suffering – so that we may know in our own lives the frankly incredible paradox that these appalling things are the very means by which God shows his love for us, and allows us to rise above our sins and selfishnesses. The Cross – Jesus's Cross, but our cross also – is the means by which the world is saved, is brought to know God's love. This is at first sight a baffling and even offensive notion; how dare the professionally religious talk to us in such a way? Even on reflection, the teaching is almost impossibly hard to accept. So we need to put it before God, honestly, in our prayer. We need to ask him to show us, to help us truly and really to know and feel, that our cross – those sufferings from which we most desire to escape – is in fact the sign and the instrument of the love that the Father has for us. Reasoned argument will not do this; prayer can.

To finish the novena on the eve of the feast, you should begin on 5th September; to finish on the feast itself, begin on 6th September.

FIRST DAY

The Roman Emperor Hadrian wanted to obliterate all signs of Christianity in Jerusalem, but in doing this he actually marked the places and preserved the relics. Even the things that seem to be absolutely against my interests can end up being the best thing for me. Give me, Lord, the grace to trust in your wisdom.

Help me to see the cross in my life and to embrace it. I ask you especially for [*here name your intention*]

Our Father - Hail Mary - Glory Be

We adore you, O Christ, and praise you because by your Holy Cross you have redeemed the world.

SECOND DAY

Legend says that when St Helena's team found the Cross, they in fact found three crosses. Nobody could tell which was the True Cross until a sick woman was brought to the place. When she touched the True Cross she was cured. Help me to discern in my life what things I should try to fight against and what is my true cross.

Help me to see the cross in my life and to embrace it.
I ask you especially for [*here name your intention*]

Our Father - Hail Mary - Glory Be

*We adore you, O Christ, and praise you because by your Holy
Cross you have redeemed the world.*

THIRD DAY

St Helena was old when she set out to find the Cross
and had suffered many injustices in her life, but she did
not let that dull her faith or make her bitter. St Ambrose
said that when Helena found the True Cross she did
not worship the Cross itself but "him who hung on that
wood. She burned with an earnest desire to touch the
guarantee of immortality." Give me the grace of a deep
faith like hers.

Help me to see the cross in my life and to embrace it.
I ask you especially for [*here name your intention*]

Our Father - Hail Mary - Glory Be

*We adore you, O Christ, and praise you because by your Holy
Cross you have redeemed the world.*

FOURTH DAY

The Protestant John Calvin said there were enough alleged pieces of the True Cross to fill a ship as he scoffed at the faith of the Church. In the nineteenth century this jibe was proved untrue: a French architect, Charles Rohault de Fleury, measured all the surviving fragments and determined they would together make up only a small part of a cross. However, pieces of the Cross were sent all over the world. They are a sign of your kingship throughout the world. Give me the grace to know your power.

Help me to see the cross in my life and to embrace it. I ask you especially for [*here name your intention*]

Our Father - Hail Mary - Glory Be

We adore you, O Christ, and praise you because by your Holy Cross you have redeemed the world.

FIFTH DAY

You have said that those who wish to follow you must pick up their cross every day. Give me the discernment to see that if I embrace my cross, you also carry it. Give me the grace to enter the life you give me, not sadly or bitterly but in hope.

Help me to see the cross in my life and to embrace it. I ask you especially for [*here name your intention*]

Our Father - Hail Mary - Glory Be

We adore you, O Christ, and praise you because by your Holy Cross you have redeemed the world.

SIXTH DAY

It is hard to understand suffering and especially the suffering of those I love. Help me to see that you love them more than I do, and to trust you with their lives. Give me the grace to help them but not to try to take away their crosses, which are their only way to you.

Help me to see the cross in my life and to embrace it. I ask you especially for [*here name your intention*]

Our Father - Hail Mary - Glory Be

We adore you, O Christ, and praise you because by your Holy Cross you have redeemed the world.

SEVENTH DAY

You showed your love by going to the Cross, by suffering, by offering up your life. Help me to see what I can do to follow you. Give me the gift of Christian love. Help me to be open to others and to offer up my suffering for the world, not forcing myself but allowing you to show me how to give.

Help me to see the cross in my life and to embrace it. I ask you especially for [*here name your intention*]

Our Father - Hail Mary - Glory Be

We adore you, O Christ, and praise you because by your Holy Cross you have redeemed the world.

EIGHTH DAY

Help me truly believe that you love me so much you died for me. You love me, as the person that I am. You see me and you still love me. This love cannot be measured. You love me more than I can imagine, and even though you love all people, you still love me as though I were the only one. Help me to believe and rejoice in that love.

Help me to see the cross in my life and to embrace it. I ask you especially for [*here name your intention*]

Our Father - Hail Mary - Glory Be

We adore you, O Christ, and praise you because by your Holy Cross you have redeemed the world.

NINTH DAY

When you were on earth everyone thought you would conquer with power, but instead you took the last place. You allowed all humiliations and evil to attack you. You accepted hatred and violence and still love us. Help me understand this. I don't look for masochism, but for humility: to be able to pass through suffering, knowing that if I follow you I, too, will overcome death.

Help me to see the cross in my life and to embrace it. I ask you especially for [*here name your intention*]

Our Father - Hail Mary - Glory Be

We adore you, O Christ, and praise you because by your Holy Cross you have redeemed the world.

Novena to St Joseph of Cupertino

FEAST DAY: 18TH SEPTEMBER

Because his father had died leaving debts and his family was consequently homeless, Joseph Desa was an unwelcome addition when he was born in Cupertino, Italy, in 1603.

As a child he was slow witted and had a habit of standing with his mouth open staring into space. He also had a terrible temper, probably born of frustration. Even his own mother thought him worthless. As a young man he joined the Capuchins but was sent away because the ecstasies he experienced made him unsuitable for work. Finally he was accepted by the Franciscans who, seeing his holiness, put him forward to train for the priesthood.

Joseph was so unintelligent that the best he could do was to study a small portion of the material he was supposed to know, and then pray that that was what he would be asked. Whilst with the Franciscans, he began to levitate in ecstasy at the mention of any holy thing, and only a command from his superior could bring him to earth. He was investigated (and exonerated) by the Inquisition because of these antigravitational activities. This also caused his superiors to move him into seclusion. He had his own room and chapel and was unable to leave them. Often those in charge even forgot to bring him food, but he accepted everything with humility. He died a holy death aged sixty. He is a patron of students doing exams and of air travellers.

FIRST DAY

You were an unwanted child and were thought worthless even by your own mother. Intercede for all unwanted children that they may come to know they were born out of God's love for them.

I ask you especially for [*here name your intention*]

Our Father - Hail Mary - Glory Be

SECOND DAY

You were an angry, frustrated child. We pray for all who struggle to express themselves, and that you help us overcome sins of anger.

I ask you especially for [*here name your intention*]

Our Father - Hail Mary - Glory Be

THIRD DAY

You experienced no love in your family, and were considered of little account by all who knew you. We pray for all who have experienced the same. May we learn to treat everyone as having the worth they possess in God's eyes.

I ask you especially for [*here name your intention*]

Our Father - Hail Mary - Glory Be

FOURTH DAY

You suffered because of your lack of intelligence. We pray for all those who struggle at school. May they take comfort from the fact that lack of intelligence did not stop you becoming a saint.

I ask you especially for [*here name your intention*]

Our Father - Hail Mary - Glory Be

FIFTH DAY

You did the best with the little intelligence you had, and put the rest in God's hands. That way, you passed all your exams and became a priest. We pray for all those struggling with exams. May we also do our best in everything and trust in God to guide our lives.

I ask you especially for [*here name your intention*]

Our Father - Hail Mary - Glory Be

SIXTH DAY

Even the thought or mention of anything holy made you levitate in ecstasy. Grant us something of the understanding and reverence for God and his saints that you had.

I ask you especially for [*here name your intention*]

Our Father - Hail Mary - Glory Be

SEVENTH DAY

Only when your superior ordered you to, were you able to come back down to earth. May we, too, have a love for and obedience to the teachings of the Church.

I ask you especially for [*here name your intention*]

Our Father - Hail Mary - Glory Be

EIGHTH DAY

You were unjustly suspected, investigated, confined to your room and neglected by those charged with looking after you. You accepted all this with humility. We pray for all those unjustly imprisoned, and that we, too, may have the humility to accept injustice for the love of Christ.

I ask you especially for [*here name your intention*]

Our Father - Hail Mary - Glory Be

NINTH DAY

Because you could levitate, you are the patron of air travellers. We pray for all those travelling by plane that they may safely reach their destinations.

I ask you especially for [*here name your intention*]

Our Father - Hail Mary - Glory Be

Novena to St Pio of Pietrelcina (Padre Pio)

FEAST DAY: 23RD SEPTEMBER

Francesco Forgione, universally known as Padre Pio (his name in religious life), was born to a peasant family in southern Italy in 1887. He became a Capuchin friar in 1903. His intense prayer life, and identification with the sufferings of Christ, took physical expression in the stigmata, or signs of the wounds of Christ's Passion (in hands, feet and side), that appeared on his body soon after he was ordained priest in 1910. He prayed for them to vanish, and they did for a time, only to re-appear permanently in 1918. His superiors were very suspicious of these phenomena, and for a time forbade him to hear confessions or celebrate Mass. They also had him investigated by sceptical doctors and by the Inquisition.

Padre Pio bore all of these humiliations without complaint. Eventually he was allowed to resume his priestly ministry, and devoted himself to hearing confessions, to spiritual direction and, founding a hospital, to works of compassion for the sick. People came in their thousands to make their confession to him and to join his celebration of Mass. He suffered persistent ill-health, and hardly seemed to need food except the Eucharist. There are many stories of his miraculous interventions in the lives of those who needed his help. He died in 1968, half a century after receiving the stigmata; but the many miracles attributed to his intercession have not ceased. He was canonised in 2002.

FIRST DAY

You were physically conformed to Christ's Passion, and bore the likeness of his wounds in your own flesh. Help us to see and accept our sufferings as a participation in Christ's sufferings for the salvation of the world.

I ask you especially for [*here name your intention*]

Our Father - Hail Mary - Glory Be

SECOND DAY

You accepted persecution and misunderstanding without complaint. Help us to be similarly patient when others do us wrong.

I ask you especially for [*here name your intention*]

Our Father - Hail Mary - Glory Be

THIRD DAY

Your witness to Christ was not bounded by time and space; help us to see that God's presence and power in our lives is similarly without limit.

I ask you especially for [*here name your intention*]

Our Father - Hail Mary - Glory Be

FOURTH DAY

You were a man of intense and constant prayer. Help us to have a real love of prayer, and to base all we do on a personal relationship with Jesus Christ.

I ask you especially for [*here name your intention*]

Our Father - Hail Mary - Glory Be

FIFTH DAY

You had a deep compassion for the sick and the suffering. Help us to see the face of Christ especially in those who suffer; and to show them something of the love the Father has for his Son; and to see our own sufferings not as a meaningless burden but as the transforming gift of the Cross.

I ask you especially for [*here name your intention*]

Our Father - Hail Mary - Glory Be

SIXTH DAY

Your compassion extended particularly to those who despair. Help us not to lose hope or fall prey to discouragement, and, like you, to be a witness to Christ's enduring love for all God's people.

I ask you especially for [*here name your intention*]

Our Father - Hail Mary - Glory Be

SEVENTH DAY

You spent long hours hearing confessions, and brought the sacrament of Christ's reconciling love to countless thousands. Help us never to be afraid to open our sins to the overwhelming mercy of God.

I ask you especially for [*here name your intention*]

Our Father - Hail Mary - Glory Be

EIGHTH DAY

You gave a great example of the humble life of a priest; intercede for all priests, and for those who may be called to this vocation, that like you they may lead truly holy lives and be living icons of Jesus Christ in love for his people.

I ask you especially for [*here name your intention*]

Our Father - Hail Mary - Glory Be

NINTH DAY

You celebrated the Eucharist with great faithfulness and devotion. Help us all to have a strong desire to meet Jesus Christ in the Eucharist, and to know and love him really present in his Word, in his Body and Blood and in the Christian assembly.

I ask you especially for [*here name your intention*]

Our Father - Hail Mary - Glory Be

*N*ovena to St Raphael

FEAST DAY: 29TH SEPTEMBER; WITH ST MICHAEL & ST GABRIEL (FORMERLY 24TH OCTOBER)

St Raphael's name means, in Hebrew, "God heals". He is first mentioned in the Book of Tobit, where he is called "one of the seven who stand before God". The Church has considered him one of the Archangels, alongside Michael and Gabriel (and others for whom we have no names). The Book of Tobit is a great image of Christian marriage, and the Archangel Raphael plays a central role in it in bringing together the young couple, Tobias and Sarah, and protecting them from the attempts of the devil to destroy their union. He is thus the particular patron of marriage, of single people looking for a marriage partner, and of those seeking God's protection against anything that might threaten their married life. He is also a patron of those undertaking journeys, particularly long or difficult ones.

FIRST DAY

You are known as the Angel of Joy; help us always to be joyful in God's service, and to see his loving hand in all the events he sends us.

I ask you especially for [*here name your intention*]

Our Father - Hail Mary - Glory Be

SECOND DAY

You are known as the Angel of Healing. Intercede for all those who need healing of mind or body, and obtain for them the consolations of God's love.

I ask you especially for [*here name your intention*]

Our Father - Hail Mary - Glory Be

THIRD DAY

You are known as a powerful protector against demons. Protect us against all the attacks of the Evil One, all his wiles and deceits, and especially the lie he tells us that we cannot be loved.

I ask you especially for [*here name your intention*]

Our Father - Hail Mary - Glory Be

FOURTH DAY

You are known as a giver of peace of mind. Help us always to live in that peace God gives to his children, whatever our outward circumstances.

I ask you especially for [*here name your intention*]

Our Father - Hail Mary - Glory Be

FIFTH DAY

You are known as the Angel of Love. Help us to know God's love for us, and to be able to have this same love for our neighbour. We particularly ask this grace for married couples, and for those discerning a vocation to married life.

I ask you especially for [*here name your intention*]

Our Father - Hail Mary - Glory Be

SIXTH DAY

You are an especial patron of youth, and the angel of happy meetings and wise choices. Help all who are young wisely to discern what God calls them to do, guide them on their path in life, and be with them in all the encounters God sends them.

I ask you especially for [*here name your intention*]

Our Father - Hail Mary - Glory Be

SEVENTH DAY

You are called the angel of everyday life. Help us all to see God's hand in our daily lives, even in events that may seem trivial to us, and to see God's loving mercy in them all; help us to make God's love present in our world.

I ask you especially for [*here name your intention*]

Our Father - Hail Mary - Glory Be

EIGHTH DAY

You are the patron of travel. Be with all who have journeys to make: protect them on their way, and bring them safely to their destination.

I ask you especially for [*here name your intention*]

Our Father - Hail Mary - Glory Be

NINTH DAY

You are known as the Angel of Last Anointing, who watches over those called from this life to God. Be with us and protect us when we make our last journey, our great Passover into the eternal country, to God's holy mountain.

I ask you especially for [*here name your intention*]

Our Father - Hail Mary - Glory Be

Here are two traditional prayers to St Raphael for the wise choice of a marriage partner. You could say any one of these over nine days as a novena for this intention.

TRADITIONAL PRAYER TO ST RAPHAEL

Glorious St Raphael, patron and lover of the young, I call upon you and ask for your help. In all confidence I open my heart to you, to beg your guidance and assistance in the important task of planning my future. Obtain for me through your intercession the light of God's grace, so that I may decide wisely concerning the person who is to be my partner through life. O Angel of Happy Meetings, lead us by the hand to find each other. May all our movements be guided by your light and transfigured by your joy. As you led the young Tobias to Sarah and opened up for him a new life of happiness with her in holy marriage, lead me to the one whom in your angelic wisdom you judge best suited to be united with me in marriage.

Amen

PRAYER OF AN ENGAGED COUPLE

St Raphael, angel of chaste courtship, bless our friendship and our love, that sin may have no part in it. May our mutual love bind us so closely that our future home may always be most like the home of the Holy Family of Nazareth. Offer your prayers to God for both of us, and obtain the blessing of God upon our marriage, just as you were the herald of blessing for the marriage of Tobias and Sarah.

Amen

Novena to St Thérèse of Lisieux

Thérèse Martin was born into a bourgeois family in France in 1873. She lost her mother at an early age; this changed her from being a happy child to one who was withdrawn and neurotic. Her close relationship with her father, however, helped her to understand the fatherhood of God. She entered the Carmelite convent in Lisieux as an enclosed nun at the age of only fifteen (after badgering the Pope, and getting special permission from her bishop), and stayed there until she died aged only twenty-three.

Under obedience, she had written a short autobiography; this was later published, and inspired many to follow her "little way" of humble confidence in God. She was proclaimed a Doctor of the Church in 1997.

St Thérèse always wanted to travel, and to be a missionary, but was unable to do so, apart from one brief trip to Rome. Since her death, however, her relics have travelled the world, and have even been into space. She promised to spend her time in heaven doing good on earth, and her many devotees know she keeps that promise.

FIRST DAY

As a small child, you were absolutely obstinate. Intercede for parents whose children are headstrong. Help them to be firm but loving.

I ask you especially for [*here name your intention*]

Our Father - Hail Mary - Glory Be

SECOND DAY

You were very close to your father. Help Christian fathers to show their children something of the loving fatherhood of God.

I ask you especially for [*here name your intention*]

Our Father - Hail Mary - Glory Be

THIRD DAY

You suffered from being neurotic and scrupulous. Help all those who suffer in this way to know God's love and mercy.

I ask you especially for [*here name your intention*]

Our Father - Hail Mary - Glory Be

FOURTH DAY

You so wanted to enter the Carmel of Lisieux that you were not afraid to ask the Pope himself, and you were ready to endure the humiliation of being removed by the Swiss Guard. Help us not to reject God's will for us because we are afraid of being humiliated.

I ask you especially for [*here name your intention*]

Our Father - Hail Mary - Glory Be

FIFTH DAY

You showed the greatest consideration for those you disliked. Help us to learn not to judge, but to be kind and understanding.

I ask you especially for [*here name your intention*]

Our Father - Hail Mary - Glory Be

SIXTH DAY

You prayed especially for priests. We pray that all who are called may accept their vocation. We ask God to keep his hand on them and protect them.

I ask you especially for [*here name your intention*]

Our Father - Hail Mary - Glory Be

SEVENTH DAY

You knew that God is a father who loves us and who keeps his promises. Help us to have that same confidence and assurance.

I ask you especially for [*here name your intention*]

Our Father - Hail Mary - Glory Be

EIGHTH DAY

You experienced the pain and suffering of tuberculosis, which was then incurable. We pray for all those who have painful or terminal illnesses. Intercede for them that they may know the comfort of their loving Father.

I ask you especially for [*here name your intention*]

Our Father - Hail Mary - Glory Be

NINTH DAY

You understood that it is not the apparent greatness or smallness of what we are called to do that is important in God's sight, but, rather, that we do whatever he sends us to do with a loving heart and with generosity of spirit. We pray to have this same understanding.

I ask you especially for [*here name your intention*]

Our Father - Hail Mary - Glory Be

Novena Prayer to St Gerard Majella

Gerard Majella was born near Naples, Italy, in 1726. His father was a tailor, and died when Gerard was twelve. Although his mother and uncle wanted him to take up the family business, Gerard was called to the religious life. He was unable to join the Capuchin order because of poor health, but was finally accepted by the Redemptorists as a lay brother when he was twenty-three. He lived only for a short time longer, dying of tuberculosis in 1755, aged twenty-nine. His life was marked by patient acceptance of suffering and injustice. Most famously, he was falsely accused by an unmarried mother of being the father of her child. He made no protest but accepted the judgements of those around him in silence and patience until, eventually, the woman admitted she had lied. For this reason, St Gerard is known as an especial patron of motherhood, of unborn children and of childbirth. He is often invoked by those who are trying to have children, and by expectant mothers.

Here are two traditional prayers to St Gerard, one for motherhood, and one for safe delivery of a child. Either could be said over nine days as a novena.

PRAYER FOR MOTHERHOOD

Good St Gerard, powerful intercessor before God and wonderworker of our day, I call on you and seek your aid. You, who on earth always fulfilled God's design, help me to do God's holy will. Beseech the master of life, from whom all parenthood comes, to make me fruitful, so I may raise up children to God in this life and heirs to the kingdom of his glory in the world to come.

Amen

PRAYER FOR SAFE DELIVERY

Great St Gerard, beloved servant of Jesus Christ, perfect imitator of your meek and humble Saviour, and devoted child of the Mother of God: enkindle within my heart a spark of that heavenly fire of charity that glowed in yours, and made you a seraph of love.

Glorious St Gerard, because when you were falsely accused of crime you bore like your Divine Master without murmur or complaint the calumnies of wicked men, you have been raised up by God as patron and protector of expectant mothers. Preserve me from danger and from the excessive pains accompanying childbirth, and shield the child which I now carry, that it may see the light of day and receive the cleansing waters of baptism; through Christ our Lord.

Amen

$\mathcal{N}$ovena to St Jude

FEAST DAY: 28TH OCTOBER

The Apostle St Jude takes only a modest role in the Gospel narratives, but he is probably the best-known intercessor of all the Twelve. According to tradition, St Jude, together with his companion the Apostle St Simon (not Simon Peter, but Simon the Zealot) who may have been his brother, preached the gospel in various parts of the Middle East (Persia, Mesopotamia, Armenia and around the Black Sea) and were eventually martyred in Georgia.

For some reason, St Jude has become known as the saint of lost causes, or of things despaired of: someone whose intercession is especially powerful in cases where all hope seems gone. Whatever the reason for this, many people can testify to the strength of his prayers for them.

FIRST DAY

O Blessed Apostle, St Jude, who laboured amongst the peoples of many lands and performed miracles in despairing cases, I ask you to take an interest in my need. You understand me. Hear my prayer, and plead for me. May I be patient in learning God's will and courageous in carrying it out.

I ask you especially for [*here name your intention*]

Our Father - Hail Mary - Glory Be

SECOND DAY

O Blessed Apostle, St Jude, grant that I may always serve the Lord as he deserves to be served, and live as he wants me to live. I ask you to intercede for me. May I be enlightened as to what is best for me now, and not forget the blessings I have received in the past.

I ask you especially for [*here name your intention*]

Our Father - Hail Mary - Glory Be

THIRD DAY

Holy St Jude, who so faithfully helped to spread the gospel, I ask you to remember me and my needs. May the Lord listen to your prayers on my behalf. May I always pray with fervour and devotion, resigning myself to God's will, and seeing his purposes in all my trials. Help me to know that God will not leave any sincere prayer unanswered.

I ask you especially for [*here name your intention*]

Our Father - Hail Mary - Glory Be

FOURTH DAY

St Jude, you were called as one of the Apostles. Listen with compassion as I ask for your help; pray that God may answer my prayer as he knows best, giving me grace to see his purpose in all things.

I ask you especially for [*here name your intention*]

Our Father - Hail Mary - Glory Be

FIFTH DAY

Holy St Jude, Apostle and companion of Jesus Christ, your life was filled with zeal for the gospel. Listen to my prayers now. May I never forget the blessings I have received in the past, and may I be resigned to God's holy will.

I ask you especially for [*here name your intention*]

Our Father - Hail Mary - Glory Be

SIXTH DAY

St Jude, Apostle of Christ and helper in desperate cases, listen to my prayer. May I seek only what pleases God and is best for my salvation. May what I desire be granted, if it is for my good; help me to know that God leaves no prayer without an answer, even if it is not what I may expect.

I ask you especially for [*here name your intention*]

Our Father - Hail Mary - Glory Be

SEVENTH DAY

Holy Apostle, St Jude, Christ chose you as one of the Twelve, and you were given the gift of martyrdom. I know you are close to God. Listen to my request; and help me to see God's purpose in all things.

I ask you especially for [*here name your intention*]

Our Father - Hail Mary - Glory Be

EIGHTH DAY

Holy St Jude, pray that I may always imitate Christ and live according to his will. Intercede for me, that I may obtain whatever I need for my salvation. Help me to accept from God whatever answer he gives to what I now ask.

I ask you especially for [*here name your intention*]

Our Father - Hail Mary - Glory Be

NINTH DAY

Holy St Jude, Apostle and martyr, help my life be pleasing to God. Intercede for me today; pray especially that I may seek God's will above all things and see his love for me in whatever trials or difficulties he sends me.

I ask you especially for [*here name your intention*]

Our Father - Hail Mary - Glory Be

$\mathcal{N}$ovena to St Martin de Porres

FEAST DAY: 3RD NOVEMBER

Martin was born in Peru in 1579, the illegitimate son of a Spanish father and a mother who was a freed slave. Rejected by his father for being too black, he grew up in poverty with his mother and sister. From an early age he had a great love of God and of the poor. He became a Dominican lay brother as he could not be accepted into the order because of his colour. He worked in menial jobs and then as an infirmarian. He became renowned for his medical ability but he eschewed the fame that came with that and remained humble and hidden. He was also known for his love of the poor and also of animals, especially dogs. He was canonised in 1962 and is the patron of interracial harmony.

FIRST DAY

You were rejected and abandoned by your father. We pray for all those who experience that same situation and for all those who are rejected for not meeting their family's expectations in some way. May they be reconciled, as you were finally reconciled with your own father.

I ask you especially for [*here name your intention*]

Our Father - Hail Mary - Glory Be

SECOND DAY

When you were a young child your mother was your only parent. We pray for all single-parent families, and ask that you help them in the particular difficulties they face.

I ask you especially for [*here name your intention*]

Our Father - Hail Mary - Glory Be

THIRD DAY

You grew up poor but you always gave to those who had even less. We ask you to help us to become generous with our goods and our time, never feeling that we have nothing to offer.

I ask you especially for [*here name your intention*]

Our Father - Hail Mary - Glory Be

FOURTH DAY

When you were eight your father reappeared and whisked you off to a prosperous life in another country before sending you back to the life you had before. We pray for all those whose family life is insecure and disrupted. May they experience, as you did, that God is their security.

I ask you especially for [*here name your intention*]

Our Father - Hail Mary - Glory Be

FIFTH DAY

You lived alone, working to support yourself from a very young age. We pray for all children who have adult responsibilities; for all children who support their families; and for all children who are carers for their parents. Intercede for them that they may receive the help they need.

I ask you especially for [*here name your intention*]

Our Father - Hail Mary - Glory Be

SIXTH DAY

You were rejected because of your colour – even by the Church. We pray for all those who suffer discrimination of any kind. May all in authority deal with everyone justly, and may we treat each other as brothers and sisters in Christ.

I ask you especially for [*here name your intention*]

Our Father - Hail Mary - Glory Be

SEVENTH DAY

You were not ashamed to do the most menial of jobs.
You were even happy cleaning lavatories. May we, too,
learn humility and come to see that all work can be holy.

I ask you especially for [*here name your intention*]

Our Father - Hail Mary - Glory Be

EIGHTH DAY

You were known for your love of animals. Help us to
love and respect all God's creation.

I ask you especially for [*here name your intention*]

Our Father - Hail Mary - Glory Be

NINTH DAY

You had great medical skill and love for other people.
We pray for all who are involved in caring for the sick.
May they share something of your compassion and
your skill.

I ask you especially for [*here name your intention*]

Our Father - Hail Mary - Glory Be

Christ the King

If Jesus Christ is a king, his kingdom, as he declares to Pilate, is not of this world. The Kingdom of God is not some theocratic state to be achieved by force of arms and a clericalised polity, as some in the past have thought. Insofar as God's kingdom is visibly present in the world, it is that thing we call the Church. But it is not by any means confined to the obvious and outward structures of the Church, although we have Jesus's assurance that the Spirit will not wholly abandon these. Outside these visible things, God is always present to his people, and acts by means we cannot see or know, except by the clear evidence of love shown and suffering accepted: of love that is stronger than death. This is the sign of God's kingdom. Any who bear this token are in some sense subjects of Christ the King. But he is a king who rules by mercy and by forgiveness. It is not for us to be jealous of his mercy to those whom we do not recognise as our fellow-subjects, or our fellow-Christians. It is enough that we ask his mercy for ourselves, and for the world.

The feast of Christ the King is celebrated on the last Sunday of the Church's year, before the start of Advent and at the end of Ordinary Time. To end on the feast, begin the novena on the Saturday before the preceding Sunday; to end on the eve of the feast, begin on the Friday of that week.

For the feast of Christ the King, the Church assigns three different Gospels, one for each year of the Sunday cycle (A, B and C). They are *Mt* 25:31–46 (A); *Jn* 18:33–37 (B); *Lk* 23:35–43 (C).

FIRST DAY
....

Mt 25:31–46

This Gospel is a parable of the End of Days. The citizens of the kingdom are the merciful. This is the sole criterion – not how hard or profoundly we have prayed, or how much we have fasted or denied ourselves, but how far we have shown mercy to those in need.

Father, help me to be merciful.
I ask you especially for [*here name your intention*]

Our Father - Hail Mary - Glory Be

SECOND DAY
....

Mt 25:31–46

The Gospel is very clear that we need to consider all those we meet who require our help as, in effect, bearers of Jesus Christ. Christ is in each person; this is another reason to show love to them, apart from their dignity as human beings made in God's image (although these facts are closely related).

I ask you especially for [*here name your intention*]

Our Father - Hail Mary - Glory Be

THIRD DAY

Mt 25:31–46

The King here acts as judge; however, the judgement
is not based on an abstract law, but born of his own
relationship with the one on trial. "How did you behave
to me?" is his question. We should not get tied up in
nice questions about whether those instances in which
we can allege we did show mercy to others will somehow
outweigh the countless occasions we have shown
neglect; rather we should try to see how, on this day, at
this moment, we can be merciful and not neglectful to
whichever of our neighbours is in need.

Father, help me to live in the present moment and not be
imprisoned by my past sins.
I ask you especially for [*here name your intention*]

Our Father - Hail Mary - Glory Be

FOURTH DAY

Jn 18:33–37

It is hard not to feel some sympathy for Pilate here,
at least as John presents him. The harassed colonial
administrator trying to keep the peace between
squabbling native holy men is not perhaps so
immediately sympathetic a figure for us as he was to
our grandparents' generation, but we can recognise,
surely, a picture of a man trying to judge fairly a quarrel
that is not his own, that he does not understand, and
that frankly rather bores him, except for the nagging
danger that it will provoke a riot, with all the tiresome
complications of destruction of property and disruption

to commerce, bother and injury to the garrison, and writing reports about it all to Rome. It was also good Roman practice to keep claimants to native kingdoms alive and compliant, in case a figurehead for a new regime was needed.

Pilate's misfortune was to be caught up in something he did not understand, and for which his standard battery of responses was simply inadequate.

Sometimes we find ourselves similarly out of our depth; we need to be careful not to be led astray by fear or expediency.

Father, help me to see things as you see them, and not be swayed by fear or self-interest at the expense of mercy. I ask you especially for [*here name your intention*]

Our Father - Hail Mary - Glory Be

FIFTH DAY

Jn 18:33–37

After much prompting, Jesus tells Pilate, "Mine is not a kingdom of this world". Pilate humours him: this is probably some species of harmless lunatic, with perhaps a certain way with words, who has got caught up in a piece of Temple politics. No need to make a fuss; flog him for his pains, and send him on his way. As we know, the religious authorities weren't willing to let the matter drop so easily, and Pilate gave in to their nagging. But his first reaction is not untypical. Many people today see religion as a harmless eccentricity, to be tolerated as long as it doesn't make a fuss or try to pretend it has anything to do with the serious business of getting on with life. We can be tempted to go along with this estimation: to avoid doing or saying anything that might be embarrassing.

Father, help me not to pretend things don't matter for the sake of a quiet life.
I ask you especially for [*here name your intention*]

Our Father - Hail Mary - Glory Be

SIXTH DAY

Jn 18:33–37

Jesus's kingdom is founded on truth, not on violence or power or political accommodation. This is an irrelevance to Pilate, as to most lazily practical men: he famously responds, "What is truth?" But "all who are on the side of truth" listen to Jesus's voice. What does it mean, to be on the side of truth? One thing it means, perhaps, is trying to live in honesty, speaking truthfully to others and hearing the truth about ourselves without reflexively defending ourselves against anything that challenges our self-delusion. It means trying to live honestly and openly, without taking refuge behind masks and conventional pieties.

We see in Jesus how the world treats those who bear witness to the truth; but we know, too, that he himself will be with those who listen to his voice.

Father, help me not to be afraid of or indifferent to the truth; help me to speak the truth in love, and hear it without fear.
I ask you especially for [*here name your intention*]

Our Father - Hail Mary - Glory Be

SEVENTH DAY

Now the King is crucified: helpless, naked and a spectacle to be mocked. Let us not suppose we would be slow to join in the mockery; most of us, if we are honest, take some pleasure in seeing the humiliation of the hitherto popular and successful, and these things are infectious. It is a poor sort of king, by all normal standards, who ends up pinned on a gibbet by the roadside. This, though, is how human beings react to the love of the merciful Father; and his answer is, always, forgiveness.

Father, help me not to delight in others' misfortune. I ask you especially for [*here name your intention*]

Our Father - Hail Mary - Glory Be

EIGHTH DAY

If you are a king, then why don't you save yourself? This question is put to Jesus by the Jewish leaders, by the soldiers of the crucifixion party and even by one of the criminals crucified with him. This is certainly not the model of heroic leadership our culture is comfortable with; a Hollywood script would have Jesus rescued by his disciples, who had somehow found courage they never knew they had, or, perhaps, wrenching himself free from his cross in an access of hitherto latent super-strength, scattering Roman soldiers like matchsticks. Or something like that. We do not like our heroes to be defeated. It seems unlikely that Jesus's contemporaries, reared on stories of the glorious victories of the Maccabees, would have been much different.

But this is what Christ's kingship looks like, and what, in the world's eyes, his followers have to look forward to. But beyond this defeat, this disappointment, is something of an altogether different order: victory over death, a victory that, unlike those of earthly kings, can never be overturned or undone.

Father, help me not to reckon success and failure as the world does.
I ask you especially for [*here name your intention*]

Our Father - Hail Mary - Glory Be

NINTH DAY

Lk 23:35–43

We should have no doubt that the men crucified with Jesus were villains; one of them admits as much. By the crude standards of the day, they got what they deserved. And yet one of them turns to Jesus (and repentance, remember, means literally a turning towards God) and asks to be remembered by Jesus when he comes into his kingdom. He is at once given a promise that he will join him in paradise. God's mercy is like this, this Gospel says. What matters is not what we have done, or how often, but that we ask to be forgiven.

Father, forgive me my sins; call me into your kingdom.
I ask you especially for [*here name your intention*]

Our Father - Hail Mary - Glory Be

❧ SCRIPTURAL NOVENAS ❧ MOSES ❧
DISCERNING & ACCEPTING OUR VOCATION ❧
ELIJAH ❧ FINDING STRENGTH IN GOD ❧
TOBIT ❧ MARRIAGE ❧ HANNAH ❧ THE GIFT OF
CHILDREN ❧ JOSEPH & HIS BROTHERS ❧ FOR
PEACE IN THE FAMILY ❧ DAVID & ABSALOM ❧

SCRIPTURAL NOVENAS ❧

❧ ESTRANGED CHILDREN ❧ MARTHA ❧
BEING THE ONE THAT DOES ALL THE WORK ❧
❧ RUTH & NAOMI ❧ FEELING ABANDONED
& FORGOTTEN ❧ DEBORAH & BARAK ❧
WHEN THINGS SEEM TOO MUCH FOR US ❧
JONAH ❧ WHEN GOD'S PLAN DOESN'T SEEM
TO MAKE SENSE ❧ JOB ❧ BEING HONEST
WITH GOD ❧ ABRAHAM ❧ OLD AGE ❧

PART II: SCRIPTURAL NOVENAS

*M*oses: Discerning and Accepting Our Vocation

SCRIPTURE: READ THE STORY OF MOSES.
(*EXODUS* 1–20, 32–4; *NUMBERS*; *DEUTERONOMY*)

Besides Abraham, Moses is perhaps the clearest example Scripture gives of God acting in one man's life. Moses is a reluctant prophet; but he accepts, eventually, that God has a purpose for him, and follows his call even though it sometimes looks to him, and to others, like plain lunacy. He is not a plaster saint – he is angry, impatient, mistrustful of God and himself, prone to doubt; yet he also trusts that God will fulfil his promises, and so becomes the means for God to achieve literally incredible things.

FIRST DAY

Now Pharaoh's daughter went down to bathe in the river ... Among the reeds she noticed the basket ... She opened it, and saw a baby boy, crying; and she was sorry for him (Ex 2:5–6).

Pharaoh planned to kill all male Hebrew children; God intervened to frustrate this plan in several ways. Moses was, ironically, rescued by Pharaoh's own daughter. God had a plan for him. We are unlikely to know all the details, but we may feel sure that God's providence has preserved us, too, from our childhood.

Father, help me to believe that you have a plan for me, too. Help me to be thankful for those parts of your plan I can already see.

I ask you especially for [*here name your intention*]

Our Father - Hail Mary - Glory Be

SECOND DAY

Moses, a man by now ... saw an Egyptian strike a Hebrew, one of his countrymen. Looking round, he could see no one, so he killed the Egyptian and hid him in the sand ... When Pharaoh heard of the matter he would have killed Moses, but Moses fled from Pharaoh and made for the land of Midian (Ex 2:11–12, 15).

Moses is a man of high status in Egypt, but he feels sympathy for his own people, who are oppressed. But his first rash effort to help them is a disaster, and he has to run away. We, too, can try to force God's hand by acting rashly; this usually turns out badly.

Father, help me to be patient, but also to remember that you can repair whatever mistakes I have made: your plans are not defeated by my impatience.

I ask you especially for [*here name your intention*]

Our Father - Hail Mary - Glory Be

THIRD DAY

Moses ... led his flock to the far side of the wilderness and came to Horeb, the mountain of God. There, the angel of the Lord appeared to him in the shape of a flame of fire, coming from the middle of a bush ... "I must go and look at this strange sight," Moses said ... and God called to him from the middle of the bush ... "Come no nearer," he said. "Take off your shoes, for the place on which you stand is holy ground." (Ex 3:1–5)

Moses did not expect to be called by God in this way, amidst his laborious daily round. Yet he was open to hearing God's voice, and knew that any place and time is made holy when God acts there.

Father, help me be attentive to the signs you send, and open to your presence and action where I do not expect it, and especially in the midst of my daily life.

I ask you especially for [*here name your intention*]

Our Father - Hail Mary - Glory Be

FOURTH DAY

And the Lord said "I have seen the miserable state of my people in Egypt ... so come, I send you to Pharaoh to bring the sons of Israel, my people, out of Egypt." Moses said to God, "Who am I to go to Pharaoh and bring the sons of Israel out of Egypt?" (Ex 3:7, 10–11)

Like Moses, we may not believe we are able to be called in the way that God seems to be calling us (as a priest, or a husband, or a mother, or whatever it might be). We need to trust that God will help us to do what we are given to do. St Catherine of Siena said, "Be what you are meant to be, and you will set the entire world alight".

Father, help me to trust that you know what you are doing.

I ask you especially for [*here name your intention*]

Our Father - Hail Mary - Glory Be

FIFTH DAY

And as Pharaoh approached ... the sons of Israel were terrified ... To Moses they said, "Were there no graves in Egypt that you must lead us out to die in the wilderness?" ... The Lord said to Moses, "... Tell the sons of Israel to march on." (Ex 14:10–11, 15)

After many miraculous signs from God, Pharaoh finally lets the people of Israel go, only to change his mind soon after and pursue them. Moses and the Israelites are caught between the impassable sea and a pursuing army. We, too, may know what it is like to feel trapped, helpless, terrified, whether by circumstances or by our own sins; but the same God who opened a way for the Israelites through the sea can open one for us, and will, if only we ask him in faith.

Father, I ask for the faith to make this prayer.

I ask you especially for [*here name your intention*]

Our Father - Hail Mary - Glory Be

SIXTH DAY

When the people saw that Moses was a long time before coming down the mountain, they gathered round Aaron and said to him, "Come, make us a god ..." ... He ... cast an effigy of a calf. "Here is your God, Israel," they cried "who brought you out of the land of Egypt!"
(Ex 32:1, 4)

God gives the Law to Moses on Mount Sinai; but the Israelites, impatient at his absence, persuade Aaron to make them a visible idol, a golden calf (a typical pagan symbol of that time). When Moses sees this, he is furious, and in his frustration throws down the tablets of the Law. Yet he does not give up on the Israelites.

Father, I am often impatient of the imperfections and faults of those I have to work with. But you have put us together for a reason; help me to trust you know what you are doing. These are never the people I would have designed or chosen, but (in the end) that is a very good thing.

I ask you especially for [*here name your intention*]

Our Father - Hail Mary - Glory Be

SEVENTH DAY

Moses pleaded with the Lord his God. "Lord," he said "why should your wrath blaze out against this people of yours whom you brought out of the land of Egypt with arm outstretched and mighty hand? ... Remember Abraham, Isaac and Jacob, your servants to whom by your own self you swore ..." So the Lord relented and did not bring on his people the disaster he had threatened (Ex 32:11, 13–14).

Despite his frustration with the people, Moses keeps praying to God on the mountain, interceding for Israel. His appeal for them turns aside God's anger, and saves them. God does not need our prayer, but he has chosen to grant us a share in his own creative and sustaining work; and one big way we do this is by praying. We need to keep praying, even if we cannot see any results, or if the thing we are praying for (for us or for someone else) seems to be constantly withheld or taken away. We cannot see more than a tiny fraction of the patterned causes that enfold the world and ourselves, let alone judge what effect our small efforts are having.

Father, help me to believe you will turn my prayers to good account, however poor or meaningless they sometimes seem.

I ask you especially for [*here name your intention*]

Our Father - Hail Mary - Glory Be

EIGHTH DAY

And the Lord said to Moses: "How long will this people insult me? How long will they refuse to believe in me despite the signs I have worked among them? I will strike them with pestilence and disown them." ... Moses answered the Lord ... "No, my Lord! It is now you must display your power, according to those words you spoke, 'The Lord is slow to anger and rich in graciousness, forgiving faults and transgressions ...' In the abundance, then, of your graciousness, forgive the sin of this people." (Nb 14:11–13, 17–19)

The journey of Israel to the Promised Land takes forty long years, and takes them through many trials and hardships. They repeatedly complain and blame Moses and the Lord for all this, and often lapse into paganism. But Moses, although frustrated, does not give up on them, and reminds God of his promise.

Father, help me likewise to persevere in what I have begun, despite the hardships of the journey, and to remember all you have done for me, and that you are faithful to your promises.

I ask you especially for [*here name your intention*]

Our Father - Hail Mary - Glory Be

NINTH DAY

"The Lord has been angry with me on your account; he has sworn that I shall not cross the Jordan or enter the prosperous land which the Lord your God is giving you as your heritage ... Take care therefore not to forget the covenant which the Lord your God has made with you ... for the Lord your God is a consuming fire, a jealous God ... But if you seek him with all your heart and with all your soul, you shall find him ... for the Lord your God is a merciful God and will not desert or destroy you or forget the covenant he made on oath with your fathers." (Dt 4:21, 23–24, 29, 31)

Moses is held responsible for the people's sins, and so cannot enter the Promised Land; he accepts this suffering for the sake of the people, and testifies to the enduring faithfulness of God.

Father, help me to accept whatever suffering you give me, for the salvation of others, as did Moses, and your Son Jesus Christ; help me to know and to trust your enduring love and mercy towards me.

I ask you especially for [*here name your intention*]

Our Father - Hail Mary - Glory Be

Elijah: Finding Strength in God

SCRIPTURE: READ THE STORY OF ELIJAH
(*1 KINGS* 17–22; *2 KINGS* 1–2).

Elijah is the great hero-prophet of the Israelite kingdom. He witnesses above all to the need to worship God alone (his name means "my God is the Lord") in a world saturated with pagan idols. He is fearless in confronting the prophets of Baal and standing up to the wickedness of King Ahab and his wife Jezebel. But after his triumph over false prophets, he is terrified by the king's threats, and overwhelmed by what God is asking him to do. He wishes he were dead. We, too, however much we have achieved, often can feel utterly crushed by the tasks that keep coming to us – work, children, elderly parents, illness, all the myriad difficulties and responsibilities we have. God renews Elijah's strength, however, and then leads him to Mount Horeb, where he hears God's voice in the gentle breeze. Then he returns to call Israel, and especially its wicked rulers, to turn to God again.

FIRST DAY

Elijah the Tishbite ... said to Ahab, "As the Lord lives, the God of Israel whom I serve, there shall be neither dew nor rain these years except at my order". The word of the Lord came to him, "Go away from here ... and hide yourself in the wadi Cherith which lies east of Jordan ... He did as the Lord had said ... The ravens brought him bread in the morning and meat in the evening, and he quenched his thirst at the stream (1 K 17:1–3, 5–6).

The people of Israel, led by their king Ahab, turned from God to the worship of idols. It was left to Elijah alone to bear witness to God, and to call the king to repent. God made Elijah a promise to keep him alive in the drought that was the sign of God's displeasure.

Father, you know how trying to live by your word is sometimes difficult, and how living as a Christian in the world can seem lonely or irrational. Help me to trust that if I witness to your love for all people, you will support me.

I ask you especially for [*here name your intention*]

Our Father - Hail Mary - Glory Be

SECOND DAY

The word of the Lord came to him, "Up and go to Zarephath, a Sidonian town, and stay there. I have ordered a widow there to give you food." (1 K 17:8–9)

God sends Elijah to live in a pagan town; there, he works great signs through him – first, he provides food for the widow, her son and Elijah; then he raises the widow's son from the dead.

Father, help me to see that you are at work amongst all people, not just those visibly within the Church; help me be a sign to them of your love that is stronger than death, and let me not forget that they, too, can be the means of your care for me.

I ask you especially for [*here name your intention*]

Our Father - Hail Mary - Glory Be

THIRD DAY

The word of the Lord came to Elijah ... "Go, present yourself to Ahab ..." So Elijah set off to present himself to Ahab ... When he saw Elijah, Ahab said, "So there you are, you scourge of Israel!" "Not I," he replied. "I am not the scourge of Israel, you and your family are; because you have deserted the Lord" (1 K 18:1–2, 17–18).

Ahab's wife, Jezebel, had killed all of the Lord's prophets she could find, and Ahab had scoured all the country and its neighbours looking for Elijah, to kill him also. But Elijah, strong in his faith in God, is fearless.

Father, help me not to be afraid to acknowledge you, to confront whatever in my life I fear to meet, and to speak the truth although I know it may not be welcome; give me faith in your saving help.

I ask you especially for [*here name your intention*]

Our Father - Hail Mary - Glory Be

FOURTH DAY

Elijah stepped out in front of all the people. "How long" he said "do you mean to hobble first on one leg then on the other? If the Lord is God, follow him; if Baal, follow him." But the people never said a word. (1 K 18:21)

The people of Israel were reluctant to trust themselves wholly to God and (like their neighbours) were prone to pay their respects as well to the gods of the locality, either following the example of their kings, or as a form of supernatural insurance policy. We should not think we are immune from this temptation.

Father, you know how hard I find it to trust your providence, your plan for my life, and how tempted I am to try to hedge my bets and make bargains with the world and its idols. Help me to trust you and to know you will not fail me.

I ask you especially for [*here name your intention*]

Our Father - Hail Mary - Glory Be

FIFTH DAY

Elijah climbed to the top of Carmel and bowed down to the earth, putting his face between his knees. "Now go up," he told his servant "and look out to the sea." He went up and looked. "There is nothing at all" he said. "Go back seven times" Elijah said. The seventh time, the servant said, "Now there is a cloud, small as a man's hand, rising from the sea." (1 K 18:42–44)

Elijah trusted in God's word to him, and persevered in looking for the sign he knew God would send that salvation – rain after drought – was coming to Israel.

Father, help me to be patient in discerning the signs of your work for myself and for others.

I ask you especially for [*here name your intention*]

Our Father - Hail Mary - Glory Be

SIXTH DAY

Elijah said, "Go and say to Ahab, 'Harness the chariot and go down before the rain stops you'". And with that the sky grew dark with cloud and storm, and rain fell in torrents. Ahab mounted his chariot and made for Jezreel. The hand of the Lord was on Elijah, and tucking his cloak he ran in front of Ahab as far as the outskirts of Jezreel (1 K 18:44–46).

Surely one of the most striking images in Scripture is this, the prophet Elijah running through a rainstorm the sixteen miles or so between Mount Carmel and Jezreel, outpacing the king's chariot, the skies dark and thunderous, rain loud on the dry earth.

Father, grant me your strength, and the faith you gave the prophet.

I ask you especially for [*here name your intention*]

Our Father - Hail Mary - Glory Be

SEVENTH DAY

Elijah went on into the wilderness ... and sitting under a furze bush wished he were dead. "O Lord," he said "I have had enough. Take my life; I am no better than my ancestors." Then he lay down and went to sleep. But an angel touched him and said, "Get up and eat."
(1 K 19:4–5)

After Elijah defeats the prophets of Baal, Ahab's queen, Jezebel, vows again to kill him. After his moment of triumph he is exhausted and terrified, and flees. But God comes to him in a simple practical way – bringing food, and sleep.

Father, help me to accept gratefully your great gifts of food and rest; help me not to give up, not to mistake fatigue, or the distorted gaze that sadness can bring, for the truth about the world and my place in it. Give me hope.

I ask you especially for [*here name your intention*]

Our Father - Hail Mary - Glory Be

EIGHTH DAY

Then he was told, "Go out and stand on the mountain before the Lord." Then the Lord himself went by. There came a mighty wind, so strong it tore the mountains and shattered the rocks before the Lord. But the Lord was not in the wind. After the wind came an earthquake. But the Lord was not in the earthquake. After the earthquake came a fire. But the Lord was not in the fire. And after the fire there came the sound of a gentle breeze. And when Elijah heard this, he covered his face with his cloak and went out and stood at the entrance of the cave. Then a voice came to him, which said, "What are you doing here, Elijah?" (1 K 19:11–13)

Elijah, as we have seen, is at the end of his tether; he is once more convinced that he alone in Israel has not abandoned God. But he follows a call to go to Horeb, the mountain of God. There, God does not show himself as a mighty force of nature, but as a quiet voice, which tells Elijah he is not alone, and has not been abandoned.

Father, help me to listen patiently for your voice, not to rush to judgement or to mistake other things for you. Help me to make time for prayer.

I ask you especially for [*here name your intention*]

Our Father - Hail Mary - Glory Be

NINTH DAY

Now as they walked on, talking as they went, a chariot of fire appeared and horses of fire, coming between the two of them; and Elijah went up to heaven in the whirlwind. Elisha saw it, and shouted, "My father! My father! Chariot of Israel and its chargers!" (2 K 2:11–12)

Elijah is taken up in a fiery chariot; in the Gospels, he is one of the witnesses to the Transfiguration, and in both Jewish and Christian tradition he will announce the Messiah's coming. He reminds us that we live in hope, not just of God's action on our behalf in this life, but of his triumphant consummation and reconciling of all things at the end of time.

Father, give me hope that you will make all things new.

I ask you especially for [*here name your intention*]

Our Father - Hail Mary - Glory Be

Tobit: Marriage

SCRIPTURE: READ THE BOOK OF TOBIT.

We may have many reasons to pray about marriage. If we are married, we may be experiencing difficulties – with our spouse or our children, with money or where we are living, or with some other aspect of our relationship. We may be unmarried, and want to ask God for a wife or a husband; we may be in a relationship, or even engaged to be married, and want God's help in discerning what to do now.

This novena draws on texts from the Book of Tobit. This book is conventionally listed amongst the historical books of the Bible, but it is actually what we would call a historical novel. It is set in the time of the Jewish exile in Babylon, although it was written much later. It tells the story of Tobit and his son Tobias, and how they are saved from various afflictions by God's angel Raphael. A big part of the story concerns Tobias's finding a wife, his distant cousin Sarah, and their triumph over adversity through God's help. Tobias and Sarah put all their difficulties into God's hands, and he does not let them down.

FIRST DAY

Do not be afraid; she was destined for you from the beginning, and it is you who will save her (Tb 6:18).

Marriage is the sacramental means God has designed for the salvation of a human couple; each is the primary means, under God, of the other's salvation. Their physical bond is a covenanted means of grace for them. Spouses are indeed "destined for each other", but not in the sense that we need search the world for some supposed ideal person, "the One". God respects and confirms the choices we make, if we have discerned them with prayer and prudence. We should remember that all circumstances and events, even the apparently trivial, are from him; we should not be so daunted by them, or so fearful of risk, as to be afraid to act. God makes what we choose generously and lovingly into our "destiny"; his grace goes before us and after us.

Father, we entrust our lives and marriage to you. Be with us in our joys and sorrows, and help us to see your hand even in what look like impossible difficulties. Take away all that stands in the way of our love for each other and for you. We ask you especially for [*here name your intention*]

Our Father - Hail Mary - Glory Be

SECOND DAY

Tobias ... fell so deeply in love with her that he could no longer call his heart his own (Tb 6:18).

Marriage calls us to a total gift of ourselves – heart, body, will – so that we no longer look first to our own good, but to that of our spouse, and (if God sends them) to that of our children. This gift of ourselves follows the pattern of the utter self-giving of the Holy Trinity, which is the very model of personhood: by living in this way, with God's grace, we become authentically human. Absolute self-giving in some form or other is part of the essential pattern of human happiness.

Father, help us to give ourselves without reserve.
We ask you especially for [*here name your intention*]

Our Father - Hail Mary - Glory Be

THIRD DAY

It was you who said, "It is not good that the man should be alone; let us make him a helpmate like himself." And so I do not take my sister for any lustful motive; I do it in singleness of heart (Tb 8:6–7).

Human beings are made to live in communion with each other. Physical attraction is a sign and an expression of this purpose, but (as fallen beings) we are sadly able to try to separate it from its proper context and make our proper physical desires just another way of being selfish. Sexuality is at the heart of any marriage, but needs to be part of our whole gift of ourselves in all our aspects ("singleness of heart").

Father, help us to live our sexuality well, in love and truth.
We ask you especially for [*here name your intention*]

Our Father - Hail Mary - Glory Be

FOURTH DAY

Be kind enough to have pity on her and on me and bring us to old age together (Tb 8:7).

The real blessing of marriage lies not in the joys of courtship, the happiness of a wedding-day, or the delight of discovering life together, real and important though all these things are. It is in the gradual growth of the couple together, through whatever circumstances God sends them, so that they can be icons of Christ to each other and to the world; for this they need to accept the events, which may seem difficult or baffling, by which God remakes them together and slowly breaks down whatever may be in them that prevents the growth of love for God and for each other. Marriage requires us to give up self-will and live for the other; any honest reflection will admit that this is a seemingly impossible task, but God is patient. For this he gives us a lifetime.

Father, help us to welcome the events you send us, every day.
We ask you especially for [*here name your intention*]

Our Father - Hail Mary - Glory Be

220

FIFTH DAY

Tobias rose from the bed, and said to Sarah, "Get up, my wife! You and I must pray and petition our Lord to win his grace and protection." (Tb 8:4)

A married couple, or an engaged couple, should pray together. The world and the devil (which the Book of Tobit personifies in the demon that afflicts Sarah before her marriage) set themselves against marriage, because a happy marriage is a living sign to the world of God's love. We need to pray for God to defend the possibility of marriage from all that would suggest to us that lifelong commitment is cruel or impossible. We should remember that, in marriage, we promise to stay with our spouse, and God promises to be with us to help us. And, unlike us, God always keeps his promises.

Father, give us the spirit of prayer.
We ask you especially for [*here name your intention*]

Our Father - Hail Mary - Glory Be

SIXTH DAY

I must be frank with you: I have tried to find a husband for her seven times among our kinsmen, and all of them have died the first evening, on going to her room. But for the present, my boy, eat and drink; the Lord will grant you his grace and peace (Tb 7:10–11).

Sarah has been intended for marriage seven times already; on each occasion, her prospective husband has died before consummating the marriage. By rights, then, Tobias – who wants to marry her – is also a dead man.

We may suppose, at times, that marriage means our death: death of that freedom to do what we want which we may think is characteristic of the single life. But Sarah's father has faith that God will protect Tobias; and he does. The "death" we may imagine lies in marriage will probably prove only an illusion; and, in any case, God has in Jesus Christ shown definitively that he is stronger than death.

Father, help us not to be afraid.
We ask you especially for [*here name your intention*]

Our Father - Hail Mary - Glory Be

SEVENTH DAY

Edna ... said to Tobias, "Dear son ... I hope to live long enough to see the children of you and my daughter Sarah ... In the sight of the Lord I give my daughter into your keeping. Never make her unhappy as long as you live ... Henceforward I am your mother" (Tb 10:12).

We should not think that relations with our parents-in-law will always be peaceful, or that it is always (or often) easy either for child or for parent to get used to the new relationships that marriage sets up. Both children and parents can find it difficult to detach, and to accept the new reality that, for the married couple, their spouse (and children, if God sends them) now holds the first place. But God is faithful, and can (and will) make all things new, if we trust him and ask him in faith.

Father, help us to accept all the people you put in our life.
We ask you especially for [*here name your intention*]

Our Father - Hail Mary - Glory Be

EIGHTH DAY

They laid [Tobit] back on his bed; he died and was buried with honour. When his mother died, Tobias buried her beside his father ... Tobias ... lived in Ecbatana with Raguel, his father-in-law. He treated the aging parents of his wife with every care and respect, and later buried them ... Much honoured, he lived to the age of a hundred and seventeen years (Tb 14:11–14).

We may think the commandment "honour your father and mother, that you may have long life in the land" is a relic of an older form of society, and hardly applies to us now; we are perhaps inclined to be mildly amused that the author of Tobit seems to take it so literally. But the duty of care we owe to our parents is part of the wider duty we have to all who, like us, are children of the one Father. The fact that we know their faults better than most other people's doesn't exclude them from this. Marriage makes us more strongly incorporate into the Body of Christ, and part of a close-woven network of love that crosses the generations.

Father, help us to live this truth.
We ask you especially for [*here name your intention*]

Our Father - Hail Mary - Glory Be

NINTH DAY

Jerusalem, Holy City, God scourged you for your handiwork yet still will take pity on the sons of the upright ... within you he may comfort every exile, and within you he may love all who are distressed, for all generations to come. A bright light shall shine over all the regions of the earth; many nations shall come from far away, from all the ends of the earth, to dwell close to the holy name of the Lord God ... Within you, generation after generation shall proclaim their joy (Tb 13:9–11).

All of our joys in this life are foretastes of the joy that God will grant us in the fuller life to come, a life the author of Tobit describes as the renewed Jerusalem. The love and mutual forgiveness that God grants, in his grace, to married couples and their children is a sign to the world of this unimagined life, where all our promise will be fulfilled, and our broken plans made whole.

Father, help us to live the happiness we are given, trusting that it is not an illusion, but a sign of what is to come; and help us to accept whatever sufferings we are sent, not as punishment but as parts of a plan we cannot yet see, but will, in your mercy, come some day to recognise.

We ask you especially for [*here name your intention*]

Our Father - Hail Mary - Glory Be

*H*annah: The Gift of Children

SCRIPTURE: READ THE STORY OF HANNAH
(*1 SAMUEL* 1:1–2:11).

The story of Hannah is found in the First Book of Samuel. She is the prophet Samuel's mother, one of the two wives of Elkanah. Elkanah's other wife, Penninah, had children, but Hannah had none. In spite of this, Elkanah loved Hannah more than he loved Penninah, and perhaps because of this Penninah hated Hannah and taunted her for her childlessness. Hannah didn't insult Penninah back, but continued to pray to God. When the prophet Eli saw Hannah praying in the Temple, he thought she was drunk; but Hannah remained humble. Finally her son Samuel was born. His name is said to mean "The Lord has heard". Hannah did not cling to the child, but gave him to serve God.

FIRST DAY ✓

Penninah had children but Hannah had none (1 S 1:2).

Father, you created me with the ability to give life. This desire is part of my being. You understand the longing I feel. Help me to trust in you: to know that you love me and do everything for my good. I bring this desire of mine before you, knowing you can fulfil it if you will; but let me enter into this novena trusting that if you do not give me what I hope for, it is out of love for me. Help me be at peace with this, not doubting your love but accepting all things in faith.

I ask you especially for [*here name your intention*]

Our Father - Hail Mary - Glory Be

SECOND DAY

Her rival would taunt her to annoy her (1 S 1:6).

Penninah had children, but she was still unhappy and jealous.

Help me not to expect all my problems to be solved by having a child. Let me not want a child for purely selfish reasons: to heal my pride; to suck love from him or her; to fulfil my needs; to have my life as I planned it. Let me learn how to love as you do.

I ask you especially for [*here name your intention*]

Our Father - Hail Mary - Glory Be

THIRD DAY

And this went on year after year; every year when they went up to the Temple of the Lord she used to taunt her (1 S 1:7).

Don't let me become jealous of those who have children.

Don't let me judge them, thinking I would be a better parent; and never allow me to judge you. Sometimes you give children to those who don't want them, or to those who mistreat them. Lord, I don't understand this. Give me the grace to know you don't make mistakes; that you love all those children more than I can understand; that their suffering grieves you deeply – but that you can bring good even out of that evil.

I ask you especially for [*here name your intention*]

Our Father - Hail Mary - Glory Be

FOURTH DAY

Then Elkanah her husband said to her, "Hannah, why are you crying and why are you not eating? Why so sad? Am I not more to you than ten sons?" (1 S 1:8)

Father, help me to see all the good things you have given me, especially my marriage. Don't let me destroy it, devaluing it because we have no children. Help me to be a loving spouse and to create a home where you can be present. Show me how to comfort my spouse so he or she does not feel judged by my disappointment. Help us to be happy together, and open to those you want to make part of our lives.

I ask you especially for [*here name your intention*]

Our Father - Hail Mary - Glory Be

FIFTH DAY

In the bitterness of her soul she prayed to the Lord with many tears and made a vow (1 S 1:10).

Lord, don't let me try to bargain with you or attempt to buy your favour. If I try to force you to do my will, it can only lead me to bitterness. Open my heart to see that your will is what can bring me true happiness.

I ask you especially for [*here name your intention*]

Our Father - Hail Mary - Glory Be

SIXTH DAY

[Eli] therefore supposed that she was drunk and said to her, "How long are you going to be in this drunken state? Rid yourself of your wine." (1 S 1:14)

Father, you know how I suffer because people think we have chosen not to have children. Sometimes they make careless jokes, not thinking how they hurt us. Help me not to become angry with them even if I don't show it. Help me not to strike back, but to be humble and (if it's appropriate) to ask them to pray for us. And help me to pray for them.

I ask you especially for [*here name your intention*]

Our Father - Hail Mary - Glory Be

SEVENTH DAY

And with that the woman went away; she returned to the hall and ate and was dejected no longer (1 S 1:18).

Father, I know you will answer my prayer in the way and at the time you choose. Give me the grace to recognise your answer. I know you will give me what is best for me because you love me. You will give me children in some way. If they are not the children of my body, perhaps they will be adopted, or children in some other way. Let me allow this to make me happy. Let me be open to your will and not cling on to the only answer I want.

I ask you especially for [*here name your intention*]

Our Father - Hail Mary - Glory Be

EIGHTH DAY

This is the child I prayed for, and the Lord granted me what I asked him. Now I make him over to the Lord for the whole of his life (1 S 1:27).

However you give me children, Lord, don't allow me to make an idol of them. You don't give them to me so that I can fulfil myself and my dreams, but for me to bring them to you. Grant me wisdom and discernment in bringing them up, and grant them faith and the knowledge of your love for them.

I ask you especially for [*here name your intention*]

Our Father - Hail Mary - Glory Be

NINTH DAY

My heart exults in the Lord, my horn is exalted in my God, my mouth derides my foes, for I rejoice in your power of saving (1 S 2:1).

Father, I trust you. Give me the grace of an open heart. Give me the gift of joy. Let the Child Jesus be the first child born in me. Then, whatever my life is like, I will have the peace only you can give.

I ask you especially for [*here name your intention*]

Our Father - Hail Mary - Glory Be

*J*oseph and His Brothers: For Peace in the Family

SCRIPTURE: READ THE STORY OF JOSEPH (*GENESIS* 37–50).

Joseph is one of twelve brothers. He is his father's favourite, and his brothers are jealous of him; he also has prophetic dreams, which sound to them like boasting. They plan to kill him, but instead at the last minute he is sold into slavery in Egypt. There his masters find him invaluable, and he rises to be adviser to Pharaoh himself. This means he is able to give his brothers food when famine comes; and their reconciliation brings safety to the whole people of Israel.

FIRST DAY

Israel loved Joseph more than all his other sons, for he was the son of his old age ... But his brothers, seeing how his father loved him more than all his other sons, came to hate him so much that they could not say a civil word to him (Gn 37:3–4).

This is a very familiar scene. We are very quick to detect slights, injustice or favouritism from our earliest days; small children soon learn to say "But it's not fair!"

Father, whatever the feelings of my heart, help me not to favour one of my children so as to be unjust to the others. Help me to know how to bring peace.

I ask you especially for [*here name your intention*]

Our Father - Hail Mary - Glory Be

SECOND DAY

*Now Joseph had a dream, and he repeated it to his brothers ...
"We were binding sheaves in the countryside; and my sheaf,
it seemed, rose up and stood upright; then I saw your sheaves
gather round and bow to my sheaf." "So you want to be king
over us," his brothers retorted (Gn 37:5–8).*

Maybe Joseph told his dream in all innocence, not
realising how it would seem to his brothers; but this was
not how it was taken by them. Miscommunication and
cross purposes can wreak havoc in family relationships;
this danger today is made stronger by myriad means of
communication, many of which, unlike old-fashioned
conversation, make no allowance for tone of voice
or context.

Lord, help us not to misinterpret each other, or read
more into statements (or into silence) than is meant.
Help us to hear each other charitably, and not to rush
to judgement.

I ask you especially for [*here name your intention*]

Our Father - Hail Mary - Glory Be

THIRD DAY

He had another dream ... "I thought I saw the sun, the moon and eleven stars, bowing to me." ... [H]is father scolded him. "A fine dream to have!" he said to him. "Are all of us then, myself, your mother and your brothers, to come and bow to the ground before you?" (Gn 37:9–10)

An unselfconscious, maybe precocious, child, or a bright and talkative young adult, may give offence without meaning it. We can recognise how annoying Joseph's talk must have been to his elders.

Lord, help us not to envy the different talents we see in others; help us, too, not to boast of what we have been given, or act or speak to put others down. Help us to trust that your plan for us is better than any plan we could devise.

I ask you especially for [*here name your intention*]

Our Father - Hail Mary - Glory Be

FOURTH DAY

They made a plot among themselves to put him to death. "Here comes the man of dreams" they said to one another. "Come on, let us kill him and throw him into some well; we can say that a wild beast devoured him. Then we shall see what becomes of his dreams." (Gn 37:18–20)

Anyone who has ever looked after small children will know that violent rage can sit easily alongside love for a brother or sister; and these hatreds and jealousies can be carried into later life. As we grow older, this is usually not as openly expressed, but is just as real; and, paradoxically, is less easily reconciled where the violence is all unexpressed or under the surface.

Father, help me to acknowledge my anger, and I ask you to turn it aside.

I ask you especially for [*here name your intention*]

Our Father - Hail Mary - Glory Be

FIFTH DAY

But Reuben heard, and he saved him from their violence ... "Shed no blood," said Reuben to them "throw him into this well in the wilderness, but do not lay violent hands on him" – intending to save him from them and restore him to his father (Gn 37:21–22).

Although Reuben had, presumably, been as angry as the other brothers about Joseph's apparent presumption and airs, he drew back from violence, and persuaded his brothers to agree.

Father, help us not to cling to plans or feelings born out of anger; help us to be merciful to each other.

I ask you especially for [*here name your intention*]

Our Father - Hail Mary - Glory Be

SIXTH DAY

Now some Midianite merchants were passing, and they drew Joseph up out of the well. They sold Joseph to the Ishmaelites for twenty silver pieces, and these men took Joseph to Egypt. When Reuben went back to the well there was no sign of Joseph. Tearing his clothes, he went back to his brothers. "The boy has disappeared" he said. "What am I going to do?" (Gn 37:28–30)

Reuben and the brothers are stricken with remorse and panic after their plan seems to have gone wrong and had terrible consequences they had not intended.

Father, help me to see that others may not have meant this situation to develop as it has; help us all not to blame each other for what may not be anyone's fault.

I ask you especially for [*here name your intention*]

Our Father - Hail Mary - Glory Be

SEVENTH DAY

Joseph gave this order to his chamberlain: "Fill these men's sacks with as much food as they can carry, and put each man's money in the mouth of his sack. And put my cup, the silver one, in the mouth of the youngest one's sack" ... When morning came and it was light, the men were sent off ... They had scarcely left the city ... before Joseph said to his chamberlain, "Away now and follow those men. When you catch up with them say to them, 'Why did you reward good with evil?'" (Gn 44:1–4)

Joseph, now a high official in Egypt, uses a series of tricks and ruses to deceive and humiliate his brothers before he makes himself known to them.

Father, help me not to take pleasure in being right or use whatever wrong has been done me as an excuse to revenge myself or humiliate others.

I ask you especially for [*here name your intention*]

Our Father - Hail Mary - Glory Be

EIGHTH DAY

So ten of Joseph's brothers went down to buy grain in Egypt ... It was Joseph, as the man in authority over the country, who sold the grain to all comers. So Joseph's brothers went and bowed low before him, their faces touching the ground ... So Joseph recognised his brothers, but they did not recognise him (Gn 42:3, 6, 8).

The brothers are able to accept and respect Joseph because they do not know it is him. Often we are so bound by our long habits of seeing and relating to a brother, sister or parent that we cannot make a fair appraisal of their qualities. Only, perhaps, if we can see them without prejudice (as if they were a stranger) can we see what may be obvious to others. God, thankfully, sees us all without prejudice.

Father, help me to see with your eyes, unclouded by the hurts and confusions of the past.

I ask you especially for [*here name your intention*]

Our Father - Hail Mary - Glory Be

NINTH DAY

I am your brother Joseph whom you sold into Egypt. But now, do not grieve, do not reproach yourselves for having sold me here, since God sent me before you to preserve your lives (Gn 45:4–5).

If God grants us reconciliation, we must pray not to dwell overmuch on whatever has now been resolved and forgiven: God takes our mistakes and sins and turns them to a good end we could not have foreseen. This is what we mean by providence.

Father, let us know hope and the joy of renewal, not fruitless regret for a past that cannot be changed, but from which you can bring some new thing.

I ask you especially for [*here name your intention*]

Our Father - Hail Mary - Glory Be

David & Absalom and the Prodigal Son: Estranged Children

David, King of Israel, had many wives and many children and there was quite a competition between them. Absalom was his third son, handsome and admired. He had a beautiful sister called Tamar, who was raped by their half-brother Amnon. David heard of this; but although he was angry, he did nothing because Amnon was his eldest son and had first place in his heart. So Absalom took matters into his own hands, and had Amnon murdered. David first exiled Absalom, but then forgave him, without, however, addressing any of the deeper questions involved. Absalom now despised his father and decided to take his throne. War broke out between them. Absalom was killed after getting his head caught in a tree and being discovered helpless by David's army. David mourned for his son.

The Prodigal Son is the younger of two sons. His father intends to divide everything equally between his two sons when he dies, but the younger son does not want to wait. He does not want to be beholden to his father but wants the money as his right. As soon as he gets the money he leaves home, goes far away and lives a life of debauchery. This doesn't work out for him, so he plans what he can say

238

to get his father to take him back. But as soon as he comes back, his father runs out to meet him and celebrates his return. The elder brother is angry, but the father is not dissuaded. He takes nothing away from the elder, while he is glad the younger has returned.

My son Absalom! Absalom, my son, my son! (2 S 19:5)

Despite his wanting to destroy him, David still loved Absalom, and when he died he was grief-stricken.

Father, you know that despite all that has happened between us, I still love my child. I suffer because I see him (her) suffer, and I really want us to be reconciled. Give me hope that this will happen.

I ask you especially for [*here name your intention*]

Our Father - Hail Mary - Glory Be

SECOND DAY

When David heard the whole story, he was very angry; but he had no wish to harm his son Amnon, since he loved him; he was his first born (2 S 13:21).

Absalom felt his father David didn't deal with injustice, so he took matters into his own hands.

Lord, open my eyes to see the times I didn't act for the best; when I was unjust and offended my son (daughter); when I treated them differently. If it is right, then let me find a way to ask their forgiveness for that. Help me also to deal with any events my son (daughter) has misunderstood or misinterpreted.

I ask you especially for [*here name your intention*]

Our Father - Hail Mary - Glory Be

THIRD DAY

Absalom sent couriers throughout the tribes of Israel saying, "When you hear the trumpet sound you are to say, 'Absalom is king at Hebron!'" (2 S 15:10)

Although we may think David had given Absalom some cause to be resentful, nothing that happened could justify him in raising rebellion against his father. Absalom made a series of deliberate decisions to do what he knew was wrong.

Lord, I know my child is an adult and so their bad choices are their responsibility. Don't let me uselessly blame myself – or worse, blame my spouse – for all that has happened. I can only pray for my son (daughter) and hope for his (her) return to the Church and to the family. Help me to leave the judgement of the past to you.

I ask you especially for [*here name your intention*]

Our Father - Hail Mary - Glory Be

FOURTH DAY

Absalom ... had taken flight and gone ... he stayed for three years. And all that time the king mourned for his son (2 S 13:37–8).

After Absalom had Amnon killed, David sent him into exile, and didn't let him come back for a while. In doing this, he was thinking of the rest of his family.

Father, give me wisdom in this situation. Help me remember that the whole family is involved and all of us must be heard. Let me (us) not gain my lost child at the expense of his (her) brother (sister). Our reconciliation must be honest.

I ask you especially for [*here name your intention*]

Our Father - Hail Mary - Glory Be

FIFTH DAY

So the father divided his property between them. A few days later, the younger son got together everything he had and left for a distant country where he squandered his money on a life of debauchery (Lk 15:12–13).

The younger son ("the prodigal") went far away, and did his own thing, living in a way very different to all he had been taught or had known.

Lord, you know how hurt I am that my son (daughter) seems to have rejected everything we taught him (her); how hurt I am by his (her) wish to have nothing to do with us. Strengthen me (us) and let me (us) not lose confidence in my (our) abilities as parents to all my (our) children.

I ask you especially for [*here name your intention*]

Our Father - Hail Mary - Glory Be

SIXTH DAY

When he had spent it all, that country experienced a severe famine, and now he began to feel the pinch ... Then he came to his senses (Lk 15:14, 17).

The younger son suffered, but that suffering brought him back.

Lord, I see that my son (daughter) suffers in the life he (she) has chosen, but I know that you can bring good out of even the worst situation. Free him (her) from his (her) poor choices and may his (her) situation spur him (her) to return to you and to us.

I ask you especially for [*here name your intention*]

Our Father - Hail Mary - Glory Be

SEVENTH DAY

....

Then he came to his senses and said, "How many of my father's paid servants have more food than they want, and here am I dying of hunger! I will … go to my father and say: Father, I have sinned …" (Lk 15:17–18)

The younger son makes a cynical calculation about his situation; he is hardly truly repentant. But even though he wasn't sincere, his father welcomed him.

Father, give me an open heart, ready to forgive if asked. Help me to push aside the rancour and blame and to try to make a new beginning.

I ask you especially for [*here name your intention*]

Our Father - Hail Mary - Glory Be

EIGHTH DAY

....

The elder son … was angry then and refused to go in, and his father came out to plead with him; but he answered his father, "Look, all these years I have slaved for you and never once disobeyed your orders, yet you never offered me so much as a kid for me to celebrate with my friends …" (Lk 15:28–29)

The elder brother is angry, but his father took nothing away from him.

Father, help me to broker peace with the rest of the family. May they not feel less loved because their sibling has returned. Let them not believe that we are less soft-hearted with them. They have stayed close to us. Let them see we value their loyalty and restraint.

I ask you especially for [*here name your intention*]

Our Father - Hail Mary - Glory Be

NINTH DAY

My son, you are with me always and all I have is yours. But it was only right we should celebrate and rejoice, because your brother here was dead and has come to life; he was lost and is found (Lk 15:31–32).

God's mercy is not limited, and does not exclude anyone; we, too, have been often in need of his mercy and compassion, and will be so again.

Finally, Lord, help me remember how many times you have forgiven me. Give me a grateful heart, and help me to show to others the mercy I have received.

I ask you especially for [*here name your intention*]

Our Father - Hail Mary - Glory Be

Martha: Being the One that Does All the Work

SCRIPTURE: READ THE STORY OF MARTHA
(LK 10:38–42 AND JN 11:1–54).

In Jesus's life on earth, he lived as we do. He had family, and he also had friends. Amongst his friends were two sisters and a brother: Martha, Mary and Lazarus. They lived in a village called Bethany, and Jesus often visited them there.

FIRST DAY

A woman named Martha welcomed him into her house (Lk 10:38).

Martha lived with her brother and sister, but Luke says that she was the one in charge of the house. She was capable and organised and it was she who took charge when Jesus visited them.

Lord, I thank you that you have given me the capabilities I have. I ask you to accept them as a gift from you without selfish pride, but without false modesty either. Please give me also the gifts of hospitality and service so that I can use my talents as you planned.

I ask you especially for [*here name your intention*]

Our Father - Hail Mary - Glory Be

SECOND DAY

Martha ... was distracted with all the serving (Lk 10:40).

Martha wanted everything to be done well, but she got so caught up in this that she missed the point of the visit.

Lord, don't let me be so keen to have things perfect that I make everything uncomfortable for everyone, and embarrass and depress the people I am supposed to be helping. Let me do what I can to the best of my abilities, but not worry about the things I can't achieve.

I ask you especially for [*here name your intention*]

Our Father - Hail Mary - Glory Be

THIRD DAY

Lord, do you not care that my sister is leaving me to do the serving all by myself? (Lk 10:40)

Martha was doing all that was needed for her visitors' comfort, and her sister was not helping her but had joined the men and was listening to Jesus.

Lord, I feel that I am left to do all the work, and people who could help me just don't do anything. Help me not to be angry with them. Have I made it difficult for them to help because of my impatience, or by insisting on doing things a particular way? Don't allow me to judge you either, or believe you do not care about me. Give me the grace to be at peace, knowing I am working in your service, and to leave the rest to you. You can take away the feeling I have of being burdened, if I give it over to you whose yoke is light.

I ask you especially for [*here name your intention*]

Our Father - Hail Mary - Glory Be

FOURTH DAY

But the Lord answered ... "Mary has chosen the better part; it is not to be taken from her." (Lk 10:41–42)

Martha hoped Jesus would tell Mary to help her – it was only fair – but he didn't. Instead, he told her she was wrong and Mary was right.

Lord, sometimes it's hard that others don't seem to see how I am taken advantage of and put upon. Nobody seems to think of me. They don't encourage others to help me; they seem to think I will just get on with things. Help me not to be resentful and full of judgement. Give me the wisdom to see the good in other people, and the good other people do.

I ask you especially for [*here name your intention*]

Our Father - Hail Mary - Glory Be

FIFTH DAY

You worry and fret about so many things, and yet few are needed, indeed only one (Lk 10:41–42).

Martha expected Jesus's support in her anger with her sister, but instead he gently rebuked her.

Lord, help me to see where your rebukes are in my life. Help me to see my life as you do; to see my own faults, not the faults of others; but also to know you love me in spite of my faults, and you are with me every day.

I ask you especially for [*here name your intention*]

Our Father - Hail Mary - Glory Be

SIXTH DAY

When Martha heard Jesus had come she went out to meet him (Jn 11:20).

When Jesus called her, Martha went out to meet him. She was not trapped in her routines or her small world of work. He called, and she went.

Lord, let me know how much you love me; how exciting life with you can be. Give me the gift of joy. I am tempted to turn in on myself, to harden my heart; but with your help I can be open to the life you give me. If I know you are with me, I can even be happy.

I ask you especially for [*here name your intention*]

Our Father - Hail Mary - Glory Be

SEVENTH DAY

I know that whatever you ask of God he will grant you (Jn 11:22).

Martha is one of the first to realise Jesus is the Christ.

Lord, give me the grace to see you, to know you, and to know you have power to help me. Let me see you are helping me: helping me in my situation in life, helping me grow in faith. Give me the trust in you that Martha had.

I ask you especially for [*here name your intention*]

Our Father - Hail Mary - Glory Be

EIGHTH DAY

Jesus wept (Jn 11:35).

When Martha's brother died, Jesus wept, even though he was going to raise him from the dead. He wept because he loved them.

Lord, I know you love me, too, and that you weep over me – not only for my sins but for my sufferings. May I feel the comfort of your closeness. May I be strengthened by the certainty that you love me.

I ask you especially for [*here name your intention*]

Our Father - Hail Mary - Glory Be

NINTH DAY

Go, therefore, make disciples of all the nations (Mt 28:19).

Tradition says that, after Pentecost, Martha went with her brother and sister to announce the gospel in Tarascon in France, and that she either destroyed a dragon or turned people away from worshipping one.

Lord, I ask you to give me hope. Let me see that the difficulties I have do not define my life. You have great plans for me if I walk with you. Even if my physical circumstances don't change, if I stay close to you I can do great things in your eyes.

I ask you especially for [*here name your intention*]

Our Father - Hail Mary - Glory Be

Ruth and Naomi: Feeling Abandoned and Forgotten

SCRIPTURE: READ THE BOOK OF RUTH.

There was a famine in Israel, so Naomi's husband sold his land and took his family to Moab. Soon afterwards, he died, leaving Naomi stranded there. Her two sons married Moabite women, but after some time the sons, too, died. Having nothing in either country, Naomi decided to return to Israel. One of her two daughters-in-law stayed in Moab, but the other, Ruth, did not want to leave the elderly Naomi to fend for herself and vowed to stay with her and live how and where Naomi did. The two women returned to Israel and Ruth worked to support them in a menial and even dangerous job. Naomi used her wisdom to find Ruth a husband. The love between mother-in-law and daughter-in-law may not be the first thing we think of when we talk about human love, but in this case, and in many others, it is a strong sign of God's acting in spite of human prejudice and limitations.

FIRST DAY

A man called Elimelech, his wife Naomi, and his two sons, Mahlon and Chillon ... came to the country of Moab and settled there. Elimelech, Naomi's husband, died ... then Mahlon and Chillon also died and the woman was bereft of her two sons and her husband (Rt 1:2–3, 5).

Naomi was in a foreign country where she had been taken by her husband.

Father, I feel so alone. I feel there is nobody to support and love me, and nobody for me to love. I am isolated from others and have nothing in common with people. Help me not to let this feeling overwhelm and destroy me. Don't let me blame others for my situation. Help me to lean on you. I know you can pull me out of this pit.

I ask you especially for [*here name your intention*]

Our Father - Hail Mary - Glory Be

SECOND DAY

The women said, "Can this be Naomi?" But she said to them, "Do not call me Naomi, call me Mara, for Shaddai has marred me bitterly. Filled full I departed, the Lord brings me back empty." (Rt 1:19–21)

Lord, my life seems such a failure. I hoped it would be so different. I see other people who seem to have everything I want and I feel so bitter. Why have you forgotten me? And yet Ruth chose you and everything she had lost was restored to her and more.

Kindle a flame of hope in me. Give me a grateful heart because I know you. Give me hope that you can enter my loneliness and comfort me. Help me to see my life as you see it: not its failures and disappointments, but what it can be, so that I, too, can be a sign of faith in you.

I ask you especially for [*here name your intention*]

Our Father - Hail Mary - Glory Be

THIRD DAY

Ruth said, "... wherever you go, I will go, wherever you live, I will live. Your people shall be my people and your God, my God." (Rt 1:16)

Ruth chose God and stuck to her choice. Ruth chose to stay with Naomi rather than remaining with her own people with a chance of marrying again. This beautiful expression of love is not between spouses but between a mother- and daughter-in-law.

Lord, help me see the love that is in my life and to value it, even if it is not the kind of love I long for.

I ask you especially for [*here name your intention*]

Our Father - Hail Mary - Glory Be

FOURTH DAY

Ruth the Moabitess said to Naomi, "Let me go into the fields and glean among the ears of corn." (Rt 2:1)

Father, show me that work is valuable in itself. It doesn't have to be high status. All work can have dignity and all work is done for your glory. Also, caring for others is not meant to be a burden. Help me to see that in loving my dependents I make it possible for you to act in my life.

I ask you especially for [*here name your intention*]

Our Father - Hail Mary - Glory Be

FIFTH DAY

Boaz said to Ruth, "Listen ... You are not to glean in any other field, do not leave here but stay with my servants ... And if you are thirsty, go to the pitchers and drink ..." And she said to him, "How have I so earned your favour?" And Boaz answered her, "I have been told all you have done for your mother-in-law since your husband's death ... May the Lord reward you for what you have done!" (Rt 2:8–12)

Boaz was kind to a foreigner, someone with no status or influence, and she became his wife.

Lord, help me to be open and kind. Give me concern for the weak and show me the way I can be some help, no matter in how small a way.

I ask you especially for [*here name your intention*]

Our Father - Hail Mary - Glory Be

SIXTH DAY

Then Naomi said to her, "Now tonight [Boaz] is winnowing the barley at the threshing-floor. Come, wash and anoint and dress yourself. Then go down to the threshing-floor." (Rt 3:1–3)

Father, help me not to become careless of my appearance and hygiene because I think my life worthless. I am not a person nobody cares for. I am deeply loved by you.

I ask you especially for [*here name your intention*]

Our Father - Hail Mary - Glory Be

SEVENTH DAY

"A son has been born for Naomi," they said; and they named him Obed. This was the father of David's father, Jesse (Rt 4:17).

No one is unimportant in the fulfilment of God's plan – each of us has a part. Naomi was old and Ruth a foreigner; both were women alone in a male-dominated world, but between them they allowed God's plan to progress. Ruth married Boaz and gave birth to Obed, who was the grandfather of King David and thus an ancestor of Jesus Christ.

Father, you can do great things with me, too. You can give me my heart's desire, but whatever my life is, I know that you can give me happiness if I allow you to. Nothing is wasted in your sight.

I ask you especially for [*here name your intention*]

Our Father - Hail Mary - Glory Be

EIGHTH DAY

So Boaz took Ruth and she became his wife. And when they came together, the Lord made her conceive and she bore a son. And the women said to Naomi, "Blessed be the Lord who has not left the dead man without next of kin this day to perpetuate his name in Israel. The child will be a comfort to you and the prop of your old age, for your daughter-in-law who loves you and is more to you than seven sons has given him birth." (Rt 4:14–16)

God can bring life out of death. When Ruth's son was born, he was counted as the son of her first husband and he was brought up by Naomi.

Lord, I see you can give life and fruitfulness to the old and the dead, and you can give me this, too.

I ask you especially for [*here name your intention*]

Our Father - Hail Mary - Glory Be

NINTH DAY

Seeing his mother and the disciple he loved standing near her, Jesus said to his mother, "Woman, this is your son." Then to the disciple he said, "This is your mother." (Jn 19:26–27)

Naomi is reckoned as a type of the Virgin Mary. She helped Ruth to find a husband and a home; to find the place God had prepared for her.

I ask you, Mary, to be my mother, to guide my life; to bring me to your son; to help me learn to love and be happy.

I ask you especially for [*here name your intention*]

Our Father - Hail Mary - Glory Be

Deborah and Barak: When Things Seem Too Much for Us

After they entered the Promised Land, the people of Israel were at first ruled by judges, who were chosen by God. The Israelites were surrounded by pagan nations and war was commonplace. The story of Deborah and Barak shows how God works through unexpected means and individuals to protect Israel, his chosen people.

FIRST DAY

At this time Deborah was a judge in Israel, a prophetess, the wife of Lappidoth (Jg 4:4).

Deborah was the only female judge of Israel (out of twelve) and lived at a time when women were secondary to men. She combined this heavy responsibility with domestic responsibilities. She was able to do this because she depended on God.

Father, I ask for your reassurance that I can live my responsibilities together with you. Even though I feel overwhelmed by what I have to do, by those I have to care for, by all the things I have to juggle, I know that you are with me. Even if I sometimes fail, I can be at peace, knowing you love me and those who depend on me, and that you will not abandon us.

I ask you especially for [*here name your intention*]

Our Father - Hail Mary - Glory Be

SECOND DAY

She sent for Barak ... She said to him, "This is the order of the Lord, the God of Israel ..." (Jg 4:6)

Barak was the person chosen by God to lead his armies, but he had to be called from far away to come and do his duty. Some Jewish rabbis say Barak is actually Deborah's husband Lappidoth. This is because Lappidoth means "torchlight" and Barak means "lightning". Before this battle he was like a small light but Deborah called him to become like lightning.

Lord, help me not to judge others who should share my burdens but who I feel are failing to do so, leaving everything to me. Let me lean on you instead of crushing them with my demands and my contempt. Give me the right way to encourage them, and give them the confidence they need to help deal with the difficulties we face.

I ask you especially for [*here name your intention*]

Our Father - Hail Mary - Glory Be

258

THIRD DAY

Barak answered her, "If you come with me, I will go; if you will not come, I will not go, for I do not know how to choose the day when the Lord will grant me success." (Jg 4:8)

Barak is willing to go, but admits he does not have Deborah's faith. Deborah chides him for his lack of trust in God but marches with him as he leads the men into battle.

Father, help me remember I have to work with others. If I lean on you, I can support them, even if they have to lean on me. Show me how to treat them with respect. Help me not to get impatient when they do things more slowly than I want, or not in the way I want. Don't let me despise and reject their help, or leave them behind and try to do everything alone. If they refuse to help me, I still have your help, but let me always respect them and be ready to accept their help.

I ask you especially for [*here name your intention*]

Our Father - Hail Mary - Glory Be

FOURTH DAY

Once again the Israelites began to do what displeases the Lord, and the Lord handed them over to Jabin the king of Canaan ... The commander of his army was Sisera (Jg 4:1–2).

The Israelites were chosen to live a godly life, but instead they often tried to live like everyone else, focusing on their own wishes and not considering what was right. God uses the consequences of this to remind them he is there, waiting to help them.

Lord, enlighten me about my own sins, about what I have done to make this situation worse – where my suffering is made worse because I don't trust you. I can't accept my weakness, and I don't accept the help of others for what it is. Give me the courage to pass this burden to you. Help me learn to walk with you.

I ask you especially for [*here name your intention*]

Our Father - Hail Mary - Glory Be

FIFTH DAY

Sisera ... called for all his chariots – nine hundred chariots plated with iron – and all the troops he had (Jg 4:12–13).

Sisera was the commander of an immense enemy army, and once Barak went out to face them, things appeared to get even worse. Sisera seemed an unbeatable foe.

Lord, when I face up to my problems and responsibilities, help me not panic even if things are worse than I feared. Keep me close to you and to the sacraments, to give me the strength and discernment I need to carry on.

I ask you especially for [*here name your intention*]

Our Father - Hail Mary - Glory Be

SIXTH DAY

Deborah said to Barak, "Up! For today is the day the Lord has put Sisera into your power." (Jg 4:14)

There was a moment when Barak had to act. He had to be ready, and act as Deborah told him. Barak was prepared, and he was able to follow the orders of a woman at a time when that was almost unknown.

May I never despair, never believe that nothing can be resolved. I know that even if the exterior situation does not change, with your help everything can change for me. Help me to recognise your voice and your hand in my life. Give me the humility to accept advice and the wisdom to know when to act on it.

I ask you especially for [*here name your intention*]

Our Father - Hail Mary - Glory Be

SEVENTH DAY

Sisera meanwhile fled on foot towards the tent of Jael, the wife of Heber the Kenite…. But Jael … took a tent peg and picked up a mallet; she crept up softly to him and drove the peg into his temple right through to the ground (Jg 4:17, 21).

When Sisera was routed in battle he fled to Heber, whom he counted as an ally, and asked help from Heber's wife. He thought he was safe; Heber's wife Jael was not someone he took any account of. But Jael was both wily and courageous. She lulled Sisera to sleep and then killed him.

Lord, I understand that the enemy I have to kill is the Evil One. Give me the wisdom to see his lies and give me the courage to turn away from them. I may be weak and disregarded, but with you I am strong. Show me the truth of my life and give me the gift of joy even in suffering.

I ask you especially for [*here name your intention*]

Our Father - Hail Mary - Glory Be

EIGHTH DAY

Barak ... went into her tent; Sisera lay dead (Jg 4:22).

Deborah had prophesied that the glory would not be Barak's, but that Sisera would be delivered into the hand of a woman. Nor was that woman Deborah, the judge and prophetess, but Jael, who was "only a housewife".

Show me that help can come from the most unexpected places, even from someone I haven't thought about. If you choose to resolve my situation without me, without warning, give me a grateful heart and help me not to doubt, but to trust that the situation is resolved.

I ask you especially for [*here name your intention*]

Our Father - Hail Mary - Glory Be

NINTH DAY

And let those who love you be like the sun when he arises in all his strength (Jg 5:31).

Lord, help me to let go of my problems when you have solved them, and not to hold on to the suffering. Let me let go of my burdens when you carry them for me and not try to grab them back. Help me to know that my sufferings and my problems are not my identity.

I ask you especially for [*here name your intention*]

Our Father - Hail Mary - Glory Be

Jonah: When God's Plan Doesn't Seem To Make Sense

SCRIPTURE: READ THE BOOK OF JONAH.

Jonah is the story of a reluctant prophet, the story of a man who runs away from what he knows God is asking him to do, because (in his well-informed opinion) what God is suggesting is preposterous. God wants Jonah to go to the great city of Nineveh, a vast metropolis, and, on his own, tell them to turn from wickedness, or they will perish. It is an obviously absurd mission, and Jonah is properly dismissive of it. God, however, will not be put off, and uses various devices (storms, sea-monsters) that we may also think ridiculous or undignified to bring Jonah back to where he wants him. God means Jonah to be the one to save the people of Nineveh from themselves; and despite his own sense of outraged dignity, Jonah eventually sees that God is right.

FIRST DAY

The word of the Lord was addressed to Jonah, son of Amittai: "Up!" he said. "Go to Nineveh, the great city, and inform them that their wickedness has become known to me." Jonah decided to run away from the Lord, and go to Tarshish (Jon 1:1–3).

Jonah heard God clearly telling him to call the people of Nineveh to convert, but he refused to obey and went off in totally the opposite direction. This was not because he was unsure about what he should do, but because he really didn't want to do it. He put a lot of effort and some money into doing the opposite of the mission God called him to.

Lord, you know there are issues in my life where I know what I should do as a Christian but it doesn't seem reasonable. Forgive me for the times I have not spoken due to fear or self-preservation, where I have not wanted to make myself vulnerable or open to ridicule. Have mercy on me for the times I have only been concerned with worldly things.

I ask you especially for [*here name your intention*]

Our Father - Hail Mary - Glory Be

SECOND DAY

The Lord unleashed a violent wind on the sea, and there was such a great storm ... that the ship threatened to break up ... The sailors rowed hard in an effort to reach the shore, but in vain ... They then called on the Lord and said "O Lord, do not let us perish for taking this man's life ..."
(Jon 1:4, 13–14)

The pagans pray and sacrifice, give up their goods and try everything to save everyone, even Jonah although they know he is to blame. The sailors didn't have the gift of faith, but they were kind. They also asked God not to blame them.

Lord, help me not to look down on those who do not know you.

I ask you especially for [*here name your intention*]

Our Father - Hail Mary - Glory Be

THIRD DAY ✓

The sailors took fright, and each of them called on his own god, and to lighten the ship they threw the cargo overboard. Jonah, however, had gone below and lain down in the hold and fallen fast asleep (Jon 1:5).

When the storm threatened the ship, all the pagans prayed and sacrificed, but Jonah, who was supposed to be a friend of God's, only slept.

There are times I have not acted, have not asked your help, have made no effort to protest about laws or actions that are against your laws. Forgive me for my apathy, for thinking first of my comfort. Forgive me for feeling indifferent, not responsible or even smug, and leaving people in their sin.

I ask you especially for [*here name your intention*]

Our Father - Hail Mary - Glory Be

FOURTH DAY

The sailors were seized with terror ... and said "What have you done?" They then said, "What are we to do with you?" ... He replied, "Take me and throw me into the sea ... for I can see it is my fault this violent storm has happened to you." ... And taking hold of Jonah they threw him into the sea; and the sea grew calm again (Jon 1:10–12, 15).

Jonah understands why the storm is raging, and knows that the only way to save the others is for him to be thrown overboard. He offers this, and persuades the others to do it. The sea is immediately calm and the ship is saved because of Jonah's sacrifice. The sailors see what happens and are converted.

Lord, you know that giving up your life for others seems like insanity or only the job of a few saints. Even if in my mind I know this is the mission of all Christians, it still seems ridiculous. Show me what "giving up my life" means in my life, and give me the desire for your spirit to fulfil this in me. Help me to do this without fear, knowing you love me.

I ask you especially for [*here name your intention*]

Our Father - Hail Mary - Glory Be

FIFTH DAY

The Lord had arranged that a great fish should be there to swallow Jonah (Jon 2:1).

When Jonah was thrown overboard into a raging sea, he did not drown as anyone would expect, but he was swallowed by a large fish.

Lord, give me faith to know that if I risk on you, if I
do the right thing, you will protect me, even if the next
thing that happens doesn't seem so perfect either. May I
see that we are moving forward together and I can rest in
your will.

I ask you especially for [*here name your intention*]

Our Father - Hail Mary - Glory Be

SIXTH DAY

*Jonah remained in the belly of the fish for three days and three
nights (Jon 2:1).*

Jonah found himself trapped in the belly of a large
fish. He was literally in the dark. He couldn't control
anything; he had to go where the fish was going. He
had to trust that God was in control. Finally, he found
himself in the place God wanted him to be without his
having made any effort to get there.

Lord, help me to be at peace if there are times in my life
when I can't move, I can't see where to go and I find myself
helpless in a situation I did not choose. Help me to believe
that you are in charge of everything that happens, and that
my life is moving towards where you want it to be.

I ask you especially for [*here name your intention*]

Our Father - Hail Mary - Glory Be

SEVENTH DAY ✔

*From the belly of the fish he prayed to the Lord, his God;
and he said, "Out of my distress I cried to the Lord and he
answered me." (Jon 2:2–3)*

Jonah understood that God had saved him, and began
a prayer of thanks even though his situation was not
immediately obviously safe. He uses the Psalms to pray.

I ask for the grace to be able to see my life as you see it,
to see where you have pulled me out of danger and to
believe that you protect me even if I can't see it. Remind
me to turn to you in the Scriptures.

I ask you especially for [*here name your intention*]

Our Father - Hail Mary - Glory Be

EIGHTH DAY

*Jonah set out and went to Nineveh ... he preached in these
words, "Only forty days more and Nineveh is going to be
destroyed." And the people of Nineveh believed in God ... God
saw their efforts to renounce their evil behaviour. And God
relented ... Jonah was very indignant at this; he fell into a
rage (Jon 3:3, 4–5, 10; 4:1).*

The large fish vomits Jonah out on the shore exactly
where he was originally asked to go. Jonah calls the
Ninevites to repentance, as he was asked to do, and the
Ninevites repent. Jonah is furious. He knew that if he
were really a prophet, this would happen; and now he
is angry. He wants to be right in doubting God and he
doesn't want the Ninevites to repent and be saved. It is
far too easy. He feels they should suffer.

Lord, you know that sometimes I feel people are given easy forgiveness, especially if they have done something against me. I don't want to forgive them and I don't want you to forgive them either. When you forgive my enemies, I feel that you don't take me seriously – or the hurt that is done to me. Help me to see that you forgive me as lovingly as you forgive my enemies, and give me the desire to forgive as you do.

I ask you especially for [*here name your intention*]

Our Father - Hail Mary - Glory Be

NINTH DAY

God said to Jonah ... "Am I not to feel sorry for Nineveh, the great city, in which there are more than a hundred and twenty thousand people?" (Jon 4:9–11)

The conversion of the Ninevites depends on God, not on Jonah. It would take three days to travel across Nineveh, let alone speak to all the inhabitants; but they convert after only one day of Jonah's preaching. God is quick to forgive those who recognise their faults and repent as the Ninevites do. He even sends Jonah to show them their faults. God pities them.

Lord, give me the gift of a merciful heart and the courage and humility not to let my own sense of dignity or self-importance stand in the way of your love for me and for others; let me be able to believe in your mercy and forgiveness, even when it comes through apparently weak or unworthy or ridiculous people (such as myself).

I ask you especially for [*here name your intention*]

Our Father - Hail Mary - Glory Be

Job: Being Honest with God

SCRIPTURE: READ THE BOOK OF JOB.

Job has always been an emblematic figure: brought low by a whim of God from happiness and prosperity to the depths of misery, his story is a showcase for the various ways people have tried to explain away human suffering. For Job, as for us, these efforts at explanation are mostly useless, where they are not actively annoying or enraging. Job, like us, is not soothed by simplistic reasonings; in the end, it is only the vision of God's transcendent majesty that allows him to move beyond his own misery. Like Job, we are less likely to be helped by argument or advice, however well-intentioned, than by an encounter with the living God; and this is why we need to pray.

FIRST DAY

"Stretch out your hand and lay a finger on his bone and flesh; I warrant you, he will curse you to your face." "Very well," the Lord said to Satan, "he is in your power." (Jb 2:5–6)

God gives Job, a righteous and God-fearing man, into the power of the Enemy for the express purpose of testing his faith. He has done nothing wrong. What happens to him is deeply unfair. Yet Job does not blame God, although he does fall into deep despair.

Father, sometimes what happens to me seems grossly unfair, and it seems as if you are punishing me without cause. Help me not to worry fruitlessly about how I may have offended you. Help me to believe you are my loving Father, however hard it may be to think so.

I ask you especially for [*here name your intention*]

Our Father - Hail Mary - Glory Be

SECOND DAY

"If we take happiness from God's hand, must we not take sorrow too?" And in all this misfortune Job uttered no sinful word ... In the end Job ... cursed the day of his birth ... : "May the day perish when I was born ..." (Jb 2:10, 3:1–3)

At first, Job utters conventional sentiments of acceptance; his wife is not convinced by this, and, before long, she is proved right when he curses the day of his birth and sees only misery and unreason. His conventional defences are down; he is at rock bottom.

Father, help me not to take refuge in simplistic pieties or a gritted-teeth acceptance that does not admit the reality or the extent of my hurt, my sadness, my disappointment. Help me not to hide from you behind rationalisations.

I ask you especially for [*here name your intention*]

Our Father - Hail Mary - Glory Be

THIRD DAY

Is not man's life on earth nothing more than pressed service, his time no better than hired drudgery? ... Lying in bed I wonder, "When will it be day?" Risen I think, "How slowly evening comes!" ... Swifter than a weaver's shuttle my days have passed, and vanished, leaving no hope behind. Remember that my life is but a breath, and my eyes will never again see joy (Jb 7:1, 4, 6–7).

Job is honest in declaring his despair at the bleak sameness he experiences; day in, day out, he finds nothing to lift his spirits or suggest God cares about him. Until we uncover our true feelings, rather than whatever pretence or façade we may show to the world, or use to get us through the day, we cannot expect God to touch us.

Father, help me to show you my true face, not the masks I put on for the world to see.

I ask you especially for [*here name your intention*]

Our Father - Hail Mary - Glory Be

FOURTH DAY

Since I have lost all taste for life, I will give free rein to my complaints; I shall let my embittered soul speak out. I shall say to God, "Do not condemn me, but tell me the reason for your assault. Is it right for you to injure me, cheapening the work of your own hands, and abetting the schemes of the wicked? ... And if I make a stand, like a lion you hunt me down, adding to the tale of your triumphs" (Jb 10:1–3, 16).

Job cannot understand what has happened to him; his pain gives him honesty, and he is baffled by the apparent futility of God's doings. Why bother to make him, and pick him up when he falls, only to knock him down again?

Father, I do not understand your ways with me. Sometimes I feel you only give me relief from my suffering to prepare me to have it again, and worse. Help me in my pain to find honesty, and tell you what I truly feel, not what I think you want me to say.

I ask you especially for [*here name your intention*]

Our Father - Hail Mary - Glory Be

FIFTH DAY

God has made my heart sink, Shaddai has filled me with fear. For darkness hides me from him, and the gloom veils his presence from me ... Fatherless children are robbed of their lands, and poor men have their cloaks seized as security. From the towns come the groans of the dying and the gasp of wounded men crying for help. Yet God remains deaf to their appeal! (Jb 23:16–17; 24:9, 12)

Job is filled with dread by what God seems to be like, if he is even there. Everywhere, evil triumphs, and the innocent and weak are oppressed without God lifting a finger to help them.

Father, you know how terror and dismay are often my companions, and how sometimes I can see only sadness and futility. Help me to know you are there, even in darkness and pain.

I ask you especially for [*here name your intention*]

Our Father - Hail Mary - Glory Be

274

SIXTH DAY

Have I been insensible to poor men's needs, or let a widow's eyes grow dim? ... Have I put all my trust in gold? ... Have I taken pleasure in my enemies' misfortunes, or made merry when disaster overtook them, I who allowed my tongue to do no wrong? ... Have I ever hidden my sins from men, keeping my iniquity secret? ... Who can get me a hearing from God? (Jb 31:16, 24, 29–30, 33, 35)

Job speaks of his righteousness, not to boast, but to ask, "What is the point? Even I, who have done all this, who have been merciful, am afflicted."

Father, let me not try to make bargains with you by doing good works; or think they are all worthless because I am suffering. Help me to be merciful.

I ask you especially for [*here name your intention*]

Our Father - Hail Mary - Glory Be

SEVENTH DAY

Then from the heart of the tempest the Lord gave Job his answer. He said: "... Where were you when I laid the earth's foundations? Tell me, since you are so well-informed! Who decided the dimensions of it, do you know? Or who stretched the measuring line across it? What supports its pillars at their bases? Who laid its cornerstone when all the stars of the morning were singing with joy, and the Sons of God in chorus were chanting praise? Who pent up the sea behind closed doors when it leapt tumultuous out of the womb, when I wrapped it in a robe of mist and made black clouds its swaddling bands

... Have you journeyed all the way to the sources of the sea, or walked where the Abyss is deepest?" (Jb 38:1, 4–9, 16–17)

God's first answer to Job does not address any of his arguments, but describes the myriad wonders of the created world, and asks, "Did you do this?" This may seem an empty answer; but simply looking at a spring sunrise may do more for our misery than a library of arguments.

Father, help me not to close my eyes to all you have made. Help me to see there is more than I can know.

I ask you especially for [*here name your intention*]

Our Father - Hail Mary - Glory Be

EIGHTH DAY

Now think of Behemoth; ... his bones are as hard as hammered iron. He is the masterpiece of all God's work ... Leviathan, too! Can you catch him with a fish-hook? ... Who dare open the gates of his mouth? Terror dwells in those rows of teeth! ... His heart is as hard as rock, unyielding as a millstone. Sword may strike him, but cannot pierce him ... He churns the depths into a seething cauldron, he makes the sea fume like a scent burner ... of all the sons of pride he is the king. (Jb 40:15, 18–19, 25; 41:6, 16, 18, 23, 26)

God's second answer is a long description of two primeval monsters of chaos, taken from the old myths of the near east: Behemoth who stalks the land, and Leviathan, the great sea-dragon. Even these, God says, are of his making; he governs and restrains them, whom no man might even look on.

Father, help me to see that you are behind all things, even the most terrifying or appalling events, and that you walk with us, unseen.

I ask you especially for [*here name your intention*]

Our Father - Hail Mary - Glory Be

NINTH DAY

This was the answer Job gave to the Lord: "I know that you are all-powerful: what you conceive, you can perform. I am the man who obscured your designs with my empty-headed words." ... The Lord turned to Eliphaz ... "I burn with anger against you ..." he said "for not speaking truthfully about me as my servant Job has done." (Jb 42:1–3, 7)

God does not rebut any of Job's accusations, or make some long speech of theological apologetics. He is angry not with Job for his honesty, but with Job's friends who have tried to give easy answers. We may quote Richard Rohr: "When Jesus was looking down on Jerusalem and weeping over it (*Lk* 19:41) the last thing he needed was a pious man running up to him and saying, 'Now, Lord, don't cry. It's all part of God's perfect plan'. No, let Jesus weep. The bigger problem is that we do not join with him in weeping ..."[5]

Father, let me not run after easy answers, but take your words into my heart. Be close to me, this day and all days.

I ask you especially for [*here name your intention*]

Our Father - Hail Mary - Glory Be

[5] *On the Threshold of Transformation* (Chicago, Loyola Press, 2010), p. 242.

braham: Old Age

SCRIPTURE: READ THE STORY OF ABRAHAM
(*GENESIS* 12–25).

Abram, who becomes Abraham, is an old man, settled in his ways, and at a deep level a disappointed man: he has no children, no one to carry on his name and his family. Without warning, God calls him to leave all this behind, and makes him frankly unbelievable promises of future happiness. Abraham risks everything on answering God's call; and despite backsliding and occasional scepticism, he sees all God's promises fulfilled. The faith he is given allows him to trust God even when he asks him to sacrifice to him the very son and heir he had longed for.

FIRST DAY

The Lord said to Abram, "Leave your country, your family and your father's house, for the land I will show you. I will make you a great nation; I will bless you and make your name so famous that it will be used as a blessing." ... So Abram went as the Lord told him ... Abram was seventy-five years old when he left Haran (Gn 12:1–2, 4).

God called Abraham when he was settled and old.

Father, you call me, too, to the Promised Land. Every day is a step nearer to heaven to be with you. But, Father, teach me to hear your voice, to know that the journey is also important. Every day is also a new beginning. Let me always be expectant so that this does not pass me by.

I ask you especially for [*here name your intention*]

Our Father - Hail Mary - Glory Be

SECOND DAY ✓

Abram's wife Sarai had borne him no child, but she had an Egyptian maidservant named Hagar. So Sarai said to Abram, "Listen, now! Since the Lord has kept me from having children, go to my slave-girl. Perhaps I shall get children through her." Abram agreed to what Sarai had said ... Hagar bore Abram a son (Gn 16:1–2, 15).

The incident of Hagar's son is a sign that Abraham has given up on God's promise to him, and is settling for second best.

Father, help me not to be disappointed, not to think "Is this all there is?" Let me see my life as you do. Help me see myself as a friend of yours. Teach me to accept with humility my failing capacities, and to rejoice that my growing weakness makes me more like you on the Cross.

I ask you especially for [*here name your intention*]

Our Father - Hail Mary - Glory Be

THIRD DAY

Abram took his wife Sarai, his nephew Lot, all the possessions they had amassed ... They set off for the land of Canaan (Gn 12:5).

Although Abraham was old, and childless, he had a wife to share his life with.

Lord, let me not forget the good things of my life – not just the life I enjoyed when I was younger, but also the life I have now.

I ask you especially for [*here name your intention*]

Our Father - Hail Mary - Glory Be

FOURTH DAY

*He looked up, and there he saw three men standing near him.
As soon as he saw them he ran from the entrance of the tent
to meet them, and bowed to the ground. "My lord," he said,
"I beg you, if I find favour with you, kindly do not pass your
servant by." (Gn 18:2–3)*

Abraham's hospitality to these three strangers by the Oak
of Mamre is, in fact, an encounter with the living God,
and brings with it future blessings for him and his wife.
His openness to others is richly rewarded.

Father, let me not turn in on myself out of grumpiness
or fear. Help me to be open to people even if I find them
hard to understand, or if they seem to think me stupid.
Help me not to set limits on the people and places
through which I am able to see your presence and action.

I ask you especially for [*here name your intention*]

Our Father - Hail Mary - Glory Be

FIFTH DAY

*God said to Abraham, "As for Sara[h] your wife ... I will bless
her and moreover give you a son by her ... kings of peoples
shall descend from her." Abraham bowed to the ground, and
he laughed, thinking to himself, "Is a child to be born to a
man one hundred years old, and will Sarah have a child at
the age of ninety?" (Gn 17:15–17)*

Abraham was called to persevere in trusting God – to
faith. He thought it was too late for him to start a new
life. But it is never too late to convert.

Father, you know me. I have my sins and some of them are very ingrained. Help me not to despair of ever conquering them, but also not to become so used to them that I see them as part of me. Don't let me guard them jealously. It is never too late to convert.

I ask you especially for [*here name your intention*]

Our Father - Hail Mary - Glory Be

SIXTH DAY

Abraham remained standing before the Lord ... [H]e said, "Are you really going to destroy the just man with the sinner? Perhaps there are fifty just men in the town. Will you really overwhelm them? ... Do not think of doing such a thing ... Will the judge of the whole earth not administer justice?" (Gn 18:22–25)

When God tells Abraham he plans to destroy Sodom, a city notorious for wickedness and sexual violence, Abraham intercedes for the Sodomites. Perhaps they are not all bad; will not God spare them, rather than blot out the righteous?

Lord, in my old age I am not useless to you. I can pray and offer my sufferings and frustrations. Abraham, like Christ, did not stand in judgement on the people of Sodom but prayed and interceded for them. Help me, too, to be someone who can talk with you and earnestly pray for the ills of the world.

I ask you especially for [*here name your intention*]

Our Father - Hail Mary - Glory Be

SEVENTH DAY

The Lord dealt kindly with Sarah as he had said, and did what he had promised her. So Sarah conceived and bore a son to Abraham in his old age, at the time God had promised. Abraham named the son born to him Isaac, the son to whom Sarah had given birth ... Abraham was a hundred years old when his son Isaac was born to him (Gn 21:1–3, 5).

Although Abraham's wife, Sarah, was understandably sceptical, God gave them a child in their old age. This event shows how God is generous and does what we cannot imagine possible; we need not think this should be understood only in terms of children in old age.

Father, help me not to think that nothing new can happen to me in my old age; you can bring new life out of me when I am old, in some way I do not expect.

I ask you especially for [*here name your intention*]

Our Father - Hail Mary - Glory Be

EIGHTH DAY

Now Sarah watched the son that Hagar the Egyptian had borne to Abraham, playing with her son Isaac. "Drive away that slave-girl and her son," she said to Abraham ... This greatly distressed Abraham ... but God said to him, "Do not distress yourself ... Grant Sarah all she asks of you, for it is through Isaac that your name will be carried on. But the slave-girl's son I will also make into a nation, for he is your child too." Rising early next morning Abraham took some bread and a skin of water, and giving them to Hagar, he put the child on her shoulder and sent her away (Gn 21:9–14).

Before Abraham could fulfil the plan God had for him, he had to leave behind those parts of his past life that could have no part in what was to come. He was very reluctant to do this; but God assured him he would care for Hagar and her son, and Abraham believed and trusted him.

Lord, teach me to know what things I have to let go of in order to move on, and to trust you to take care of the things I can't. Give me discernment to know what these things are.

I ask you especially for [_here name your intention_]

Our Father - Hail Mary - Glory Be

NINTH DAY

---

*Isaac spoke to his father Abraham, "Father" he said ... "Look
... here are the fire and the wood, but where is the lamb
for the burnt offering?" Abraham answered, "My son, God
himself will provide the lamb" ... Then looking up, Abraham
saw a ram caught by its horns in a bush. Abraham took the
ram and offered it as a burnt offering in place of his son.
(Gn 22:7–8, 13)*

The sacrifice of Isaac shows how we must hand over to
God everything we love most, full of faith that God will
restore to us all things.

Father, give me a Christian death and welcome me into
the land you have promised me, knowing that you have
already provided the Lamb of God to take away my sins.

I ask you especially for [*here name your intention*]

Our Father - Hail Mary - Glory Be

❧ SCRIPTURAL NOVENAS ❧ MOSES ❧
DISCERNING & ACCEPTING OUR VOCATION ❧
ELIJAH ❧ FINDING STRENGTH IN GOD
TOBIT ❧ MARRIAGE ❧ HANNAH ❧
THE GIFT OF CHILDREN ❧ JOSEPH & HIS
BROTHERS ❧ FOR PEACE IN THE FAMILY
❧ DAVID & ABSALOM ❧ ESTRANGED
CHILDREN ❧ MARTHA ❧ BEING THE
ONE THAT DOES ALL THE WORK ❧

❧ *FOUR LONGER*
NOVENAS ❧

❧ RUTH & NAOMI ❧ FEELING ABANDONED
& FORGOTTEN ❧ DEBORAH & BARAK ❧
WHEN THINGS SEEM TOO MUCH FOR US
❧ JONAH ❧ WHEN GOD'S PLAN DOESN'T
SEEM TO MAKE SENSE ❧ JOB ❧ BEING
HONEST WITH GOD ❧ ABRAHAM ❧ OLD
AGE ❧ FOUR LONGER NOVENAS ❧ THE
HOLY SPIRIT ❧ PENTECOST ❧ THE VIRGIN
MARY ❧ OUR LADY UNTIER OF KNOTS ❧

PART III: FOUR LONGER NOVENAS

A NOVENA TO THE HOLY SPIRIT

BY FR PHILIP G. BOCHANSKI

$\mathcal{A}$ Novena to the Holy Spirit

FRUITS OF THE HOLY SPIRIT

Gathered with his Apostles in the Upper Room, Jesus reminded them that he had chosen and appointed them to "go and bear fruit that will remain" (*Jn* 15:16). At that same Last Supper, he promised them that they would not be alone in accomplishing this mission: "I will ask the Father," he said, "and he will give you another Advocate to be with you always, the Spirit" (*Jn* 14:16–17). The story of the early church related in the Acts of the Apostles shows just how Jesus kept his promise: the Holy Spirit descended on the Apostles at Pentecost, and they went out to accomplish great things in the mission of evangelising the world.

Although we have all heard of the Holy Spirit, he can sometimes be the most difficult of the three Persons of the Trinity to understand. Jesus himself compares the Holy Spirit to the wind: we cannot see the wind, which is invisible, but we recognise it because we can feel it blowing on our skin, and we can see its effects on the objects around us. In the same way, although the Spirit himself is invisible, and often works in hidden ways, we can recognise his presence in the works that he accomplishes in those who believe. St Paul calls these works – "love, joy, peace, patience, kindness, generosity, faithfulness, gentleness, self-control" – the fruits of the Spirit (*Ga* 5:22–23).

In the *Summa Theologica* (I-II, Q. 70), St Thomas Aquinas explains that these spiritual qualities in a person are called "fruits" because they are the result of one's co-operation with the Holy Spirit. They are different from the theological virtues (faith, hope and love) and the gifts of the Holy Spirit (wisdom, knowledge, understanding, counsel, fortitude, piety and holy fear), which are infused, that is, poured into the heart directly by God. Rather, the fruits of the Spirit come about in the soul when we receive the virtues and gifts of the Spirit, and let them change the way we live – in other words, when we put them into practice. The gifts are graces: purely the initiative of God, the giver of all good gifts. The fruits are evidence of our response to God's gift. They combine our own efforts with the Spirit of God working in us, and show the world the power of God at work in our lives.

✓ PRAYING TO THE HOLY SPIRIT

Before he ascended into heaven, Jesus instructed the Apostles to remain in Jerusalem and to pray for the coming of the Holy Spirit. If we wish to receive the power of the Holy Spirit that will help us to bear his fruits, we, too, must follow this command and example of fervent prayer.

These prayers and devotions may be used to make a novena of prayers to the Holy Spirit, seeking help that we may bear his fruits. Certainly, a good time to pray such a novena would be on the nine days between Ascension and Pentecost, but there are many other reasons to pray for the Spirit's fruits during the whole year. A new job, a new school year, a move to a new location are all good times to pray for the guidance and support of the Advocate that Jesus promised to his disciples. Or perhaps we have recognised that peace, love, joy, or some of the other fruits are missing from our lives. Prayer for the action of the Holy Spirit is the necessary first step if these fruits are to grow in our lives. Whatever the reason, we can be sure that the Holy Spirit hears our prayers and will pour out his graces on us so that we can bear fruit in abundance.

VESSEL OF THE HOLY SPIRIT

When the Apostles made the original novena to the Holy Spirit, they were not alone. Because we belong to the Communion of Saints, we too can be sure that as we pray, we are in the company of the Blessed Mother and the Apostles, as well as myriads of saints from every time and place. In our meditations during this novena, we will pay particular attention to one saint, a sixteenth-century Roman priest who has come to be known as the "vessel of the Holy Spirit".

Around the year 1533, a young man from Florence entered the gates of the city of Rome, drawn there by a special attraction, what he perceived to be a call from God himself. He soon found employment as a tutor to the two sons of a fellow Florentine who was director of the custom-house – a job that provided him with a roof and a bed, food and drink, and a great deal of free time, which he put to good use. Sometimes he would go to volunteer in the hospitals, and often he would spend long hours in prayer in one of Rome's many churches. Nearly every day he would walk around the city, seeking out young men like himself who also had time on their hands, and striking up conversations with them.

From this humble beginning, Philip Romolo Neri built a lifestyle and a ministry that would lead to his being called "The Second Apostle of Rome". For out of the friendships he made in these early days would come his own vocation to the priesthood, and the gathering of a community of lay people for prayers and fellowship each afternoon in a chapel – also called an "oratory" – above the aisle of his church of San Girolamo della Carità. Soon these afternoon exercises became known as "The Oratory", and gave a name also to the congregation of priests and brothers that was established to conduct them. Through it all, Philip Neri had an impact on thousands of people – paupers and popes, men and women of every class and career – over a lifetime of eighty years. Everyone agreed that there was something special about this humble, unassuming man, which drew people to him "as the magnet draws iron".

HEART OF FIRE

To depict this special quality that people experienced in their contact with him, St Philip is often described in art, poetry and prayers as having a heart of fire. But this is not merely a metaphor. During his lifetime many people noticed that he seemed always to be warm; he was often flushed, and would walk around with his cassock unbuttoned at the chest, even in the middle of winter. Not only that, but several of his disciples reported that his heart used to beat violently when he prayed or preached, sometimes enough to shake the bench on which he was sitting. Some people could hear his heart beating across the room, and others experienced unspeakable peace and joy when he embraced them and held their heads to his breast. Typical of St Philip, although so many people witnessed this incredible warmth and palpitation of his heart, no one knew where it came from until St Philip was on his deathbed. There he told one of his favourite disciples, Pietro Consolini, who waited until he himself lay dying, in 1643, before he revealed the secret of St Philip's personal Pentecost.

Over a period of about ten years, while St Philip was in his twenties and still a layman, he used to spend many nights in prayer, either on the porticos of Roman churches, or in the catacombs, the underground burial places of the martyrs outside the walls of the city. On the vigil of Pentecost in 1544, St Philip was praying in the Catacombs of St Sebastian, on the Via Appia, as he had done many times, and asking God to give him the Holy Spirit. As the night passed, St Philip was suddenly filled with great joy, and had a vision of the Holy Spirit, who appeared to him as a ball of fire. This fire entered into St Philip's mouth, and descended to his heart, causing it to expand to twice its normal size, and breaking two of his ribs in the process. He said that it filled his whole body with such joy and consolation that he finally had to throw himself on the ground and cry out, "No more, Lord! No more!"

This mystical experience was a defining moment in St Philip's life. But he did not make much of its extraordinary nature, and he would not want us to do so either. "As for those who run after visions," he would say, "we must lay hold of them by the feet and pull them to the ground by force, lest they should fall into the devil's net." Rather, its importance lay in the fact that, from that moment on, St Philip was convinced and constantly aware of the presence and action of the Holy Spirit in him and through him. This mystical experience of the Spirit gave him great confidence in living his vocation and carrying out what he saw to be his special mission. He was sure that he had received the gifts of the Holy Spirit, and this assurance set him free to bear the Spirit's fruits.

The world in which we live today is not terribly different from the materialistic, self-centred, overly sensual Rome that St Philip evangelised in the sixteenth century. He was a driving force for renewal in his own day, and his example and advice are as relevant and necessary in our day as they were in his. Above all, St Philip shines forth as a sign of hope – of the great things that become possible when a person co-operates with the power of the Holy Spirit working in him, and dedicates himself to bearing spiritual fruit. The saint of gentleness and kindness, who practised perfect chastity and tireless generosity, is an example of patience who draws us to celebrate the peace, joy and love that come from the presence and work of the

Holy Spirit in each human heart. Let us pray with him for an outpouring of the same Holy Spirit that set his heart on fire, that we may imitate him in bearing the fruits of the Spirit.

DAY ONE — LOVE

HYMN

(May be taken from the hymns printed after Day Nine below)

ANTIPHON

Come, Holy Spirit, fill the hearts of your faithful, and kindle in them the fire of your love. Send forth your Spirit, and they will be created.

- And you will renew the face of the earth.

PRAYER

God our Father, your love for us gives us strength to accomplish your will. Fill us, as you filled St Philip, with the love of your Holy Spirit, so that like him we may share your love with others. We ask this through Christ our Lord. Amen.

READING | 1 JN 4:7–9

Beloved, let us love one another, because love is of God; everyone who loves is begotten by God and knows God. Whoever is without love does not know God, for God is love. In this way the love of God was revealed to us: God sent his only Son into the world so that we might have life through him.

RESPONSORY | CF. RM 5:5; 8:11

The love of God has been poured into our hearts (alleluia).

- By his Spirit living in us (alleluia).

MEDITATION

> *I love, and loving must love ceaselessly,*
> *So whole a conquest in me love hath won;*
> *My love to Thee, Thy love to me dost run;*
> *In Thee I live, and Thou dost live in me.*

These words, from one of the two sonnets that survive from St Philip, summarise well the way that he experienced and understood the love of God and neighbour. "We must give ourselves to God altogether," he insisted, for God has already given himself completely to us. As St Thomas says, in the fruit of love "the Holy Spirit is given in a special manner, as in his own likeness, since he himself is love." Such a total gift of self on God's part demands a response that is likewise total, and leaves no room for any rival. "As much love as we give to creatures," St Philip says, "just so much do we take from the Creator."

Yet he will insist over and over that the fruit of our love for God must be visible in the love we have for our neighbours, and in our concern for them in their need: "God never comes where there is no love of neighbour." From the very beginning of his days in Rome, long before his ordination as a priest, and even before his Pentecost, St Philip organised charitable groups and institutions in the city. Later, during the Holy Year of 1550, he established the Confraternity of the Holy Trinity (*Santissima Trinità dei Pellegrini*) to serve the pilgrims who came to Rome for the Jubilee. This work continued in subsequent Holy Years, and in the interim the confraternity devoted itself to caring for the sick in hospitals and convalescent homes. St Philip frequently joined in their work, even in his old age, and constantly sent his penitents to the hospitals as well. "A diligent charity in ministering to the sick," he advised them, "is a compendious way to the acquisition of perfect virtue."

This was dirty, exhausting, thankless work, but he performed it with cheerfulness and an evident love – and expected his disciples to come to it with the same attitude. Many found it a great mortification, especially those who in their own lives were used to being cared for and waited on, rather than the other way around. But this mortification of self-will and pride is at the heart of St Philip's spiritual approach, and was for him the measure of all spiritual progress: "The greatness of our love for God must be tested by the desire we have of suffering for his love." He was not oblivious to the sacrifices that works of charity involved, but he knew that real charity would overcome these obstacles. "The love of God makes us do great things."

LITANY

(Optional; some are printed below, after Day Nine)

Our Father - Hail Mary - Glory Be

CONCLUDING PRAYER

*H*eavenly Father, hear the prayers that we make in the name of your Son, and give us the Paraclete whom he promised you would send. May your love for us give us strength to respond to you, and to bear fruit in our love for you and for our neighbour. We ask this through Christ our Lord. Amen.

DAY TWO — JOY

HYMN

ANTIPHON

Come, Holy Spirit, fill the hearts of your faithful, and kindle in them the fire of your love. Send forth your Spirit, and they will be created.

- And you will renew the face of the earth.

PRAYER

*F*ather, the presence of your Holy Spirit gives joy to your people. Open our hearts to receive your Spirit, that like St Philip we may rejoice in his presence every day of our lives. We ask this through Christ our Lord. Amen.

READING | 1 P 1:8–9

Although you have never seen [Christ] you love him; even though you do not see him now you believe in him, you rejoice with an indescribable and glorious joy, as you attain the goal of your faith, the salvation of your souls.

RESPONSORY

The love of God has been poured into our hearts (alleluia).

- By his Spirit living in us (alleluia).

MEDITATION

"The necessary result of the love of charity is joy: because every lover rejoices at being united to the beloved." So teaches St Thomas, and this fruit of the Spirit was so evident in the life of St Philip that it has become almost synonymous with his name. "Light of Holy Joy" Cardinal Newman calls him, and a contemporary author who wrote a philosophical treatise on the subject titled his work simply "Philip: or Christian Joy". Many eyewitness accounts give testimony to the great spiritual joy that seemed to overflow from St Philip's heart and was evident to everyone who met him.

Often this joy would have physical manifestations: some witnesses report seeing St Philip levitate at the altar while saying Mass, and the servers who assisted at his Mass later in his life tell us that, when he came to the elevation of the Host before Communion, he would sometimes be lost in contemplation for hours at a time. People who came to his room early in the morning for Confession often found him lost in prayer, perhaps standing in the middle of the room with his shirt half-buttoned, so distracted by love and joy that he had forgotten what he was doing.

We have seen already, though, that St Philip did not put much stock in these ecstatic gifts and manifestations in his own life, and he positively discouraged them in others. "He who desires ecstasies and visions does not know what he is desiring," he would say, and he meant it. The raptures that used to come upon him while he was preaching or celebrating Mass were a source of great embarrassment and distress for him, and he would do anything he could think of to distract himself so that his emotions did not overpower him. With others he was equally cautious. "Philip did not make much account of this warmth and acuteness of feeling, for he said that emotion was not devotion, that tears were no sign that a man was in the grace of God; neither must we suppose a man holy merely because he weeps when he speaks of religion."

Still, the holy joy that filled St Philip's heart was difficult to hide, and in many cases was positively contagious. "What St Paul says of himself seemed to be fulfilled in Philip," Newman tells us, quoting the second letter to the Corinthians: "I am filled with consolation – I over-abound with joy." His penitents often felt joyful simply being in his room, even if he were not there, and some who were in distress only needed to stand at the door of his room, without going in, to feel better. Though some people are naturally outgoing and expressive, it seems that this was not the case with St Philip, and he was always ready to attribute the joy he felt and shared with others to its real source. "The Holy Spirit is the master of prayer and causes us to abide in continual peace and cheerfulness, which is a foretaste of Paradise. We ought to pray God fervently to increase in us every day the light and heat of his goodness."

LITANY

Our Father - Hail Mary - Glory Be

CONCLUDING PRAYER

*H*eavenly Father, hear the prayers that we make in the name of your Son, and give us the Paraclete whom he promised you would send. May we rejoice always in the presence of your Holy Spirit, and become living signs of his action in the world. We ask this through Christ our Lord. Amen.

DAY THREE — PEACE

HYMN

ANTIPHON

Come, Holy Spirit, fill the hearts of your faithful, and kindle in them the fire of your love. Send forth your Spirit, and they will be created.

- And you will renew the face of the earth.

PRAYER

*F*ather of mercy, your Holy Spirit is the sign and instrument of your peace in the world. Fill our hearts with this peace, so that, like St Philip, we may conform our lives to your holy will. We ask this through Christ our Lord. Amen.

READING | PH 4:5–7, 9

The Lord is near. Have no anxiety at all, but in everything, by prayer and petition, with thanksgiving, make your requests known to God. Then the peace of God that surpasses all understanding will guard your hearts and minds in Christ Jesus ... Keep on doing what you have learned and received and heard and seen in me. Then the God of peace will be with you.

RESPONSORY

The love of God has been poured into our hearts (alleluia).

- By his Spirit living in us (alleluia).

MEDITATION

"He who wishes for anything but Christ does not know what he wishes; he who asks for anything but Christ does not know what he is asking; he who works, and not for Christ, does not know what he is doing." Such single-mindedness lies at the heart of St Philip's approach to life and ministry, and gives us insight into the source of the peace which pervaded his personality. St Thomas says that the peace that is a fruit of the Holy Spirit involves two things: "freedom from outward disturbance", since our hearts are so fixed on God that they do not attend to external things, and perfect calm, since "our desires rest altogether in one object", namely, doing God's will. St Philip was aware that God required not only all of his love, but also his full attention and complete confidence; because he was able to give them, he enjoyed real peace. "To be entirely conformed and resigned to the divine will is truly a road in which we cannot go wrong, and is the only road which leads us to taste and enjoy that peace which sensual and earthly men know nothing of."

But how does someone know he is truly resigned to the divine will? For St Philip the answer lay in distrusting the self, and putting complete confidence in one's spiritual director. He insisted that the primary relationship in the life of anyone striving for virtue is one of obedience to the spiritual father. "He always asked advice, even on affairs of minor importance. His constant counsel to his penitents was that they should not trust in themselves, but always take the advice of others, and get as many prayers as they could." "They who really wish to advance in the way of God," he said, "must give themselves up into the hands of their superiors always and in everything … There is nothing which gives greater security to our actions, or more effectively cuts the snares the devil lays for us, than to follow another person's will, rather than our own, in doing good."

One anecdote shows how seriously St Philip took his own counsel in regard to obedience. He was on friendly terms with Ignatius of Loyola, who came to visit him often with letters from a fellow Jesuit, Francis Xavier, who was working as a missionary in India and the Far East. As he listened to St Ignatius read these letters, St Philip found himself burning with desire to follow in St Francis's footsteps, and there came a time when he had gathered twenty or so men and was ready to set sail with them for pagan territories. But he would not go until he had consulted a priest whom he had come to trust. This priest told St Philip, "Your Indies are in Rome", and he accepted the advice with peaceful resignation. This conversation took place in 1556; for the next forty years, St Philip worked diligently in Rome and never left the city.

As a spiritual director himself, St Philip often shared this gift of peace with those who turned to him for guidance. Some "recovered their lost peace of mind by simply looking Philip in the face. To dream of him was enough to comfort many. In a word, Philip was a perpetual refreshment to all those who were in perplexity and sadness." Because of this he was in great demand as a counsellor and confessor, and his penitents gave him little rest, even when he was sick. But he held nothing back from those who needed to know God's peace; indeed, Newman tells us, "When he was ill, he did not so much receive as impart consolation."

LITANY

Our Father - Hail Mary - Glory Be

CONCLUDING PRAYER

*H*eavenly Father, hear the prayers that we make in the name of your Son, and give us the Paraclete whom he promised you would send. May the peace that your Holy Spirit brings transform our lives, remove anxiety and teach us to be obedient to you. We ask this through Christ our Lord. Amen.

305

DAY FOUR — PATIENCE

HYMN

ANTIPHON

Come, Holy Spirit, fill the hearts of your faithful, and kindle in them the fire of your love. Send forth your Spirit, and they will be created.

- And you will renew the face of the earth.

PRAYER

*F*ather, the grace of your Holy Spirit gives us courage to endure all things. Strengthen our hearts, that like St Philip, we may patiently endure every trial, and persevere in doing your will. We ask this through Christ our Lord. Amen.

READING | JM 5:7–8

Be patient, therefore, brothers, until the coming of the Lord. See how the farmer waits for the precious fruit of the earth, being patient with it until it receives the early and the late rains. You too must be patient. Make your hearts firm, because the coming of the Lord is at hand.

RESPONSORY

The love of God has been poured into our hearts (alleluia).

- By his Spirit living in us (alleluia).

MEDITATION

The way that St Philip dealt with his own illnesses, which were many, points us to another fruit that the Spirit bore in his life, namely patience. The Vulgate translation of the Scriptures adds another fruit here, called long-suffering, and St Thomas distinguishes the two in this way: each, he says, refers to the ability of the mind not to be disturbed. Patience, properly so-called, endures when evil threatens; long-suffering perseveres when good things are delayed. Both aspects of patience were central to St Philip's spirituality. "The great matter," he insisted over and over, "is to persevere."

Certainly patience is necessary in the midst of physical suffering – "Resignation is all in all to the sick man" – but it applies equally to spiritual tribulations, persecutions and misunderstandings as well. St Philip was no stranger to this kind of suffering: on more than one occasion those who misunderstood his efforts or were jealous of his success (often the same people) went out of their way to make life difficult for him, even going so far as to report him to the Holy See as a suspected heretic. Each time he was vindicated and given reassurance, often by the Holy Father himself, but the hurt was real. Still, he saw everything he suffered as part of God's plan, and welcomed it with love. "There is no surer or clearer proof of the love of God than adversity," he advised. "Tribulations, if we bear them patiently for the love of God, appear bitter at first, but they grow sweet when one gets accustomed to the taste."

He likewise advised his penitents to make patience and long-suffering a part of their prayer life: "We must not give up praying because we do not receive what we ask for all at once." Not only did they need to have patience when asking something from God and waiting for it to be fulfilled, but they ought, he said, to make perseverance itself the object of their request. "Among the things we ought to ask of God is perseverance in well-doing and in serving the Lord, because, if we only have patience and persevere in the good life we have begun to lead, we shall acquire a most eminent degree of spirituality. We must often remember what Christ said, that not he who begins, but he who perseveres to the end, shall be saved."

LITANY

Our Father - Hail Mary - Glory Be

CONCLUDING PRAYER

*H*eavenly Father, hear the prayers that we make in the name of your Son, and give us the Paraclete whom he promised you would send. May that Holy Spirit be our strength when we are weak, and help us to bear patiently whatever you ask of us. We ask this through Christ our Lord. Amen.

DAY FIVE — KINDNESS

HYMN

ANTIPHON

Come, Holy Spirit, fill the hearts of your faithful, and kindle in them the fire of your love. Send forth your Spirit, and they will be created.

- And you will renew the face of the earth.

PRAYER

Merciful Father, your kindness endures forever. May the same Holy Spirit who filled the heart of St Philip fill our hearts also, and make himself known in the kindness we show to those around us. We ask this through Christ our Lord. Amen.

READING | EP 4:31–32

Do not grieve the Spirit of God, with which you have been sealed for the day of redemption. All bitterness, fury, anger, shouting, and reviling must be removed from you, along with all malice. And be kind to one another, compassionate, forgiving one another as God has forgiven you in Christ.

RESPONSORY

The love of God has been poured into our hearts (alleluia).

- By his Spirit living in us (alleluia).

MEDITATION

The words that St Thomas uses to discuss the fruit of kindness – also called benignity – are particularly apt in this discussion of the saint with the "heart of fire". Kindness disposes a person to treat other people well, "for the benign are those in whom the salutary flame (*bonus ignis*) of love has enkindled the desire to be kind to their neighbour." The flame of love in St Philip showed itself constantly in the cheerful kindness which he showed to all those around him, so much so that Newman can call him "winning saint" and "sweetest of fathers" without exaggeration. A poem that the cardinal wrote about his patron has become a favourite hymn of the Oratory, and begins, "This is the saint of gentleness and kindness".

"Cheerfulness strengthens the heart," St Philip says, and so "in dealing with our neighbour we must assume as much pleasantness of manner as we can, and by this affability win him to the ways of virtue." He was convinced that the way to win someone over was by kindness, rather than harshness, and so far this approach seems obvious. He advised priests hearing confessions to be compassionate, and dozens of his penitents bear witness that he followed his own advice. But St Philip's kindness was not affected or insincere; rather, we find its source in his real humility, and in his basic conviction that he was addressing Christ in every person whom he encountered. He was kind to friends and strangers alike: "Philip welcomed those who consulted him with singular benignity, and received them, though strangers, with as much affection as if he had been a long time expecting them."

In dealing with others, benignity requires that we always assume the best of them, and not impute bad motives to the things we see them do. "We should never remind anyone of his natural defects," St Philip counsels, and "we must sometimes bear with little defects in others. We should not be quick at correcting others; we ought to hate no one." Several centuries later, Cardinal Newman would incorporate these and similar sentiments into his definition of a gentleman (in *The Idea of a University*). Kindness is at the heart of the community life that is the essence of the Congregation of the Oratory, and a necessary protection against the dangers that threaten fraternal love. "Our enemy, the devil, who fights with us in order to vanquish us, seeks to disunite us in our houses and to breed quarrels, dislikes, contests, and rivalries ... While we are fighting with each other, he comes and conquers us and makes us more securely his own."

But cheerful kindness was not something St Philip advised merely for the sake of winning others. It likewise strengthens the heart of the one who practises it, for by being cheerful we are co-operating with the Spirit of kindness, and allowing the "salutary flame of love" to bear fruit in our actions. "The true way to advance in holy virtues is to persevere in a holy cheerfulness," he says, and "the cheerful are much easier to guide in the spiritual life than the melancholy." The connection between cheerful kindness and growth in spirituality is found in the freedom that comes with humility, and St Philip saw a lack of cheerfulness to be connected with too much self-concern. "Excessive sadness," he insisted, "seldom springs from any other source than pride."

LITANY

Our Father - Hail Mary - Glory Be

CONCLUDING PRAYER

*H*eavenly Father, hear the prayers that we make in the name of your Son, and give us the Paraclete whom he promised you would send. Set our hearts on fire with your Holy Spirit, and help us to share this flame of love with our brothers and sisters. We ask this through Christ our Lord. Amen.

DAY SIX — GOODNESS

HYMN

ANTIPHON

Come, Holy Spirit, fill the hearts of your faithful, and kindle in them the fire of your love. Send forth your Spirit, and they will be created.

- And you will renew the face of the earth.

PRAYER

*L*oving Father, your generous love overflows in the outpouring of your Holy Spirit. Fill us, as you filled St Philip, with the Spirit of generosity, and teach us to make a gift of ourselves to others. We ask this through Christ our Lord. Amen.

READING | 1 TM 6:17–19

Tell the rich in the present age not to be proud and not to rely on so uncertain a thing as wealth, but rather on God, who richly provides us with all things for our enjoyment. Tell them to do good, to be rich in good works, to be generous, ready to share, thus accumulating as treasure a good foundation for the future, so as to win the life that is true life.

RESPONSORY

The love of God has been poured into our hearts (alleluia).

- By his Spirit living in us (alleluia).

MEDITATION

Like kindness and cheerfulness, the spiritual fruit of goodness also disposes us well towards our neighbour; here, the Spirit is at work to produce not only good thoughts towards others, but a willingness to do good things for those around us. "Do not let a day pass without doing some good during it," St Philip advised his disciples. "We must not delay in doing good, for death will not delay its time." He felt an urgency about making the love of God and neighbour visible in the form of good works, and this was a watchword with him from the very beginning of his time in Rome. When he met young men on his walks during those early days in Rome, his greeting was always the same: "Well!" he would say, with a grin on his face, "When shall we have a mind to begin to do good?"

This goodness requires a generous spirit, one that is sincerely detached from the world and its material delights. "Give me ten men who are really detached from the world, and wish for nothing but Christ," St Philip once exclaimed, "and I have the heart to believe I could convert the world with them." But the freedom and power that come with detachment are completely squelched by the bonds of avarice. "He who wishes for material possessions will never have devotion ... He who wishes for perfection must have no attachments to anything of this world." Anecdotes abound of the counsels he gave and the penances he assigned, to gently but firmly lead those who were greedy to renounce their connections to material things.

Generosity for St Philip applied not merely to money and objects – he had few enough of them as it was, and often showed his gratitude for gifts by giving one to the donor that was double the value of the one he had received. More important for him was a commitment to be generous with his time and energy. "If we wish to help our neighbour," he taught, "we must reserve for ourselves neither place, nor hour, nor time." When one of the fathers of the Congregation refused to answer the door to those who came for Confession or alms, because he was saying his prayers, St Philip would have none of it. He admonished him and the other fathers and brothers that when they were called for, they were to come immediately, no matter if they were praying or anything else, for in doing so they would be "leaving Christ for Christ".

LITANY

Our Father - Hail Mary - Glory Be

CONCLUDING PRAYER

Heavenly Father, hear the prayers that we make in the name of your Son, and give us the Paraclete whom he promised you would send. Let the love of your Holy Spirit abound in our hearts, and help us to bear fruit in good works and generous service to our neighbour. We ask this through Christ our Lord. Amen.

DAY SEVEN — FAITHFULNESS

HYMN

ANTIPHON

Come, Holy Spirit, fill the hearts of your faithful, and kindle in them the fire of your love. Send forth your Spirit, and they will be created.

- And you will renew the face of the earth.

PRAYER

*H*oly Father, your love for us is everlasting and always true. By the gift of your Holy Spirit keep us faithful to you, that in imitation of St Philip we may serve you with integrity. We ask this through Christ our Lord. Amen.

READING | RV 2:10B, 25–26

Remain faithful until death, and I will give you the crown of life ... You must hold fast to what you have until I come. To the victor, who keeps my ways until the end, I will give authority over the nations.

RESPONSORY

The love of God has been poured into our hearts (alleluia).

- By his Spirit living in us (alleluia).

MEDITATION

St Thomas tells us that the spiritual fruit of fidelity, or
faithfulness, has two aspects. On the one hand, fidelity
towards our neighbour keeps us from offending him
through fraud or deceit. Faithfulness towards God is
closely connected with the supernatural virtue of faith,
and leads us to subject our intellect, and all that we have,
to God. St Philip bore the spiritual fruit of faithfulness
equally towards God and his neighbour, providing an
example and instruction for his disciples to do the same.

We have seen how gentle and kind St Philip always
was towards those around him. He also demanded
absolute honesty and integrity in his relationships. "He
could not bear two-faced persons," Cardinal Newman
tells us, and "as for liars, he could not endure them,
and was continually reminding his spiritual children to
avoid them as they would a pestilence." Lying to avoid
embarrassment was even worse; he insisted that his
followers accept the crosses that came to them daily,
since "he who runs away from the Cross the Lord sends
him" through daily humiliations "will meet a bigger one
on the road". The faithfulness that St Philip practised
and demanded of others was not relaxed in the face
of adversity or hardship. On the contrary, he insisted,
"poverty and tribulations are given us by God as trials of
our fidelity."

St Philip recognised how difficult it is to maintain
this fidelity, especially towards God, in the face of trials.
"Everyone is willing to stand on Mount Tabor and
see Christ transfigured, but few are willing to go up to
Jerusalem and accompany Christ to Mount Calvary."

Therefore he counselled his followers that the best
way to be faithful was to start slowly and focus on
perseverance, rather than try to take on too much at the
beginning, and burn out quickly. "We must not be too
ready to trust young men who have great devotion,"
he said, speaking from experience. "We must wait till
their wings are grown and then see what sort of a flight
they make." When someone came to him full of fire and
enthusiasm, he did not crush their good intentions, but
he urged them to proceed with moderation. "It is well
to choose some one good devotion and stick to it," he
advised. "We must not wish to do everything at once, or
become a saint in four days, but gradually, little by little."

LITANY

Our Father - Hail Mary - Glory Be

CONCLUDING PRAYER

*H*eavenly Father, hear the prayers that we
make in the name of your Son, and give
us the Paraclete whom he promised you would
send. Keep us faithful to you, that filled with
your grace we may serve and worship you in
Spirit and in truth. We ask this through Christ
our Lord. Amen.

DAY EIGHT — GENTLENESS

HYMN

ANTIPHON

Come, Holy Spirit, fill the hearts of your faithful, and kindle in them the fire of your love. Send forth your Spirit, and they will be created.

- And you will renew the face of the earth.

PRAYER

Gentle Father, your justice is revealed in mercy, and your power in forgiveness. May the same Holy Spirit who filled the gentle heart of St Philip teach us to reach out to others with his tender love. We ask this through Christ our Lord. Amen.

READING | EP 4:1–4A

I, then, a prisoner for the Lord, urge you to live in a manner worthy of the call you have received, with all humility and gentleness, bearing with one another through love, striving to preserve the unity of the spirit through the bond of peace: one body and one Spirit.

RESPONSORY

The love of God has been poured into our hearts (alleluia).

- By his Spirit living in us (alleluia).

MEDITATION

Gentleness allows a person to suffer "with equanimity the evils which his neighbour inflicts on him", says St Thomas, and to curb anger. This meekness and gentle spirit was evident in St Philip throughout his life, even when he had become the first Provost or father of the newly formed Congregation of the Oratory. He did not allow himself to get puffed up with pride because of the authority which he exercised – his advice was that "he who wishes to be perfectly obeyed should give but few orders" – and advised his followers that in all things "a man should keep himself down, and not busy himself *in mirabilibus super se* [in marvels beyond his power]."

St Philip's gentleness allowed him to remain calm even when those around him – sometimes even those closest to him – did not treat him with the respect that he deserved. A famous story is related about Father Talpa, one of the first Oratorians. As Newman tells it, "Once, when he was Superior of the Congregation, one of his subjects snatched a letter out of his hand; but the saint took the affront with incomparable meekness, and neither in look, nor word, nor in gesture betrayed the slightest emotion." Although this may have amazed his other disciples, St Philip demanded that they always follow his example when it came to this kind of mortification. "He who wishes to become a saint must never defend himself ... He who cannot put up with the loss of his honour can never advance."

In order to instil this attitude in his disciples, St Philip insisted on the mortification of the *razionale*, the reasoning part of the mind that always wants to have its way, to be given explanations and consulted on matters. To mortify this part of the self was, for St Philip, much more important than external mortifications like fasting, vigils and bodily penances. Whenever someone asked him why his disciples did not fast, "he was accustomed to say, 'The sanctity of a man lies within the space of three fingers,' and, while he said it, he would touch his forehead, and add, in explanation of his words, 'The whole point lies in mortifying the understanding ... since perfection consists in leading captive our own will and following that of our superiors" (from *The Excellences of the Oratory*).

The penances that St Philip assigned to some of those who came to him for Confession are legendary; for example, those who struggled with vanity often found themselves ordered to dress in their best attire and carry St Philip's dog in their arms through the city streets, with a procession of street urchins mocking them all the way. In this manner he hoped to teach his penitents not to be worried about the opinion others had of them, and to "keep down and thwart [that] touchiness of mind" that is a sure sign of pride, and that leads to unkind and ungentle behaviour. Above all else, the struggle to bear the spiritual fruit of meekness and gentleness requires a sense of humour, especially regarding ourselves and our own status. "To persevere in our cheerfulness amid ... troubles is a sign of a right and good spirit."

LITANY

Our Father - Hail Mary - Glory Be

CONCLUDING PRAYER

Heavenly Father, hear the prayers that we make in the name of your Son, and give us the Paraclete whom he promised you would send. May your Holy Spirit teach us to conquer our pride, and to spend our lives in humble, gentle service to our brothers and sisters. We ask this through Christ our Lord. Amen.

DAY NINE — SELF-CONTROL

HYMN

ANTIPHON

Come, Holy Spirit, fill the hearts of your faithful, and kindle in them the fire of your love. Send forth your Spirit, and they will be created.

- And you will renew the face of the earth.

PRAYER

*F*ather, the wisdom and strength of your Holy Spirit made St Philip a model of chastity to inspire those around him. May that same Spirit strengthen us in mind and body, and teach us to serve you with pure hearts. We ask this through Christ our Lord. Amen.

READING | GA 5:16–17, 24–25

I say, then: live by the Spirit and you will certainly not gratify the desire of the flesh. For the flesh has desires against the Spirit, and the Spirit against the flesh ... Now those who belong to Christ have crucified their flesh with its passions and desires. If we live in the Spirit, let us also follow the Spirit.

RESPONSORY

The love of God has been poured into our hearts (alleluia).

- By his Spirit living in us (alleluia).

MEDITATION

The spiritual fruit of continence, or self-control, is closely connected with the virtue of temperance, and means that the Holy Spirit working in us gives us power to control our bodily desires, and to keep both soul and body in their proper relationship. The Vulgate translation of the letter to the Galatians adds two more spiritual fruits here – modesty and chastity – which further specify the self-control which continence involves, and draw our attention to the importance of integrity and vigilance with regard to sexuality. In St Philip's time, as in our own, chastity was not a "fashionable" virtue, as the art and philosophy of the late Renaissance humanists seemed to revive all of the excesses of ancient paganism. The continence that St Philip displayed in his own life, and encouraged in the lives of others, gives evidence of the power of the Holy Spirit at work in him.

Those who gave testimony during the process of St Philip's canonisation noted over and over the great purity which was evident in his whole demeanour – so much so that, as Cardinal Newman tells us, "it shone out of his countenance. His eyes were so clear and bright, even to the last years of his life, that no painter ever succeeded in giving the expression of them … Moreover, his body, even in his old age, emitted a fragrance which refreshed those who came near him." All of his biographers relate that St Philip maintained his virginity throughout his life, despite many attempts by those who were jealous of him to trip him up. His constant approach was to avoid the source of the temptation; he always said that "in the warfare of the flesh, only cowards gain the victory; that is, those who flee."

This was his advice to his penitents as well, for he believed that "in the matter of purity, there is no greater danger than not fearing the danger." "When a person puts himself in the occasion of sin, saying, 'I shall not fall, I shall not commit it,' it is an almost infallible sign that he will fall, and with all the greater damage to his soul." And so he gave his followers some very practical rules for daily living, which were no doubt drawn from years of his own experience: they needed good friends, but should avoid bad company; they were not to retire to their rooms immediately after the mid-day meal; they must avoid idleness. When faced with a sudden temptation, they should fix their minds on something else, no matter what, and use little prayers like "God, come to my assistance. Lord, make haste to help me." Above all, he insisted, frequent use of the Sacrament of Reconciliation was central to the battle for chastity. "A most excellent means of keeping ourselves pure is to lay open all our thoughts, as soon as possible, to our confessor, with the greatest sincerity, and keep nothing hidden in ourselves. To acquire and preserve the virtue of chastity, we have need of a good and experienced confessor."

This was St Philip's special ministry, and in the confessional he used every gift and fruit of the Spirit to bring souls back to God. It is said that he had a supernatural ability to know who had committed sins against chastity by their smell, and at times he would tell a penitent who was embarrassed and hesitant to confess, "My son, I know your sins already." Notwithstanding his own strict virtue, and this ability to detect the stench of sin, he treated those who came to him to confess sins of impurity with the utmost compassion. "One of the most efficacious means of keeping chaste," he said, "is to have compassion for those who fall through their frailty, and never to boast in the least of being free." He insisted that his disciples treat each other with the same patient understanding, and he used to say that "not to have pity for another in such cases was a forerunner of a speedy fall in ourselves; and that when he found a man censorious, and secure of himself, and without fear, he gave him up for lost".

By his tender guidance St Philip helped many young men to make a good Confession and to be set free from years' worth of bad habits and serious sins, and their connection with him enabled them to persevere in chastity. "Many confessed that they were at once delivered from temptations by his merely laying his hands on their heads. The very mention of his name had a power of shielding from Satan those who were assailed by his fiery darts."

LITANY

Our Father - Hail Mary - Glory Be

CONCLUDING PRAYER

*H*eavenly Father, hear the prayers that we make in the name of your Son, and give us the Paraclete whom he promised you would send. May your Holy Spirit cleanse our hearts and strengthen our bodies. May the purity of our lives bear witness to the power of your love. We ask this through Christ our Lord. Amen

HYMNS

COME, HOLY GHOST

Come Holy Ghost, Creator blest,
And in our hearts take up thy rest;
Come with thy grace and heav'nly aid
To fill the hearts which thou hast made,
To fill the hearts which thou hast made.

O Comforter, to thee we cry,
Thou heav'nly gift of God most high;
Thou fount of life and fire of love,
And sweet anointing from above,
And sweet anointing from above.

O Holy Ghost, through thee alone
Know we the Father and the Son;
Be this our firm unchanging creed:
That thou dost from them both proceed,
That thou dost from them both proceed.

Praise be to thee, Father and Son,
And Holy Spirit, three in one;
And may the Son on us bestow
The gifts that from the Spirit flow,
The gifts that from the Spirit flow.

(*The* Veni Creator Spiritus*, translated by
Fr Edward Caswall of the Oratory*)

HYMN TO ST PHILIP

This is the saint of gentleness and kindness,
Cheerful in penance, and in precept winning;
Patiently healing of their pride and blindness
Souls that are sinning.

This is the saint who, when the world allures us,
Cries her false wares, and opes her magic coffers,
Points to a better city, and secures us
With richer offers.

Love is his bond; he knows no other fetter,
Asks not our all, but takes whate'er we spare him,
Willing to draw us on from good to better,
As we can bear him.

When he comes near to teach us and to bless us,
Prayer is so sweet that hours are but a minute;
Mirth is so pure, though freely it possess us,
Sin is not in it.

Thus he conducts by holy paths and pleasant
Innocent souls, and sinful souls forgiven,
Towards the bright palace where our God is present,
Throned in high heaven.

This is the saint of gentleness and kindness,
Cheerful in penance, and in precept winning;
Patiently healing of their pride and blindness
Souls that are sinning.

(John Henry Newman)

VENI CREATOR SPIRITUS

Come, Holy Spirit, Creator come,
From your bright heavenly throne!
Come, take possession of our souls,
And make them all your own.

You who are called the Paraclete,
Best gift of God above,
The living spring, the living fire,
Sweet unction, and true love!

You who are sevenfold in your grace,
Finger of God's right hand,
His promise, teaching little ones
To speak and understand!

O guide our minds with your blessed light,
With love our hearts inflame,
And with your strength which never decays
Confirm our mortal frame.

Far from us drive our hellish foe
True peace unto us bring,
And through all perils guide us safe
Beneath your sacred wing.

Through you may we the Father know,
Through you the eternal Son
And you the Spirit of them both
Thrice-blessed three in one.

All glory to the Father be,
And to the risen Son;
The same to you, O Paraclete,
While endless ages run.

Amen.

Veni, creátor Spíritus,
mentes tuórum vísita,
imple supérna grátia,
quæ tu creásti péctora.

Qui díceris Paráclitus,
altíssimi donum Dei,
fons vivus, ignis, cáritas,
et spiritális únctio.

Tu septifórmis múnere,
dígitus patérnæ déxteræ,
tu rite promíssum Patris,
sermóne ditans gúttura.

Accénde lumen sénsibus,
infúnde amórem córdibus,
infírma nostri córporis
virtúte firmans pérpeti.

Hostem repéllas lóngius
pacémque dones prótinus;
ductóre sic te prǽvio
vitémus omne nóxium.

Per te sciámus da Patrem
noscámus atque Fílium,
teque utriúsque Spíritum
credámus omni témpore.

Deo Patri sit glória,
et Fílio, qui a mórtuis
surréxit, ac Paráclito,
in sæculórum sæcula.

Amen.

(Attributed to Rabanus Maurus (c.776–856))

LITANIES

LITANY OF THE HOLY SPIRIT

Lord, have mercy.	*Lord, have mercy.*
Christ, have mercy.	*Christ, have mercy.*
Lord, have mercy.	*Lord, have mercy.*
Christ, hear us.	*Christ, graciously hear us.*

God the Father of heaven,   *Have mercy on us.*
God the Son, Redeemer of the world,
God the Holy Spirit,
Holy Trinity, One God,

Holy Spirit, proceeding from the Father and the Son,
Holy Spirit, co-equal with the Father and the Son,
Promise of the Father, most bounteous,
Ray of heavenly light,
Author of all good,
Source of living water,
Consuming fire,
Burning love,
Spiritual unction,

Spirit of truth and power,
Spirit of wisdom and understanding,
Spirit of counsel and fortitude,
Spirit of knowledge and piety,
Spirit of fear of the Lord,
Spirit of compunction,
Spirit of grace and prayer,
Spirit of love, peace and joy,
Spirit of patience,
Spirit of longanimity and goodness,
Spirit of benignity and mildness,

Spirit of fidelity,
Spirit of modesty and continence,
Spirit of chastity,
Spirit of adoption of sons of God,

Holy Spirit, our Comforter,
Holy Spirit, our Sanctifier,
You who in the beginning moved upon the waters,
You through whom spoke holy men of God,
You who overshadowed the Virgin Mary,
You by whom Mary conceived Christ,
You who descend upon men at Baptism,
You who on the day of Pentecost appeared through
    fiery tongues,
You by whom we are reborn,
You who dwell in us as in a temple,
You who govern and animate the Church,
You who fill the whole world,
That you will renew the face of the earth,
We beseech you, hear us.

That you may shed your light upon us,
That you may pour your love into our hearts,
That you may inspire us to love our neighbour,
That you may teach us to ask for the graces we need,
That you may enlighten us with your heavenly inspirations,
That you may guide us in the way of holiness,
That you may make us obedient to your commandments,
That you may teach us how to pray,
That you may always pray with us,
That you may inspire us with horror for sin,
That you may direct us in the practice of virtue,
That you may make us persevere in a holy life,
That you may make us faithful to our vocation,
That you may grant us good priests and bishops,
That you may give us good Christian families,

That you may grant us a spiritual renewal of the Church,
That you may guide and console the Holy Father,

Lamb of God, who takes away the sins of the world:
Spare us, O Lord.
Lamb of God, who takes away the sins of the world:
Graciously hear us, O Lord.
Lamb of God, who takes away the sins of the world:
Have mercy on us.
Holy Spirit, hear us. *Holy Spirit, graciously hear us.*

Lord, have mercy. *Lord, have mercy.*
Christ, have mercy. *Christ, have mercy.*
Lord, have mercy. *Lord, have mercy.*

Create a clean heart in us, O Lord.
Renew a right spirit in us, O Lord.

Let us pray:

O God, who enlighten the hearts of the faithful by the
light of the Holy Spirit, grant to us the same Spirit, that
we may be truly wise and ever rejoice in his consolation.
We ask this through Christ our Lord. Amen.

THE LITANY OF ST PHILIP

Lord, have mercy. *Lord, have mercy.*
Christ, have mercy. *Christ, have mercy.*
Lord, have mercy. *Lord, have mercy.*
Christ, hear us. *Christ, graciously hear us.*

God the Father of heaven, *Have mercy on us.*
God the Son, Redeemer of the world,
Have mercy on us.
God the Holy Ghost, *Have mercy on us.*
Holy Trinity, one God, *Have mercy on us.*
Holy Mary, *Pray for us.*
Holy Mother of God, *Pray for us.*
Holy Virgin of virgins, *Pray for us.*

St Philip, *Pray for us.*
Vessel of the Holy Ghost, *Pray for us.*
Child of Mary, *Pray for us.*
Apostle of Rome, *Pray for us.*
Counsellor of Popes, *Pray for us.*
Voice of prophecy, *Pray for us.*
Man of primitive times, *Pray for us.*
Winning saint, *Pray for us.*
Hidden hero, *Pray for us.*
Sweetest of fathers, *Pray for us.*
Flower of purity, *Pray for us.*
Martyr of charity, *Pray for us.*
Heart of fire, *Pray for us.*
Discerner of spirits, *Pray for us.*
Choicest of priests, *Pray for us.*
Mirror of the divine life, *Pray for us.*
Pattern of humility, *Pray for us.*
Example of simplicity, *Pray for us.*
Light of holy joy, *Pray for us.*
Image of childhood, *Pray for us.*

Picture of old age,	*Pray for us.*
Director of souls,	*Pray for us.*
Gentle guide of youth,	*Pray for us.*
Patron of thine own,	*Pray for us.*

Who didst observe chastity in thy youth,	*Pray for us.*
Who didst seek Rome by divine guidance,	*Pray for us.*
Who didst hide so long in the Catacombs,	*Pray for us.*
Who didst receive the Holy Ghost into thy heart,	*Pray for us.*
Who didst experience such wonderful ecstasies,	*Pray for us.*
Who didst so lovingly serve the little ones,	*Pray for us.*
Who didst wash the feet of pilgrims,	*Pray for us.*
Who didst ardently thirst after martyrdom,	*Pray for us.*
Who didst distribute the daily word of God,	*Pray for us.*
Who didst turn so many hearts to God,	*Pray for us.*
Who didst converse so sweetly with Mary,	*Pray for us.*
Who didst raise the dead,	*Pray for us.*
Who didst set up thy houses in all lands,	*Pray for us.*

Lamb of God, who takest away the sins of the world,
Spare us, O Lord.
Lamb of God, who takest away the sins of the world,
Graciously hear us, O Lord.
Lamb of God, who takest away the sins of the world,
Have mercy on us.
Christ, hear us. *Christ, graciously hear us.*

V. Remember thy Congregation,
R. *Which thou hast possessed from the beginning.*

Let us pray:

O God, who hast exalted blessed Philip, thy confessor, in the glory of thy saints, grant that, as we rejoice in his commemoration, so we may profit by the example of his virtues, through Christ our Lord.

R. Amen.

A NOVENA FOR PENTECOST

TAKEN FROM *THE ROAD TO PENTECOST*

BY THE NATIONAL SERVICE COMMITTEE FOR
CATHOLIC CHARISMATIC RENEWAL IN ENGLAND

Novena for Pentecost

Each day of the novena, which ends on the vigil of Pentecost, focuses on a particular intention, which is accompanied by a passage of Scripture, a reflection, and a prayer. It is important is to keep this attitude of prayer and intercession in your heart through each of these nine days, interceding for the Church and the world – that the Holy Spirit can renew both with his powerful love.

FIRST DAY:

FOR ISRAEL, THE PEOPLE OF THE COVENANT

SCRIPTURE

Is it possible that God abandoned his people? Out of the question. God never abandoned his own people to whom years ago he gave recognition ... on the contrary their failure has brought salvation to the Gentiles, in order to stir them to envy (Rm 11).

REFLECTION

God revealed himself to the Jewish people in a special way in history and prepared them to receive the Messiah. Jesus Christ, who was a Jew, was the fulfilment of all the Old Testament prophecies. When he came, however, people rejected him because he was not the kind of Messiah they were expecting.

PRAYER

*F*ather, we thank you for the Jewish people. We thank you for their devotion and fidelity to you over the centuries. We repent of any sins of anti-Semitism on our part. We ask for your blessing upon them. Send them your Holy Spirit.

SECOND DAY:

FOR THE RENEWAL OF THE CHURCH

SCRIPTURE

And now I am sending upon you what the Father has promised. Stay in the city then, until you are clothed with power from on high (Lk 24:49).

REFLECTION

The Christian Church is the body of Christ on the earth. It is both human and divine. We are called to show the love and power of Christ to our world. Often our witness is marred, however, by our sins as individuals and as a body and this stops people seeing Jesus or listening to our message.

PRAYER

*L*ord, we thank you for your Church on earth, the abiding expression of your love and reminder of your presence amongst us. We are sorry for the times we have let you down, as a Church and as individuals. You know how weak we are. We pray that we as a body would reflect your face, your priorities and your values. We pray for all Church leaders, especially the Pope; grant them the wisdom and holiness they need to lead your people at this time in our history. Please send us your Holy Spirit, O Lord, and renew us. Fill us with your love and power and zeal for the gospel. May our Church become alive with the Spirit of Pentecost once again.

THIRD DAY: FOR THE UNITY OF CHRISTIANS

SCRIPTURE

May they all be one, just as, Father, you are in me, and I am in you, so that they also may be one in us, so that the world may believe it was you who sent me (Jn 17:21).

REFLECTION

Right from the beginning the Christian body has been marred by divisions. There were arguments and jealousies amongst the Apostles and in the early Christian community between Gentile Christians and Jewish believers. This has continued to this day. There are not only divisions between the different denominations and churches but within our own parishes, communities and fellowships. Our divisions and lack of love for each other, however, impair our common witness as followers of Christ and are confusing to others outside the Church.

PRAYER

*F*ather, we thank you for all Christians, for their love and devotion to you. Help us to love and respect each other and to think the best of each other. Help us to support each other when we can and not to judge the different ways we might do things, knowing that you are at the heart of everything. Purify us, Lord, and help us to keep you at the centre, as the closer we are to you, the closer we will be to each other.

FOURTH DAY: FOR THE RENEWAL OF SOCIETY

SCRIPTURE

Look, here God lives among human beings ... He will wipe away all tears from their eyes. There will be no more death, and no more mourning or sadness or pain. The world of the past has gone. Then the One sitting on the throne spoke: "Look, I am making the whole of creation new." (Rv 21:3–5)

REFLECTION

Jesus came to bring about the kingdom of God on earth – a world of love and peace and joy. He showed us the way to do this, by turning away from selfishness, giving our lives to him and drawing on his power as the Son of God. The temptation of humankind, however, is always to reject God and his authority and to try and build utopia on our own strength – to create a world where we are in charge. When we do this, however, everything always crumbles into nothing.

PRAYER

*F*ather, we lift up to you our world and our society with all its brokenness and problems. We lift up to you our governments and leaders. Guide them by your Holy Spirit to make good decisions for the benefit of all. In our own lives we suffer and inflict suffering on others because of our sinfulness. Transform us in the power of your Holy Spirit so that we may be agents of building a civilisation of love and of your kingdom.

FIFTH DAY: FOR CONVERSION AND HOLINESS

SCRIPTURE

Anyone who does not take up his cross and follow in my footsteps is not worthy of me. Anyone who finds his life will lose it, anyone who loses his life for my sake will find it (Mt 10:37–39).

REFLECTION

There is a danger of thinking holiness means human perfection, which we know from our own lives is impossible as we constantly fall. Holiness, however, means being set apart for God. Conversion is that primary decision we make in our life when we decide to live for God instead of ourselves. God uses all the events of our life, if we let him, to help us to become more and more dependent on him and his Holy Spirit, and less and less on ourselves and our own strength. This is holiness – the growing presence of the Spirit of God within us directing our every thought and action, which will show itself in growing virtue and love of others.

PRAYER

O Lord, so often we try and deal with life using our own limited vision and gifts. Help us to see people and events through your eyes. Fill us with your love. May we die to our egos and desires and grow in our knowledge and dependence on you. May all men and women be given the grace of conversion to know, love and follow you.

SIXTH DAY: FOR RECONCILIATION AND HEALING

SCRIPTURE

How delightful it is to live as brothers, all together! (Ps 133:1)

REFLECTION

God has revealed to us that he is our Father and he calls us to love everyone as brothers and sisters. So often we find this so hard, particularly with those who hurt us the most – often those nearest to us – our families, work colleagues and fellow Christians. We hurt each other, justifying ourselves, condemning the other, in an endless cycle of pain and recrimination which slowly but surely destroys us. Jesus tells us that the only way out of this destructive cycle is to forgive. Because of what Jesus has done on the Cross, we can draw on the strength of his Holy Spirit to do the things we cannot do on our own, particularly to forgive our enemies, not just as individuals but as peoples and nations.

PRAYER

O Jesus, you know all the people who have hurt me in my life. You know how hard I find it to forgive them. I lift up to you the wounds that exist, not just in my life but in the lives of my friends, my family and my country. Nothing is impossible for you. May your reconciliation and peace and healing come to us all.

SEVENTH DAY:

FOR EMPOWERMENT FOR EVANGELISATION

SCRIPTURE

And now I am sending upon you what the Father has promised. Stay in the city until you are clothed with the power from on high (Lk 24.49).

REFLECTION

The Apostles spent three years with Jesus. They saw his miracles, experienced his love and heard his teaching. They loved him, yet in his moment of trial they ran away. They were not ready for the task to which Jesus was calling them. They still needed the empowerment of the Holy Spirit. We are the same today. If we are to share the gospel message with others we, too, need the empowerment of the Holy Spirit. The only way that the Holy Spirit becomes truly effective in our lives is if we make a personal decision to repent of our sins and self-sufficiency and ask God to take control over our lives.

PRAYER

Father, I acknowledge my sinfulness and pride. I repent of all self-sufficiency and I want to rely on you alone. Send down your Holy Spirit on me with all the charisms and gifts I need to be the effective Christian you want me to be. I lift up to you my prayer group, my parish community, my church. Send us your Spirit of love and power so that we may be instruments of the Kingdom of God.

EIGHTH DAY:

FOR THE VICTORY OF THE HOLY CROSS

SCRIPTURE

May the God of our Lord Jesus Christ, the Father of glory, give you a spirit of wisdom and perception of what is revealed, to bring you to full knowledge of him. May he enlighten the eyes of your mind so that you can see what hope his call holds for you, how rich is the glory of the heritage he offers among his holy people, and how extraordinarily great is the power that he has exercised for us believers (Ep 1:17–20).

REFLECTION

Jesus could have come in strength and overcome evil by his almighty power but he chose a different way. He seemingly allowed himself to be overcome by evil and died on a cross. But through the power of the Holy Spirit he rose again and demonstrated for all time the power of love to overcome evil. This truth has been shown again and again down through the ages.

PRAYER

O Lord, help me to recognise those moments of death and resurrection in my own life. Those times when you are calling me to lay aside my strength and my power and to die to my own opinions for the good of unity, so that your will be done. May I never become depressed by the evil I see around me, but know that you are able to use all things for your purposes. Give me faith in the power of your love, that through your Cross your kingdom will come on the earth.

NINTH DAY: FOR A NEW OUTPOURING

OF THE HOLY SPIRIT AND HIS GIFTS

SCRIPTURE

Do not leave Jerusalem, but wait there for what the Father has promised. It is, he said, what you have heard me speak about. John baptised with water but not many days from now you are going to be baptised with the Holy Spirit (Ac 1:4–5).

REFLECTION

For the Church to do its job and be an effective agent for the Kingdom of God, it needs a continual empowerment of the Holy Spirit with all its charisms and gifts. Throughout history there have been outpourings of the Holy Spirit, and this novena asks for another outpouring today to equip all God's people so that we can implement God's work of salvation on earth.

PRAYER

*L*ord, I humbly pray that you would send your Holy Spirit down on me in the same way you did on the Apostles in the Upper Room at Pentecost. Jesus, I give my life to you. Give me the grace to turn away from anything in my life that is an obstacle in my relationship with you. Help me to put you first in my life. Amen.

Reflect upon the following words of Pope Benedict XVI on the Solemnity of Pentecost (May 2008):

> We read in the Acts of the Apostles that the disciples were praying all together in the Upper Room when the Holy Spirit descended upon them powerfully, as wind and fire. They then began to proclaim in many tongues the Good News of Christ's Resurrection (cf. 2:1–4). This was the "Baptism of the Holy Spirit" which had been foretold by John the Baptist: "I baptise you with water," he said to the crowds, "but he who is coming after me is mightier than I … he will baptise you with the Holy Spirit and with fire" (*Mt* 3:11).

> In fact, Jesus's entire mission aimed at giving the Spirit of God to men and women and baptising them in his regenerative "bath". This was brought about with his glorification (cf. *Jn* 7:39), that is, through his death and Resurrection: then the Spirit of God was poured out in super-abundance, like a cascade capable of purifying every heart, extinguishing the fire of evil and kindling the flame of divine love in the world … Pentecost [is] the fulfilment of this promise and hence the culmination of Jesus's entire mission.

A NOVENA TO THE BLESSED VIRGIN MARY

BY FR WALTER MACKEN

$\mathcal{N}$ovena to the Blessed Virgin Mary

A PRESENTATION

This novena is designed to help us think more consistently about what Our Lady did at different moments of her life. We are trying to make a space for her each day of this novena. That implies that we need to reserve that space for God. It can be simply done by reading the comment for each day in the early morning before setting out for work. It can be done in the quiet of the evening around the fire with our family or friends. Many people have derived benefit from reading it together. The object is to help us think our way into the life of the Blessed Virgin. We have to imagine ourselves beside her. We have to watch her as she gathers water from the well, or washes the clothes in the stream. We will look at her for those few moments, and we will be delighted and charmed by how ordinary she is, and still she is the Mother of God. There is the use of a novena like this one. We will get to know Our Lady better, become more familiar with her lifestyle. And in that way we will grow in understanding her Son. As she did, we will learn to listen to him to ponder on what he said.

This type of novena is a legacy of St Josemaría Escrivá, the founder of Opus Dei. He taught us to develop a personalised conversational devotion to Our Lady. Thus we learn to listen to her as she guides us towards the Gospels, the Word of God himself. While designed originally for use in the lead-up to the Feast of the Immaculate Conception on 8th December, these reflections can be used in preparing a novena before any feast day of Our Lady. It is always a chance to make a clearer path towards love of Jesus for each of us. Pope Francis pointed to Our Lady pondering these things, the reality of Christ, in her heart in his homily on St Joseph the Worker's feast day on 1st May 2013. That is what we are all trying to do!

September 2013

DAY ONE: FAITH

1. It was a winter's day when they brought St Andrew face to face with the cross in Northern Greece, around the year AD 60. The apostle was an old man then, and he had walked many miles explaining Christ to people. There is a great story that when he saw the cross from a distance, propped up there waiting to take him out of this life, he began to talk to it in poetic terms. "I have long desired you," he said, "you through whom my Master redeemed the world, you are now going to unite me with him." The cross for him was an object of delight, even though he knew he was going to have to suffer for a long time on it. The story says that he spent two days on the cross, all the time talking in a cheerful voice about his Master who had died on a cross to save the world. The pagans thought he was crazy. He was, too. He was crazy with love for Christ our Lord. He did not really see the cross. He only saw Jesus.

2. The purpose of this novena is to help us see Jesus more clearly. We want to do that through Mary. She is the short cut. "If it is true," Pope St John Paul II said, "as the Council itself proclaims that 'only in the mystery of the Incarnate Word does the mystery of man take on light', then this principle must be applied in a very particular way to that exceptional 'daughter of the human race,' that extraordinary 'woman' who became the Mother of Christ. Only in the mystery of Christ is her mystery made clear." (*Redemptor Hominis*, 4) We are looking towards the light at this time of the year (December), preparing our minds for the birth of the Incarnate Word. The best way to do that is through Mary, to follow her path as she prepared her mind for

the moment Christ would be born. At the Council of Ephesus, in the year AD 431, the Church declared that Mary was the Mother of God. The people waited outside the Council chambers, and when the declaration of Mary's motherhood was made public, there was great cheering. They carried the Fathers of the Council shoulder-high to a Mass of thanksgiving in the cathedral. They were particularly pleased since they knew Our Lady had lived for some years at Ephesus with St John before her Assumption. Because she is God's Mother, Mary can lead us by the hand in faith, since she believed before anyone else did.

3. She believed:

> Indeed, at the Annunciation Mary entrusted herself to God completely, with the "full submission of intellect and will", manifesting "the obedience of faith" to him who spoke to her through his messenger. She responded therefore with all her human and feminine "I", and this response of faith included both perfect co-operation with "the grace of God that precedes and assists" and perfect openness to the action of the Holy Spirit, who "constantly brings faith to completion by his gifts" (*Redemptoris Mater*, 13).

In this passage, John Paul II was quoting the Second Vatican Council. When Jesus replied to a compliment paid his mother with the sentence: "Still happier those who hear the word of God and keep it!" (*Lk* 11:28), it was further praise of Our Lady, since no one kept God's word as closely as she did. She preceded everyone in her belief in the Incarnate Word. She was the very first person to believe.

St Augustine says: "Mary was more blessed in possessing Christ through faith than in conceiving the flesh of Christ. Her maternal bond with God would not have got her anywhere if she was not happier to carry Christ in her heart than to carry him in her womb." Day after day Our Lady carried out the ordinary jobs of a busy housewife in a small town. She looked at Jesus, working beside St Joseph at the carpenter's bench, and she knew he was the Son of God. He had to earn his living like any other man. For those hidden years Jesus did nothing out of the ordinary. He worked. There were no outward signs of his divinity. His mother still had to walk down to the well for water. She had to bring the clothes to the stream and beat the dirt out of them with flails – they had no soap then. She had to look after the sick relatives and children with runny noses, and listen to the complaints of the older people. She was the same as any other busy housewife anywhere in the world. And she was the Mother of God, and she knew it too. When she saw Jesus working at the carpenter's bench, she rejoiced in God's presence so close to her everyday tasks.

4. We need to look at Our Lady so as to increase our faith and see God more clearly. She helps us see God's face. The novena gives us a chance to cultivate our Lady's friendship. After nine days of thinking about the life of Jesus and Mary, we will have got to know God better. Getting to know God means learning to talk to him. Let each person pick the prayers that suit them best. Here I will only be recommending the prayers everyone knows, and particularly the Holy Rosary, that contemplative prayer, which helps us see into the lives of Jesus and Mary.

5. St John Paul II said at Knock in 1979:

> "Do whatever he tells you." What Jesus tells
> us, through his life and by his word, has been
> preserved for us in the Gospels, and in the
> letters of the Apostles and of St Paul, and
> transmitted to us by the Church. We must make
> ourselves familiar with his words. We do this by
> listening to the readings from Sacred Scripture
> in the liturgy of the word, which introduce
> us to the Eucharistic sacrifice; by reading the
> Scriptures on our own, in the family, or together
> with friends; by reflecting on what the Lord tells
> us when we recite the Rosary and combine our
> devotion to the Mother of God with prayerful
> meditation on the mysteries of her Son's life
> (*Knock Homily*, par. 5).

6. Saying the Rosary well requires struggle. Sometimes
we are waiting for the flashing light that will make our
prayer easier. We wait in vain! I'm sure you have laughed
at those people in the television ads. They seem never to
have a hair out of place. Their kitchens are effortlessly
spotless. Every job is made look easy. Paint simply walks
onto walls. Doors and windows shrug off dirt. One pint
of whatever, and one bite of something else, and you
become an immediate success. The television ads create
a mentality suggesting that success can be achieved
without a struggle. A clean kitchen takes a great amount
of elbow grease. We have to work hard to improve our
Rosary. The most important point is to keep up the
effort. We can go out of training, particularly if we are
expecting God to make it easy. The Rosary is never easy.
That is why it is such a great help to our faith.

7. We have to make a constant effort to improve our faith, by trying to see what we can do to pray more effectively each day. That is a help the novena gives. We take a nine-day run at improving our prayer. Let's try to be a little more attentive every day of this novena. Let's try to fight distractions in our Rosary today, simply by turning all the stray thoughts that come into our minds into a conversation with Our Lady. Let's set out to get used to talking to her about all the ordinary affairs that worry us. She is there ready to listen. What is more, she is there ready to speak to Our Lord about us. She intensifies our faith in the nearness of Christ. She helps us have real faith.

DAY TWO: SIMPLICITY

1. He was a well-established businessman. He was clever. He was well off. He knew about financial deals, how to get the best interest for his investments, how to get the most work out of his employees. Even in those days, back in the sixties, he was looking forward to the world of computer technology. He used to speak of electronic devices for speeding up the accounting. He was a sophisticated man. He got cancer, and I met him in the last period of his life. He was only fifty-three, and dying with great cheerfulness. "Look," he said to me, one day when I came into the room. "What?" "Look at the picture on the wall," he said, pointing with a terribly thin arm. It was a line drawing of Our Lady, playing with the child, making Jesus laugh. "That's the way I like to see her," said the man on the bed, "she played with the child, she laughed and danced with him." And he smiled contentedly.

The same man died on the eve of Our Lady's birthday, with a smile on his face. He had a virtue that we can easily admire, because it led him to a clear view of God, through Mary. He had simplicity. That virtue is related to the gifts of the Holy Spirit, the gifts of wisdom and understanding, of knowledge and piety, of strength and counsel and fear of the Lord. These are the gifts Isaiah mentions when he is speaking about the spirit which will rest on the Root of Jesse, the one who is to come, the Incarnate Word himself (cf. Is 11:1–9). We received these gifts at Confirmation, so the wisdom that leads us to be simple in our approach to God lies within our reach.

2. Listen to that conversation between the angel Gabriel and Our Lady (*Lk* 1:26–38). Mary was perhaps reading, or working around the house talking to God in her own quiet way. Tradition tells us she was only sixteen years old. The angel entered and greeted her with the astonishing words: "Hail, full of grace, the Lord is with you." St John Paul II linked that grace the angel sees in her with the blessings of sanctification St Paul explained to the Ephesians. God has blessed us all in Christ, but God has blessed her first.

> It is a spiritual blessing which is meant for all people and which bears in itself fulness and universality ("every blessing"). It flows from that love which, in the Holy Spirit, unites the consubstantial Son to the Father. At the same time, it is a blessing poured out through Jesus Christ upon human history until the end: upon all people. This blessing, however, refers to Mary in a special and exceptional degree: for Elizabeth greeted her as "blessed among women" (*Redemptoris Mater*, 8).

The angel Gabriel recognises the Holy Spirit within Mary. He acknowledges her, a human creature, as on a level above his own. The Lord is with her in a special way. She is queen of the angels and still a human being, a woman. Mary is a person of surpassing beauty because God is within her, creating the loveliness of that abode which is to become the dwelling place of God on earth for nine months. When St Bernadette saw Our Lady for the first time at Lourdes she said that her "Lady" was so beautiful she would be happy to die in order to see her again. And for the first half-hour of her appearing to Bernadette, Our Lady said nothing. She only smiled.

3. The angel was struck by the source of that beauty in Mary our mother: he saw God shining through. The third person of the Blessed Trinity, the Holy Spirit, will give us simplicity as part of his wisdom, as he gave it to Our Lady. Look how she reacts to the angel's first words. She is perplexed. She wonders what kind of greeting this could be. Maybe it was the first time she ever thought about herself. She is not one to complicate her life by continually analysing what people think of her, or what the reaction will be to the next comment she makes. We lack the wisdom of the Holy Spirit that Mary had, and instead of fixing our attention on God, we are all the time thinking about ourselves, and so getting more complicated. Our Lady serenely waits for the angel to explain himself.

4. Simplicity implies an ability to recognise our virtues and defects. If we think we have no good qualities we are being complicated. I doubt if we could ever think we have no defects, which would be much too complicated altogether. Our problems are usually small ones, and with God's grace we will not be found committing grave sin. But we are to be found gossiping, and thinking badly of one another. We do tend to harbour resentment for old insults, and we can very easily sulk when we don't get our own way. All these are "normal" defects. But we have to be simple in order to see them as such, and start again each day to get over them.

If we are simple we will never say: I know it all, there is nothing you can teach me. We won't think of ourselves as wise. We will avoid saying: "Me? I have been around for a long time now, I have seen everything." I'm sure you have all realised that in the same way as a person can be young and foolish, a person can be old and foolish. Age by itself does not bring wisdom. Look at Mary. She was only sixteen and full of the Holy Spirit. Of her the sentence from the Psalm could be said: *super senes intellexi, quia mandata tua quaesivi* – I have more understanding than the aged because I keep your precepts (*Ps* 119:100).

5. Simplicity helps us to see ourselves as we are, in the clear light cast over human nature by the Mother of God. She is so straight that the Holy Spirit can use her for his great work of the Incarnation. We can see in her the advantages of being simple and direct in our lives, avoiding being convoluted, or fussy, or devious. All these defects stop the light of God coming into our souls. It follows that the closer we get to God, the more aware we are of his near presence, as Our Lady was, and the more we will lead simple and straightforward lives: the more cheerful we will be.

6. Devotion to Mary brings us towards simplicity because we see in her a creature like ourselves. As Blessed John Henry Newman pointed out, those who accuse us of making Mary divine do not understand the divinity of Jesus. "Our Lord cannot pray for us as Mary prays." Mary is a creature. We can go to her and chat easily. In the presence of the second person of the Blessed Trinity, we must first of all adore, since he is the Word through whom the world was made, and whose thought holds us in existence.

7. The simpler a person is, the happier she is. Why are we so fussed about human success, about whether we are well off or not, or whether we win or lose? It all passes away anyhow. I'm sure you have heard people lament their past failures in sport or business with a victim-like air? A simple person is never a victim. If they lose a match or a race or some money, they smile, offer it to God and carry on. They have no time to waste on complicated lamentations.

DAY THREE: SERENITY

1. The angel Gabriel explained to Our Lady the job God wanted her to do. He wanted her to be mother of the Messiah, the long awaited messenger from God, descendant of King David. Our Lady answers with a question: "How can this be since I know not man?" In other words, how can I be a mother and a virgin at the same time? She had committed herself to virginity already, and wanted to know how this act of dedication to God's will could fit in with this new command to be a mother.

The angel was waiting for the question. He answered it with the blinding revelation of the Trinity. "The Holy Spirit will come upon you, and the power of the most High will cover you with its shadow. And so the child will be holy and will be called Son of God" (*Lk* 1:35). With the simplicity of divine things, a shattering mystery is presented to a teenage girl, and what is more, God *waits* for her answer.

The human mind by itself cannot realise that God has the power to become incarnate. God tells her through the angel that the Messiah is going to be none other than the Son of God. And she is going to be the mother of the Word Incarnate. As we watch the scene unfold before our eyes we would not be surprised if Our Lady got a little fussed at this point. She could have asked for time to think it over. I am tempted to think that if she were from these islands she would have asked for time to consult her family! But she does not. There comes about her that unshakeable serenity which we notice all through her life. "Behold the handmaid of the Lord; let it be done unto me according to your word." This is not a feeble and frightened "yes". This is an expression of complete abandonment to God's will. Whatever God wants, God gets!

2. Mary always gave an example of serenity. Her calm attitude contrasts with the fuss we often make. From the moment of her conception she had the grace of God within her, and as soon as she was able she spoke to God intimately. Here is the key to her serenity. God surrounds Our Lady, and this explains why she is so tranquil. It also explains why we are often so excited and worried about unimportant things. We get all worked up about our everyday concerns because we do not see God standing near. Mary was always keyed up to God's presence, no matter what she was doing. We have so much noise in our heads we do not hear God's gentle voice.

3. Have you ever experienced a storm? One minute the sea is all serene, and the next it is as if a big fist came bursting up from the depths and tore the calm surface asunder. Chapter eight of St Matthew's Gospel tells us how this happened to the disciples. They were crossing the Lake of Galilee, normally a calm stretch of water, when suddenly a storm blew up from the northwest. They found themselves thrown from side to side by the waves, their shouts deafened by the howling wind, sopping wet, trying to bail the water pouring into the boat. And there lies Jesus, at the back of the boat, his head on a cushion, sound asleep.

4. This world is full of storms. There are antagonisms everywhere, as people fall out over land or politics or inheritances. Some families never learn to forgive and are always fighting. Fury arises in the hearts of many. They feel insulted, or their good name smeared. They

can lose their peace – grow angry when they realise how hard a world it is. They are in the eye of the storm and don't know what to do. When this happens we do as the Apostles did, we rouse Jesus.

5. "Master," they said, "do you not care? We are going down!" And what does Jesus do? The gale is howling. The water is pouring into the boat. The sails are flapping and the sky is black. Jesus stands up in the boat, looks out over the sea and says "Quiet now! Be calm!" (*Mk* 4:39) At the beginning of that sentence, everything was full of the noise. At the end, the whole world went quiet. There was a great calm, the Gospel writers say, and it came immediately. The Apostles – fishermen, well used to the vagaries of the sea – looked about them amazed. Jesus said quietly: "Why are you afraid, men of little faith?" The boat had been so unstable they were convinced it was sinking. And here is Jesus, a carpenter, asking them – the true sailors – why had they been fearful, where was their faith. Did they not realise who was there with them in the boat?

Whenever there is a storm in our lives, we have to go, hand in hand with Mary, to Jesus. With him everything becomes still and quiet. That is what Jesus brings to the soul. His is never a deathly silence. The great calm comes. We hear St Paul's sentence: "For those who love God, everything works out for the best" (*Rm* 8:28). We talk over our difficulties with Jesus, and we can tackle them serenely.

6. We learn to trust in God more fully as we frequent the sacraments. There the maternal concern of Our Lady makes itself evident: she keeps leading us to the Eucharist and to Penance. St John Paul II has reminded us of that in Dublin in 1979.

In faithfully observing the centuries-old
practice of the Sacrament of Penance – the
practice of individual Confession with a
personal act of sorrow and the intention to
amend and make satisfaction – the Church
is therefore defending the human soul's
individual right: man's right to a more personal
encounter with the crucified forgiving Christ,
with Christ saying, through the minister of the
Sacrament of Reconciliation: "Your sins are
forgiven; go, and do not sin again" (*Phoenix
Park Homily*, 6).

He went on to make a dramatic plea to anyone who was
still hesitating.

Remember this: the person who knows how
to acknowledge the truth of guilt and asks
Christ for forgiveness enhances his own human
dignity and manifests spiritual greatness.

Late on that very evening at the end of September,
there was a priest sitting in a confessional in a church in
Dublin. An older man came in. It had been thirty years
since his last Confession. When the priest asked him what
had made him come on that day, his reply was: "I could
not refuse that man." He had been watching the Pope on
television, and had received the grace to go to Confession.
He said he went home tranquil for the first time in several
decades. He had made his peace with God.

7. When we get to know Jesus through frequent use of
the sacraments, we discover God who forgives. We are
not only inspired to forgive others any real or imaginary
injury they may have done to us, but we are inspired to
tackle our daily chores with greater optimism. Mary, our

mother, is looking after each of us all the time. Whatever panics the next few weeks hold for us, we can go to her, talk them over with her, ask her to keep us calm, even when there is plenty of complex Christmas shopping to be done, even when we have relations and friends dropping in at all hours. And the best way is to have our conscience cleared by regular Confession. It gets the dust of our guilt cleared away. It makes it easier for us to say to our mother: "Please, Mary, conceived without sin, keep me serene today."

DAY FOUR: MISSIONARY SPIRIT

1. The feast of St Francis Xavier occurs on 3rd December. Let us take a look at a scene from the life of Our Lady which at first sight seems to have little to do with the great missionary. One day Mary is invited to a wedding. It is to be in Cana, a few miles down the road: I imagine it was a relation or a close friend. Jesus and his disciples are also invited to the wedding.

A wedding in those days was a very lively affair. It was always an "at home" wedding. There were weeks of preparations; the women had to get ready all the food for the week the festivities lasted. Everyone around was invited. There was colour, lights, music, laughter. The guests gathered around the bridegroom's house. There were children running about everywhere, people sitting down, usually on the warm earth, eating and drinking. When the solemn section, the bringing of the bride to her new home, was completed they got down to the real business. In Aramaic a wedding feast was called a *mistita*, which means "drink festival". So there was always a big crowd at a wedding like this one.

And then disaster struck. Perhaps during the second or third day, the wine ran out. Somebody had made a mistake. The person in charge of collecting wine over the previous months had forgotten. There was plenty of wine available in Galilee since it was a wine-growing area. And so there was no excuse. But it was a serious failure. If a remedy were not found, this event would go down in the annals of the town to the eternal shame of the family concerned. For months afterwards, they would have been making jokes about the famous "dry" wedding.

Who is the first person to realise something is wrong? Our Lady! Who else? She is a guest, but she has a sharp eye, and she was probably helping anyway in her unobtrusive manner. What does she do? She turns to Jesus. "They have no wine," she says. She does not ask for anything. She does not blame anybody. She states the facts as she sees them, in her usual sympathetic way. She expects that Jesus will find the solution, as he always does.

2. St Francis Xavier died on the island of Sancian, near the coast of China, on 3rd December 1552. He was forty-six years of age. In ten years he had preached the gospel to thousands of people in India, the Molucca Islands and Japan. He died with his eyes on the vast fields for conversion China presented. He gave his entire life cheerfully for the spread of the gospel. We admire a man like him so much that we think his is the only type of valuable missionary work. St Josemaría Escrivá makes us think more personally, so that our admiration for St Francis will find a practical outlet in the way each of us can be a missionary at home.

> A missionary – you dream of being a missionary. Another Francis Xavier ... And you long to conquer an empire for Christ. Japan, China, India, Russia ... And the peoples of the North of Europe, or America, or Africa, or Australia?
>
> Stir up that fire in your heart, that hunger for souls. But don't forget that you are more of a missionary "obeying". Geographically distant from those apostolic fields, you work both "here" and "there": don't you – like Xavier – feel your arm tired after administering Baptism to so many? (*The Way*, n. 315)

In our daily lives, without moving away from home, we can be missionaries, we can lead others to God through our friendship and affection.

3. There you can see the link between Our Lady and the idea of the missions. Helping others does not mean only bringing new peoples to the faith, or giving assistance to those in material need. It means helping everybody around you. Our Lady drew a miracle from Jesus to provide wine for a country wedding. It was the first of his miracles. St John Paul II commented on this scene and said:

> Even though Jesus's reply to his mother sounds like a refusal (especially if we consider the blunt statement "My hour is not yet come" rather than the question), Mary nevertheless turns to the servants and says to them "Do whatever he tells you". Then Jesus orders the servants to fill the stone jars with water, and the water becomes wine, better than the wine which has previously been served to the guests. What deep understanding existed between Jesus and his mother! That event outlines the new dimension of Mary's motherhood ... Mary's solicitude for human beings (*Redemptoris Mater*, 21).

Our Lady made a maternal suggestion. Jesus looks up to heaven and says: "Well, this is not in the plan, you know, the time for doing miracles has not come yet ..." And then he must have smiled, so Our Lady knew he was changing his timetable simply because she asked.

4. At Mass in St Paul-outside-the-Walls on 15th April 2013, Pope Francis underlined the need of proclaiming the Resurrection of Christ. "The proclamation made by Peter and the Apostles does not merely consist of words; fidelity to Christ affects their whole lives, which are changed, given a new direction and it is through their lives that they bear witness to the faith and to the proclamation of Christ." Further on he states that this applies to everyone:

> We all have to proclaim and bear witness to the Gospel. In God's great plan, every detail is important, even yours, even my humble little witness, even the hidden witness of those who live their faith with simplicity in everyday family relationships, work relationships, friendships. There are the saints of every day, the "hidden" saints, a sort of "middle class of holiness" as a French author said, that "middle class of holiness" to which we can all belong.

5. Pope Francis presents us with a target to aim at in our everyday lives. We can start by being affectionate and cheerful to everyone near us. And this is a truly demanding apostolate. We may find it easy to face the duties of our state in life cheerfully on a Saturday or Sunday! But then Monday comes along, and we are confronted by all that washing to be done, or a pile of work at the office, or that first hard class of the day to be given or attended. We can let ourselves go moody, or cranky.

6. Part of Our Lady's maternal care is to keep on presenting our needs to Jesus: "They have no wine"; that is, they are in bad humour, they are in a selfish mood, they are not seeing God in their neighbours, their lives are dull as dishwater, because they do not see you all the time. Jesus hears her, because he always hears his mother. As St John Paul II wrote:

> At Cana of Galilee, there is shown only one concrete aspect of human need, apparently a small one and of little importance. But it has a symbolic value. Mary places herself between her Son and mankind in the reality of their wants, needs and sufferings. She acts as mediatrix and not as an outsider, but in her position as mother (*Redemptoris Mater*, 21).

7. Imagine a person who every single day is in good humour! This person never has a bad word to say about anyone. They don't complain. They are always smiling, early in the morning or late at night. They never flop into chairs and say they are exhausted, looking for sympathy, but always ask about the other people first. They never demand their television programmes, or insist on their own special chair.

They may become like the old Irish widow. The local ruffian had died. He was laid out with a set of rosary beads in his hands for the first time in his misled existence. Mrs Murphy came in to pay her respects. The locals were waiting, because there could be nothing good to say about this man. He had been a villain all his life. She came into the room where the body was laid out. She knelt down and said a decade of the Rosary in a quiet voice. Then she stood up and sighed: "Ah," she said, "I will miss his cheerful whistling in the morning!"

She managed to pick out something positive from a misspent life.

Imagine a person like that and then imagine the effect they have on others. They radiate an atmosphere of cordiality. They bind people together. They make us look up from our selfishness and see the beauty around us. They are true apostles.

DAY FIVE: PRACTICAL HUMILITY

1. People dream about succeeding. They imagine themselves conquering all before them. The world loves success and denounces failure. "You say you've failed? We never fail. You placed your confidence wholly in God. Nor did you neglect any human means. Convince yourself of this truth: your success – this time, in this – was to fail. Give thanks to our Lord and try again" (*The Way*, n. 404). This positive view of failure is based on the practical humility Our Lady discovers for us. If we can recognise our failures quickly then they can always be offered to God as a sign of our dependence on him. We need not be put off by failures. They can help us sharpen our sense of the greatness of God and our nothingness. Our Lady did not experience success from a human point of view. She lived a hidden life. Nobody understood what it meant to be the Mother of God until after she had been assumed into heaven. So our Lady's life on earth was unobtrusive.

2. A friend once told me he had discovered the practical meaning of another point of *The Way*. It is the first one in the chapter 'Humility', and reads: "When you hear your success being applauded, let there also sound in your ears the laughter you provoked with your failures" (*The Way*, n. 589). This friend is a vet, expert on dealing with horses. He was very successful in fixing up racehorses with broken bones and getting them out to stud. He is well-known in the horse industry. He was at a conference in England a number of years ago, asked to deliver a paper on his experiences to the British veterinary surgeons. It was a big conference. They expected to hear an account of my friend's latest

success. Instead he began by quoting that point of *The Way*, and then gave them a run down on the failures he had experienced, and all the knowledge he had garnered from these many and often hilarious mistakes. At the end of his lecture the people at the conference were weeping with laughter. He made a laugh of his failures, but I think they were impressed with his practical humility.

3. It is at the Visitation that Mary pronounces the *Magnificat* poem, which is a chant in honour of humility. Her mind is full of God. There is no room there for self-love. God is so mighty, she says, because he regards the lowliness of his handmaiden. All generations are going to call her blessed because the magnificence of God has been expressed in her already, since God is at that moment in her womb. How mighty is God! How fantastic is his name! Look at God, Mary is saying. Isn't he marvellous?

St John Paul II wrote of the Visitation:

> When Mary enters, Elizabeth replies to her greeting and feels the child leap in her womb, and being "filled with the Holy Spirit", she greets Mary with a loud cry: "Blessed are you among women, and blessed is the fruit of your womb". Elizabeth's exclamation or acclamation was subsequently to become part of the Hail Mary, as a continuation of the angel's greeting, thus becoming one of the Church's most frequently used prayers. But still more significant are the words of Elizabeth in the question which follows: "And why is this granted me, that the mother of my Lord should come to me?" Elizabeth bears witness to Mary: she recognises and proclaims that

before her stands the mother of the Lord,
the mother of the Messiah. The son whom
Elizabeth is carrying in her womb also shares in
this witness: "The babe in my womb leaped for
joy". This child is the future John the Baptist,
who at the Jordan will point out Jesus as the
Messiah (*Redemptoris Mater*, 12).

4. Mary's mind is full of God; she has no time to think
about herself. What about us? How many times do we
tell a story to our own advantage? How many times do
we share a piece of gossip to show how superior we are
to others? How many times do we get cross because we
have not been praised for something we did at home?
How we search for compliments! How offended we
get when the new outfit or the new car is not praised
as it should be! Often, if we ask ourselves why we feel
annoyed it is because we want thanks and no one said
anything. And again, how difficult we find it to admit we
were wrong. We tend to disguise our failures, forgetting
them. We have a selective memory. It blots out what we
have done badly, and exalts what we do well.

5. God, as Mary points out in the *Magnificat*, raises the
lowly from the dust. He lowers the proud from their
mighty seat. The mighty are those people with great
plans. They make big promises. They say: "Don't you
worry, I'll have that done for you by next Friday." And
next Friday never comes. Let's stop dreaming about far-
away fields and strange soap opera adventures that only
happen on the internet! Get down to reality. Let's clear
that room. Go and finish that exercise. Write that email.
Make those phone calls. Dig that garden. Finish those
accounts. Clear out that cupboard. Do the ironing now,
not tomorrow.

6. Humility enables us to see the greatness of God in everyday life. Holiness is accessible to ordinary people. Everyone is called to find Jesus in their daily work, just like Mary found him. This requires humility, because otherwise we will be looking for ourselves in our daily work. Pride holds us back from God.

When Mary visited Elizabeth she spent three months with her, helping her prepare for the birth of John the Baptist. Mary hid so that Jesus could stand out clearly. Mary reveals Christ as man, and she leads us to him as God.

Mary spent all her life carrying out ordinary duties. For someone who loves God, every day is important. Our Lady shows us how valuable it is for our holiness that each of us should get on with what we are doing at this moment, and do it as well as we can. Each task is a chance to love God more, and a chance to ask for his help; because we need God's help for everything. To know that is to begin to be humble.

DAY SIX: DISTRACTIONS

1. Some people think Our Lady had an easy life. All she had to do was do the housework, look after two people. She had God beside her so prayer was so easy. St Joseph while he was there made all the big decisions; all she had to do was follow on. This false image of Our Lady has her living in a small mountain cabin, with everything laid on, angels arriving regularly to solve major problems. All she had to do was pray. The Second Vatican Council sees Mary as "a model of the Church in the matter of faith, charity and perfect union with Christ" (*Lumen Gentium*, 63). Our Lady advanced through her life on a pilgrimage of faith, the same document stresses. Our Lady precedes us in faith; she is the first to believe in the Incarnation.

2. One glance at the Gospel is enough to dispel the image of a detached airy person, living in a quiet mountain cabin. Follow the Holy Family as they make their way up to Jerusalem for the Passover celebrations. After a week in the city, probably staying with relations, and attending all the ceremonies in the Temple, they set off for Nazareth with the caravan of people from home. They did not miss the twelve-year-old Jesus until they had gone a day's journey. At the age of twelve in those days a boy was regarded as grown-up. That first evening was an anxious one for Our Lady and St Joseph. They went back to the city and after three days searching they found him at one of the schools attached to the Temple, "sitting among the doctors, listening to them and asking them questions" (*Lk* 2:47). They were amazed. Our Lady said: "My child, why have you done this to us? See how worried your father and I have been, looking for you." "Why were you looking for me?" Jesus answered. "Didn't you know that I must be busy with my Father's

affairs?" They did not understand him, says St Luke, but he went down to Nazareth with them, and lived in subjection to them until the moment came for him to begin his public life.

The sentence "But they did not understand what he meant" (*Lk* 2:50) can be confusing until you realise its source. We know that St Luke got his information about these events from Our Lady herself. It is easy to imagine her telling him about the finding in the Temple after perhaps thirty years. Think how far she must have progressed in knowledge of God during that time ... When she looked back, she would say in her lively way to St Luke: "We understood nothing, not a thing." Compared to how much she grasped the divinity of Jesus afterwards, her understanding at the time of the Finding in the Temple seemed quite dull to her. Now both Mary and Joseph appreciated from the very beginning that Jesus was the Son of God. However, this Son of God had acted so naturally, had been such an ordinary child that she had been surprised by his statement of divine independence. Our Lady grew in awareness of God all through her life, as she pondered these things in her heart, as St Luke reminds us on two occasions (*Lk* 2:19, 51). If God, in the person of Jesus, felt it necessary to awaken in Mary and Joseph a deeper sense of the unfathomable mystery of God, what about us?

3. John Paul II wrote in his Marian encyclical:

> When the Holy Family returns to Nazareth, after Herod's death, there begins the long period of the hidden life ... Mary knows that the Son to whom she gave birth in a virginal manner is precisely that "Holy One", the Son of God, of whom the angel spoke to her. ...

During the years of Jesus's hidden life in the house at Nazareth, Mary's life too is "hid with Christ in God" (cf. *Col* 3:3) through faith. ...

However it is not difficult to see in that beginning a particular heaviness of heart, linked with a sort of "night of faith", to use the words of St John of the Cross – a kind of "veil" through which one has to draw near to the Invisible One and live in intimacy with the mystery. And this is the way that Mary, for many years, lived in intimacy with the mystery of her Son, and went forward in her "pilgrimage of faith" while Jesus "increased in wisdom, in stature, and in favour with God and with men" (*Lk* 2:52). (*Redemptoris Mater*, 17)

See then how Mary had to struggle to appreciate every day more profoundly the great mystery of God who lived and worked beside her? She, too, had to grow in wisdom and grace by dint of a daily effort to keep her mind on God.

4. Sometimes we live with God far from our minds. We continue at our prayers out of force of habit. It is a good habit, as it is better to keep at our prayers rather than give them up because we feel they are automatic, since the light of God can break through at any time. However, even if we are good at our prayers, and keep them up, we can still seek to grow in understanding of God every day as Mary did. We can try to start thinking more about our prayers while we say them. What are you thinking about while you are at Mass? What are you thinking about when you are saying the Rosary, or praying the stations? Has it ever occurred to you to talk to Our Lady?

It is so easy, though, to get distracted. There are many things on our minds that seem to interfere with our ability to talk to God. We often get the feeling there is not much we can do. We think that conversation with God is for special people. Our minds are full of bills to be paid, presents to be bought, exams to be done. In the middle of Mass we can find ourselves making out a menu for the next few days, or a shopping list. What can we do with these distractions?

5. St Luke tells us that Our Lady kept all the events of Our Lord's birth and life "pondering them in her heart" (*Lk* 2:19, 51). That must mean that over the years, as she went up from the well, with the pitcher of water balanced on her elegant head, she thought about Jesus. As she baked the family bread, grinding the flour at one of the wooden or stone mills they used, she planned the next few days' housework, and thought about God. God and work were equally on her mind. Since she spent most of her life running a home, Our Lady had no difficulty in speaking to God about ordinary things. Jesus, would you fix this door for me? Jesus the roof is leaking, does it need new straw? Jesus, what present will we give the cousins for Passover? Our Lady asked Christ for domestic favours all the time. And she was never disappointed. We can learn from her to tell Our Lord about our worries. We can start off the day with a morning offering, through the heart of Mary, and looking at the day, we will say: "Please Jesus, keep me calm today, with all the relations coming, or the shopping to be done, or that exam to be sat, or those phone calls to be made." We have to learn how to think of God *through* the things we are doing. In this way distractions are no more than another topic of conversation with God.

6. Of course in order to speak to God about everyday things, we have to get to know him better.

> The Church wishes to serve this single end:
> that each person may be able to find Christ, in
> order that Christ may walk with each person
> the path of life, with the power of the truth
> about man and the world that is contained
> in the mystery of the Incarnation and the
> Redemption, and with the power of the love
> that is radiated by that truth (*Redemptor
> Hominis*, 13).

We must discover Christ at the centre of our everyday lives as Our Lady did. Talk to Jesus about all your worries, and gradually you will learn to talk to him about himself. You will learn to turn your distractions into prayer, going from talking to God about your ordinary affairs, to talking to him about his mysteries and his marvels. You will gradually find out what a fantastic person Christ is: with Our Lady's encouragement, you will also discover the magnificence of the Father, the hidden humour of the Holy Spirit. And then slowly, step by step, we learn to listen to what we are saying when we do pray ...

DAY SEVEN: CHARITY

1. St Nicholas was bishop of a place called Myra in
Asia Minor. He died on 6th December around the year
346. That is a long time ago, and considering that we
know very little about his life, the fact that he is patron
of so many countries (Russia and Greece, as well as the
city of Naples and island of Sicily) suggests something
special about the man. It is his charity that echoes down
through the centuries, since during the last few hundred
years St Nicholas has become Santa Claus in these
northern countries. All the legends told about him stress
his generosity with those in need, and he is shown in a
painting in Brescia in Italy bringing some children to Our
Lady. His remains were taken to Bari in Italy in the Middle
Ages by some Italian merchants. When he gave the last few
bags of gold he had, to help some girls have a dowry so
that they could marry, he little imagined this action would
earn him a reputation lasting for more than a thousand
years. He certainly must find it very amusing to be known
as a man in a funny red suit, sweeping down from the
northern lights on a sleigh with reindeer. But I bet he likes
the idea, because like all the saints, he would be happy to
give, and keep on giving. He is the patron of children so
his fictional Santa Claus personality is based in reality.

2. As we approach Our Lady's feast we should offer
her the gift of an improved life. Could we be generous
towards others, as St Nicholas was? During the days
before Christmas, the Church in her liturgy presents
us with John the Baptist. He emerged from the desert,
preaching a baptism of repentance; his was the voice
crying in the wilderness, preparing people for the coming
of Jesus. When Jesus began his public life, St John

pointed him out to all who would listen. Many did not bother. They found St John exotic enough for their tastes, but Jesus seemed very much of an ordinary person. In the end they rejected Jesus. When St Peter was writing his second epistle, not long before his martyrdom, he reminded the early Christians that Christ's kingdom was a true one, not a "cleverly invented myth" (2 P 1:16). People were expecting Our Lord's kingdom to sweep all enemies before it, establishing God's reign over all men. But this kingdom is like a light shining in a dark place, waiting for the dawn to come. And where that light has to shine, is in our souls. Our Lord does not wish to conquer empires. He wants to reign in our hearts.

3. Look at Mary again. The Mother of God leads a very quiet life indeed. She rarely leaves Nazareth during the first thirty years of Our Lord's life. She spends her days in ordinary tasks. "Mary the most holy Mother of God," says St Josemaría Escrivá in *The Way* (n. 499), "passes unnoticed, as just one more among the women of her town. Learn from her how to live with 'naturalness'." We have to keep reminding ourselves that Our Lady had to walk down to the well for water every day. She had to go to the stream to wash the clothes with the other women. Her life is hidden and silent.

4. There is a moment in Our Lord's life when his relations come to him – cousins, perhaps, uncles and aunts – and they give him some advice (*Jn* 7:3). Go up to Jerusalem, they said; don't stay here in this quiet backwater. Go and let your deeds be seen. Jesus went up to Jerusalem then, but quietly. It was not in their style, which would have been in a big procession with bands blaring: Jesus went not publicly, but as if he would

keep himself hidden (cf. *Jn* 7:10). His relations did not understand Jesus. They wanted a spectacular victory so they would boast about his fame! The next time we meet them is in the Acts of the Apostles, when the gathering of Our Lord's followers await the coming of the Holy Spirit. St Luke gives a list of the Apostles, and then says: "All these joined in continuous prayer, together with several women, Mary the Mother of Jesus, *and his brethren.*" (*Ac* 1:14) There they are again, Our Lord's relations! How did they get in at the beginning of the Church? Weren't they the same people who had been complaining about Christ a few months previously?

5. There is only one explanation. St Luke mentions the relations of Jesus immediately after Our Lady, so she was the reason for their being there; they had been won over by her. She listened to them, talked to them, sympathised with them, and so loved them. She bore witness to the reality of Jesus, explaining him again to them in her quiet voice.

John Paul II writes in the Marian Encyclical (26):

> The Church is born and then grows through
> the testimony that Peter and the Apostles bear
> to the Crucified and Risen Christ. Mary did
> not directly receive this apostolic mission. ...
> But she was in the Upper Room, where the
> Apostles were preparing to take up this mission
> with the coming of the Spirit of Truth: she was
> present with them. [They] knew that ... she was
> ... a unique witness to the mystery of Jesus ...
> Thus from the very first moment, the Church
> "looked at" Mary through Jesus, just as she
> "looked at" Jesus through Mary.

Mary's mission is the charity of personal friendship and affection.

6. Charity means understanding. St Paul teaches us this in his First Letter to the Corinthians. They had been worried about the importance of special gifts – such as speaking in strange languages and prophesying. St Paul explains the use of gifts in the Church, and then points out the greatest gift of all, without which our knowledge of strange languages is no more than noise. Your faith may move mountains, but without charity, it goes for nothing. You can even be burnt at the stake, but if it is not for love, it is a waste of time (cf. *1 Co* 13:1–3). But what is this gift, what does it imply? St Paul goes on: "Love is always faithful and kind; it is never jealous; love is never boastful or conceited; it is never rude or selfish; it does not take offence, and is not resentful. Love takes no pleasure in other people's sins but delights in the truth; it is always ready to excuse, to trust, to hope and to endure whatever comes" (ibid., 4–7). Can we examine ourselves on these points?

7. We should ask Our Lady for patience, understanding and kindness every day. We must try to be calm when we see the failures of others. Thomas à Kempis in *The Imitation of Christ* shows how charity demands humility as a base.

> We would willingly have others perfect, and yet we amend not our own faults. We will have others severely corrected, and will not be corrected ourselves. The large liberty of others displeases us, and yet we will not have our own desires denied us. We will have others bound down by rules, and we will in no way endure any regulations ourselves. And so it appears how seldom we weigh our neighbour in the same balance with ourselves.

Are you always kind to people whom you find boring or tactless? Are you always trying to be more courteous? It should not cost that much of an effort to be better humoured and patient in a street busy with traffic. We should be able to be more kind in asking for something in a shop. It is a clear expression of charity to make life more agreeable for others, without being overbearing or sentimental.

DAY EIGHT: CONFESSION

1. Let us begin this second last day of the novena accompanying Our Lady at the foot of the cross. As John Paul II said:

> John's description is concise: "Standing by the cross of Jesus were his mother, and his mother's sister, Mary the wife of Cleophas, and Mary Magdalene. When Jesus saw his mother and the disciple whom he loved standing near, he said to his mother: 'Woman, behold your son'. Then he said to the disciple: 'Behold, your mother'. And from that hour the disciple took her to his own home" (*Jn* 19:25–27). The Mother of Christ, who stands at the very centre of this mystery – a mystery which embraces each individual and all humanity – is given as mother to every single individual and all mankind (*Redemptoris Mater*, 23).

Mary bears each of us in pain and sorrow. When Our Lady came close to the cross of Jesus, he was being insulted by the passers-by. They shook their heads, they shouted at him: "Come down from the cross, come down, and we will then believe you" (*Mt* 27:42). People have been shouting the same sentence at Jesus ever since. Come off the cross, they say. Give us an easy Christianity, a pleasant and easygoing morality, and we will follow you. Cut out this harsh demand for holiness. Take away sorrow and pain from life. The main thing is to have a good time, and be nice to others, isn't that all that is required of us? The only reply of Jesus is silence. For three hours he hung upon the cross in agony. He did speak a few well-chosen words. He forgave all those who crucified him, he promised paradise to the good thief and he gave us his last most treasured possession: his mother. "Mary's motherhood," St John Paul II said, "which becomes man's inheritance is a gift: a gift which Christ himself makes personally to every individual" (*Redemptoris Mater*, 45). Our Lady stood at the foot of the cross, her heart pierced by sorrow, but she was showing Jesus that there was someone there who would not run away from the cross. Such strength Mary had!

2. Where does Our Lady get that courage? We think of her as a gentle person, which indeed she was. But her gentleness and quietness are of hardened steel, as she stands silent under the cross. Her source of strength is the Holy Spirit within her, giving her the grace to stand firm and steady. "Youth itself may weaken," says Isaiah (40:30–31), "the warrior faint and flag, but those who trust in the Lord will renew their strength, like eagles new-fledged; hasten, and never grow weary of hastening, march on, and never weaken on the march." If we want to imitate the strength of our Mother and stand up to the difficulties of life, we have to go to the same source: God's grace. This extra power to the soul comes mainly through the sacraments. They are footsteps of the Incarnate Word, channels through which God's grace comes from the Cross to each of us.

3. One day Jesus sat down teaching in a house in Capernaum. He had just started his public life. The power of the Lord was there, St Luke says, to grant healing (cf. *Lk* 5:17–25). The house was packed, everyone, even the Pharisees and scribes, hanging on every word Jesus said. Along came some friends with a paralysed man on a stretcher. They could not get into the house because of the crowd: so they climbed on the one-storey flat roof, took

away some of the tiles, and let the paralysed man down on his stretcher, "into the middle of the gathering, in front of Jesus". Everybody waited breathless for something marvellous to happen. But what Jesus said was: "Man, your sins are forgiven." That was an unexpected comment. People were surprised. The important men in the front row began to murmur. "Who is this man? Who can forgive sins but God alone?" Jesus with his quiet humour waited for that thought to cross their minds. "Which is it easier to say: rise and walk, or your sins are forgiven?" They don't answer that question, since it is obvious that a human being could do neither. A magician might pretend to forgive sins, but could never tell a paralysed man to walk. So Jesus underlined his divine power. "To prove to you that the Son of Man has power on earth to forgive sins," he turned to the paralysed man, "I order you, get up, pick up your stretcher and go home." The man proceeded to do just that, marching off, the stretcher under his arm, walking with tentative steps at first, and then as he realised his new found freedom, running along and thanking God in a loud voice; then people there realised that Christ could forgive sins. And that power he passed on to his disciples: "Whose sins you shall forgive they are forgiven, whose sins you shall retain, they are retained" (*Jn* 20:23).

4. Sin is a reality. In his apostolic exhortation on Penance, John Paul II lamented the loss of the sense of sin. We have tended to forget that mortal sin is a personal offence against God, and leads to eternal death. We have even tended to regard venial sin as something unimportant, when it, too, shares in the deathlike quality of all sin, a turning away from the creator of the world. Christ makes his way to each soul through the grace of the sacraments, necessary means for salvation established by Our Lord himself.

> Just as at the altar where he celebrates the
> Eucharist and just as in each one of the
> sacraments, so the priest, as the minister of
> Penance, acts *in persona Christi*. The Christ
> whom he makes present and who accomplishes
> the mystery of the forgiveness of sins is the
> Christ who appears as the brother of man, the
> High Priest, faithful and compassionate, the
> Shepherd intent on finding the lost sheep, the
> Physician who heals and comforts, the one
> Master who teaches the truth and reveals the
> ways of God, the Judge of the living and the
> dead, who judges according to the truth and
> not according to appearances (*Reconciliatio et
> Paenitentia*, 29).

It is God who forgives us in Confession. When we
kneel there and humbly confess our sins, saying we are
sorry, and the priest gives us absolution, those sins are
cleansed. In the eyes of God they are gone. The evil in
our souls is replaced by the grace of the Holy Spirit. If
we are in the state of mortal sin, we are dead to God.
It is therefore an awesome power the priest has been
given. He can bring us back to life, in God's name. He
can gain for us entry into heaven, whereas if we do die
with a mortal sin on our souls, we will find ourselves
hating God.

5. There are some basic convictions about the Sacrament
of Penance that John Paul II stated in 1984. First,
after repeating his faith in the divine institution of the
sacrament, he says that for a Christian, the Sacrament
of Penance is the ordinary way of obtaining forgiveness
of the serious sins committed after Baptism. Second,
since Confession is both a judgement and a healing

of a medicinal character, then, "it requires knowledge of the sinner's heart, in order to be able to judge and absolve, to cure and heal. Precisely for this reason the sacrament involves, on the part of the penitent, a sincere and complete confession of sins" (ibid., 31). Third, he outlines the parts of the sacrament: examination of our consciences so as to admit our guilt, contrition that is a real conversion to Our Lord, and the actual confession of our sins. "We understand why the confession of sins must ordinarily be individual and not collective, just as sin is a deeply personal matter." Then come absolution and the satisfaction imposed on the penitent. John Paul II rounds off his summary of the workings of the sacrament by insisting on its personal and intimate character, on the reconciliation with God and with the Church that it implies and, finally, on the need priests have of going to Confession frequently themselves.

6. The key to making good use of the Sacrament of Confession is the examination of conscience. What can I say, we often think, I've had no time to do anything bad? This is an excuse for putting off Confession for long periods, and we miss the grace that is going with the sacrament, the build-up and strengthening of our interior lives, the development of virtue that is made possible by the grace we gain at Confession. We may be under the illusion of not being sinners. Well, there are always the sins of our past life, which we should mention if we go to Confession frequently, as they provide material for the sacrament, although forgiven already. Then we can try to pick out the particular points that are not going well for us at this moment. Ask yourself, for example, how you have treated God in prayer since the last Confession. Did you lose your temper? Did you let your imagination stray

too far? Did you use your time well? Did you help your neighbours in need? These are practical questions, and they usually show us our current defects. When we are sorry for those, and for the venial sins they often bring with them, then God's grace can help us improve. The grace of the sacrament is quite capable of turning our defects into virtues.

Remember the grace of Confession was won for us on the Cross. Our Lady stood there, sharing in that outflow of grace from the broken Heart of Jesus. The power of the Lord is there to grant healing every time you approach the sacrament. Let us ask Our Lady that we would not let ourselves become lukewarm, mediocre, simply because we are not using the divine power that is there for the asking.

DAY NINE: THE IMMACULATE CONCEPTION OF

THE BLESSED VIRGIN MARY AND FAMILY LIFE

1. We come to the end of this nine days' meditation on the reality of Our Lady. We finish with the same Gospel scene with which we began. We listen to the angel again, as he greets Our Lady: "Hail, full of grace, the Lord is with you." We have already thought about her humility, her serenity, in accepting this embassy from God. Today I would like to think on some further implications of the phrase "full of grace", beginning with the words of John Paul II in his Marian Encyclical (8):

> When we read that the messenger addresses
> Mary as "full of grace", the Gospel context,
> which mingles revelations and ancient promises,
> enables us to understand that among all the
> "spiritual blessings in Christ" this is a special
> "blessing". In the mystery of Christ she is
> present even "before the creation of the world"
> as the one whom the Father "has chosen" as
> Mother of his Son in the Incarnation.

2. In 1854 Pope Pius IX asked the bishops of the Catholic Church, all two thousand of them, if they thought the time had come to declare that Our Lady was free from the stain of original sin from the moment of her conception, by the merits of her Son's cross being applied to her by anticipation. They all said YES. They were quite definite about it. So, on the 8th December 1954, the Pope declared it a dogma of the Catholic faith. This was not a new dogma suddenly discovered. It was the culmination of many centuries of thought. It took time for the theologians to realise that the merits

of Christ could be applied to his mother before his actual death on the cross. This is another example of the Church growing in understanding of the mysteries revealed by God.

3. Imagine being born without sin: doesn't this make Our Lady somebody impossible to imitate? All of us are descendants of Adam and Eve. We come into the world with our soul turned away from God. We need God's special grace to be able to reach our heavenly home, and to be balanced people here on earth. Isn't she too perfect for us then? Not at all! We have seen through this novena that Our Lady is far from being a glacial model, an ice queen. Her beauty is not that of a distant and undisturbed lake in the mountains. She is not like a silent valley bathed in the afterglow of a winter's sunset.

First of all we know that it is great to have somebody as perfect as she is and she a human being like each one of us. She is someone who will never have to come down from a heroine's pedestal. We can admire many saints in history, but all of them have their flaws, even the holiest. Look at St Paul, roaring at the early Christians. Look at St Peter, denying Our Lord at the crucial moment. But Mary has no sins at all. She is the perfect model. We can always rely on her virtues, because she never allowed sin to get into her soul in any way.

4. Mary is the great model; she is the first to believe in the Incarnate Word of God. "For every Christian, for every human being," John Paul II said (*Redemptoris Mater*, 46):

> Mary is the one who first "believed", and precisely with her faith as Spouse and Mother she wishes to act upon all those who entrust

themselves to her as her children. And ... they recognise more and more clearly the dignity of man in all its fulness and the definitive meaning of his vocation, for "Christ fully reveals man to man himself" (*Gaudium et Spes*, 22).

The Pope then outlined the specific role Our Lady plays in regard to the significance of femininity.

It can thus be said that women, by looking to Mary, find in her the secret of living their femininity with dignity and of achieving their own true advancement. In the light of Mary, the Church sees in the face of women the reflection of a beauty which mirrors the loftiest sentiments of which the human heart is capable: the self-offering totality of love; the strength that is capable of bearing the greatest sorrows; limitless fidelity and tireless devotion to work; the ability to combine penetrating intuition with words of support and encouragement.

These are the high ideals Our Lady presents to both men and women. All of the virtues mentioned have a clear bearing on family life. There is where we must give ourselves all the time. There is where the "self-offering totality of love" often comes up against fickleness, complaints, limiting of our self-surrender to when we feel up to it. That is also the testing ground for strength to bear sorrow. Women give birth in sorrow, so they understand pain well enough. But real sorrows are much more than physical. Do we help carry the loneliness, the hurt of all those in our own house?

John Paul did not ask for an occasional burst of looking after others when we feel charitable, he asked for limitless fidelity. "Fidelity" means forever, for always, for God. The only real love is one that lasts into the next life. When we say yes, we must try and mean "Yes!" How often we tend to qualify that "Yes" with a "perhaps" or a "depending on how I feel". "Tireless devotion to work": that's a hard one, since as soon as we get tired we are inclined to flop into a chair and tell everyone how much a victim we are! "Intuition" and "encouragement": how important those two words are. Women can often see much farther ahead than men, which is why they worry so much. If you do happen to be farsighted, then the best thing is to offer whatever you do see to God. We will try and learn to depend on him, on his Blessed Mother, and we will be then the ones who know how to encourage others. Where do we go when we are down? A man goes to his wife, a woman to her husband. We all go to our mothers looking for encouragement. That's part of the maternal instinct we can all acquire from our Mother Mary. We can all go to her and ask for a maternal heart like hers. And that will enable us willingly to carry one another's burdens (cf. *Ga* 6:2).

5. You can bring those ideals to family life during the time leading up to Christmas or any other holiday in the year. We try to look after each other better. We can all do jobs around the house, particularly the husband and the children. Mothers can keep up their task of being more encouraging and positive, even when they are getting hassled in shops and supermarkets, and by children demanding large presents. Many husbands are so busy earning their living that they can be tempted to leave all the decisions on their children to their wives: that is a

lack of dedication. Or a working mother can come home from a long day and find the housework hard, and maybe become too harsh. We can be bad-humoured easily within the family. As soon as we are asked to lift a finger, we groan like martyrs. We can tend to sulk when the last unforeseen job comes up. Let's try and catch ourselves out and look at our houses and see how much more we can willingly do to make life agreeable for others. Let's not nag. Let's not sulk. Let's think of Our Lady: how real her beauty is, and how we must imitate her.

6. When Jesus came to Nazareth to preach in the synagogue, soon after he began his public life, the locals were expecting great things. After all, he had already done miracles at Capernaum. What would happen in his own village? He read a passage from the Prophets, which foretold the coming of the Messiah, one who would make the blind see and the lame walk. Then he sat down, and "all the eyes in the synagogue were fixed on him" (*Lk* 4:20). That sentence came from Our Lady. Then Jesus explained the spiritual dimension of his task: he was coming to ask people to repent, to change their lives. This was not what they wanted. Immediately they started to complain and said to each other: "Is not this the son of Joseph?" (*Lk* 4:23) while they admired the words he spoke. At that apparent lack of regard for St Joseph, Jesus pointed out their lack of faith: they had less than the pagans. They got mad and tried to throw him over a cliff. He must have looked at them with those divine eyes of his. They stood back. He walked through the midst of them, and went on his way.

What that means is that Jesus spent thirty years of hidden life living exactly like everyone else in Nazareth. He did nothing different. If he had spent one night out on the mountain praying, they would have remembered it. But no! Jesus hid his divinity effectively. He sanctified ordinary family life. Our Lady hid her holiness during her lifetime. Nobody noticed how close to God she was, since God himself was hidden also. They could not grasp the importance of St Joseph either, that silent patriarch whom God chose as his father on earth, the one to represent God the Father, no less. Perhaps we can make up to Our Lord for that neglect by the way we create a family air around us, by means of a silent self-giving.

We can look to Our Lady for that grace she has in abundance for each of us. She is willing to help us change a little each day. We, too, like Jesus, must grow in wisdom and grace at the heart of the family to which we belong. To improve our family lives day by day is a demanding task, since it means trying to be better NOW. We cannot wait until tomorrow to smile. We have to smile today, and if we follow Our Lady we will learn how to build a world of smiles out of a world of tears.

NOVENA TO OUR LADY UNTIER OF KNOTS

BY MIGUEL CUARTERO SAMPERI

Novena to Our Lady Untier of Knots

Begin each day as follows:

Sign of the Cross - Our Father - Hail Mary - Glory Be

Make an act of contrition, such as:

O my God, I am heartily sorry for having offended you and I detest all my sins, because I dread the loss of heaven and the pains of hell, but most of all because they offend you, my God, who are all good and deserving of all my love. I firmly resolve, with the help of your grace, to confess my sins, to do penance and to amend my life. Amen.

Recite the first three decades of the Holy Rosary.

MEDITATION FOR THE FIRST DAY

Holy Mother, my beloved, Holy Mary, who untie the "knots" that oppress your children, reach out your merciful hands to me.

I give you today this "knot" [name it if possible ...] and every negative consequence that it provokes in my life. I give you this "knot" that torments me, makes me unhappy and prevents me from uniting myself with you and your Son Jesus the Saviour.

I turn to you, Mary, who untie knots, because I trust in you and know that you have never disdained a sinful child who pleads with you to help him. I believe that you can untie these knots because you are my Mother. I know that you will do so because you love me with eternal love.

Thank you, my beloved Mother.

Mary, untier of knots, pray for me.

Those who seek grace will find it in the hands of Mary.

Recite the last two decades of the Holy Rosary.

MEDITATION FOR THE SECOND DAY

Mary, mother most beloved, full of grace, my heart turns to you today. I acknowledge that I am a sinner and need you. I have not kept in mind your graces because of my egoism, my rancour, my lack of generosity and humility.

I turn to you today, Mary untier of knots, that you may ask for me from your Son Jesus purity of heart, detachment, humility and trust. I will live this day with these virtues. I will offer them to you as proof of my love for you. I place this "knot" [name it if possible ...] in your hands because it is preventing me from seeing the glory of God.

Mary, untier of knots, pray for me.

Mary offered to God every instant of her life.

Recite the last two decades of the Holy Rosary.

MEDITATION FOR THE THIRD DAY

Mother Mediatrix, Queen of Heaven, in whose hands are the riches of the king, turn to me your eyes of mercy. I place in your holy hands this "knot" of my life [name it if possible ...] and all the rancour that results from it.

God the Father, I ask you to forgive my sins. Help me now to forgive every person who knowingly or unknowingly has provoked this "knot". Thanks to this decision you will be able to untie it.

My beloved Mother, before you, and in the name of your Son Jesus my Saviour, who has been so greatly offended, and who has been able to forgive, I now forgive these persons, and also myself, forever. Mary, untier of knots, I thank you because you untie in my heart the "knot" of rancour and the "knot" that I present to you today.

Mary, untier of knots, pray for me.

Anyone who wants graces should turn to Mary.

Recite the last two decades of the Holy Rosary.

MEDITATION FOR THE FOURTH DAY

My beloved Holy Mother, who welcome all those who seek you, have pity on me. I place in your hands this "knot" [name it if possible ...]. It prevents me from being happy, from living in peace; my soul is paralysed and it prevents me from walking towards my Lord and serving him. Untie this "knot" of my life, O my Mother.

Ask Jesus to heal my paralysed faith that stumbles over the stones in my path. Walk with me, my beloved Mother, that I may be aware that in reality these stones are for my benefit; may I cease to complain and learn to give thanks, to smile at every moment, because I trust in you.

Mary, untier of knots, pray for me.

Mary is the sun and the whole world benefits from her warmth.

Recite the last two decades of the Holy Rosary.

MEDITATION FOR THE FIFTH DAY

"Mother who unties knots", you who are generous and full of compassion, I turn to you to place, once again, this "knot" into your hands [name it if possible ...]. I ask you for the wisdom of God, that I may succeed in the light of the Holy Spirit in untying this tangle of difficulties. No one has ever seen you angry; on the contrary, your words are so full of sweetness that in you we meet the Holy Spirit. Free me from the bitterness, from the anger and hatred, that this "knot" has caused me.

My beloved Mother, give me your sweetness and your wisdom; teach me to meditate in the silence of my heart; and, just as you did on the day of Pentecost, intercede with Jesus that I may receive the Holy Spirit.

Mary, untier of knots, pray for me.

Mary is powerful in the presence of God.

Recite the last two decades of the Holy Rosary.

MEDITATION FOR THE SIXTH DAY

Queen of Mercy, I give you this "knot" of my life [name it if possible ...] and I ask you to give me a heart that may know how to be patient until you untie this "knot".

Teach me to listen to the Word of your Son, to confess, to receive communion; stay with me, Mary. Prepare my heart to celebrate with the angels the grace that you are obtaining for me.

Mary, untier of knots, pray for me.

You are most beautiful, Mary, and there is no stain in you.

Recite the last two decades of the Holy Rosary.

MEDITATION FOR THE SEVENTH DAY

Mother most pure, I turn to you today: I beseech you to untie this "knot" of my life [name it if possible ...] and to free me from the influence of evil. God has granted you great power over all the demons. Today I renounce the demons and all of the ties I have had with them. I proclaim that Jesus is my only Saviour and my only Lord.

O Mary, untier of knots, crush the head of the devil. Destroy the traps caused by these "knots" in my life. Thank you, Mother most beloved.

Lord, free me with your precious blood!

Mary, untier of knots, pray for me.

You are the glory of Jerusalem, you are the honour of our people.

Recite the last two decades of the Holy Rosary.

MEDITATION FOR THE EIGHTH DAY

Virgin Mother of God, rich in mercy, have pity on me, your child, and untie the "knots" [name them if possible ...] of my life. I need you to visit me, as you did with Elizabeth. Bring to me Jesus, bring to me the Holy Spirit.

Teach me courage, joy, humility and, like Elizabeth, fill me with the Holy Spirit. I want you to be my mother, my queen, and my friend. I give you my heart and all that belongs to me: my home, my family, my spiritual and material possessions. I belong to you forever. Give me a heart like yours so that I may do all that Jesus tells me to do.

Mary, untier of knots, pray for me.

Let us walk full of trust towards the throne of grace.

Recite the last two decades of the Holy Rosary.

MEDITATION FOR THE NINTH DAY

Mary Most Holy, our Advocate, you who untie knots, I come to you today to thank you for having untied this "knot" [name it if possible ...] in my life. You know the sadness it has caused me. Thank you, my beloved Mother; I thank you because you have untied the "knots" of my life. Enfold me in your mantle of love, protect me, illuminate me with your peace.

Mary, untier of knots, pray for me.

Recite the last two decades of the Holy Rosary.

This volume has been compiled from material previously published under the following titles:

Handbook of Novenas to the Saints
Handbook of Scriptural Novenas
Handbook of Novenas for Feasts and Seasons
Novena to the Blessed Virgin Mary
Novena to the Holy Spirit
Novena for Pentecost, taken from *The Road to Pentecost*
Novena to Our Lady Untier of Knots, taken from
Our Lady Untier of Knots